The Architectural Models of Theodore Conrad

The Architectural Models of Theodore Conrad

The "miniature boom" of mid-century modernism

TERESA FANKHÄNEL

BLOOMSBURY VISUAL ARTS
LONDON • NEW YORK • OXFORD • NEW DELHI • SYDNEY

BLOOMSBURY VISUAL ARTS
Bloomsbury Publishing Plc
50 Bedford Square, London, WC1B 3DP, UK
1385 Broadway, New York, NY 10018, USA
29 Earlsfort Terrace, Dublin 2, Ireland

BLOOMSBURY, BLOOMSBURY VISUAL ARTS and the Diana logo are trademarks of
Bloomsbury Publishing Plc

First published in Great Britain 2021

Copyright © Teresa Fankhänel, 2021

This work was accepted as a PhD thesis by the Faculty of Arts and Social Sciences, University of Zurich
in the spring semester 2016 on the recommendation of the Doctoral Committee:
Prof. Dr. Martino Stierli [main supervisor] and Prof. Dr. Barry Bergdoll

Teresa Fankhänel has asserted her right under the Copyright,
Designs and Patents Act, 1988, to be identified as Author of this work.

For legal purposes the Acknowledgments on pp. xi–xiv constitute an extension of this copyright page.

Cover design by Namkwan Cho
Cover image © The Museum of Modern Art, New York / Scala, Florence

All rights reserved. No part of this publication may be reproduced or transmitted
in any form or by any means, electronic or mechanical, including photocopying, recording,
or any information storage or retrieval system, without prior permission in writing from the publishers.

Bloomsbury Publishing Plc does not have any control over, or responsibility for,
any third-party websites referred to or in this book. All internet addresses given in
this book were correct at the time of going to press. The author and publisher
regret any inconvenience caused if addresses have changed or sites have ceased to exist,
but can accept no responsibility for any such changes.

A catalogue record for this book is available from the British Library.

Library of Congress Cataloging-in-Publication Data
Names: Fankhänel, Teresa, author.
Title: The Architectural Models of Theodore Conrad: The "miniature boom" of
mid-century modernism / Teresa Fankhänel.
Identifiers: LCCN 2020046860 (print) | LCCN 2020046861 (ebook) | ISBN
9781350152830 (paperback) | ISBN 9781350152847 (hardback) | ISBN
9781350152854 (pdf) | ISBN 9781350152861 (epub) | ISBN 9781350152878
Subjects: LCSH: Conrad, Theodore, 1910-1994--Criticism and interpretation.
| Architectural models--United States--History--20th century.
Classification: LCC NA2790.F36 2021 (print) | LCC NA2790 (ebook) | DDC 720.22--dc23
LC record available at https://lccn.loc.gov/2020046860
LC ebook record available at https://lccn.loc.gov/2020046861

ISBN: HB: 978-1-3501-5284-7
       PB: 978-1-3501-5283-0
       ePDF: 978-1-3501-5285-4
       eBook: 978-1-3501-5286-1

Typeset by RefineCatch, Bungay, Suffolk NR35 1EF, UK
Printed and bound in India

To find out more about our authors and books, visit www.bloomsbury.com
and sign up for our newsletters.

Contents

List of Illustrations   vii
Acknowledgments   xi

Introduction   1
    The Dean of Models   3
    Objects in Their Own Right   6
    The Postwar Modeling Boom   8
    Editing out   10

1   Architectural Model Making as a Profession   13

    From Ghostwriters to Co-Authors   13
    A New Generation of Model Makers   16
    The Introduction of Large-Scale Modeling Operations   22
    Model Makers for the War Effort   26
    Industrialization and the Division of Labor   30
    Competition, Collaboration, and Co-Authors   34
    Model Making and the Architect   40

2   Modeling Materials   51

    Model and Building   51
    Material Diversity in the 1920s   55
    Imitating Modern Architecture   69
    The Postwar Modeling Boom   80
    From Miniature Buildings to the Idea as Model   88

3   Model Drawings   95

    The Three-Dimensional Shift   95
    Translations and Gaps   97
    Drawing Models   98

4 Model Photography   111
    Realism   111
    Camera and Model   113
    Models, Photos, and Drawings   117
    Faking versus Honesty   124
    Photo Models   128
    The Magazine Era   133
    Model Photos in Architectural Practices   138

5 Model Displays   145
    Selling an Idea   145
    The Modeling Craze   149
    Architectural Exhibitions   156
    Interactive Displays   162

Notes   173
References   193
Index   203

Illustrations

0.1 Lever House model in the exhibition *The Architectural Model: Tool, Fetish, Small Utopia*, DAM German Architecture Museum, 2012. — 2
0.2 Theodore Conrad with final Lever House model, *c.* 1953. — 2
0.3 Theodore Conrad in his first workshop, *c.* 1934. — 4
1.1 Hand tools used in Harvey Wiley Corbett's office in the 1920s. — 17
1.2 Floor plan of Conrad's Griffith Street workshop in Jersey City, *c.* 1934. — 20
1.3 Wood lathe (left) and metal lathe (right) in Conrad's workshop, *c.* 1934. — 21
1.4 Electric sander in Conrad's workshop, *c.* 1934. — 21
1.5 Tool cabinet for hand tools in Conrad's workshop, *c.* 1934. — 22
1.6 Conrad with his model of the *Fortune Naval Base*, *c.* 1940. — 28
1.7 Blueprint for the *Fortune Naval Base*. — 28
1.8 Photo of model airplanes for military training. — 29
1.9 Louis Checkman and his model of the Fort Myers airbase, *c.* 1945. — 30
1.10 Conrad's postwar workshop separated wood and metal working. — 31
1.11 Conrad's employees and photographer Louis Checkman (standing on the right). — 32
1.12 Self-portrait of Conrad's employees with hand tools. — 33
1.13 Conrad and his employees assembling the ground floor of a large model. — 34
1.14 Devon Dennett with a model of the Pan American air terminal. — 35
1.15 Landscape architect and model maker Thomas Salmon using an electrical saw. — 36
1.16 Checkman with view camera. — 37
1.17 Checkman photographing a high-rise model after the war. — 38
1.18 Checkman's photo of Conrad's model for the American Pavilion at the Brussels Expo 1958 on a three-cent stamp. — 39
1.19 Conrad (left) disassembling a model in his studio together with photographer Eric Schaal (center). — 41
1.20 Designers standing inside the large-scale model of the Radio City Music Hall auditorium, *c.* 1931. — 44
1.21 Celebration at Edward Durell Stone's office on the occasion of the publication of his biography in 1962. Conrad can be seen far right. — 46
1.22 Changed representation of the architectural profession: the architect hands a model to his clients. — 49
1.23 Stanley Tigerman, Crown Hall model depicted as the Titanic, photo montage, 1978. — 50
2.1 "Zoning and the Envelope of the Building," published in *Pencil Points*, 1923. — 57
2.2 Drawing of model parts before assembly. — 58
2.3 Making a cardboard model with a razor blade. — 59
2.4, 2.5, 2.6 Massing models of the Metropolitan Life North Building, *c.* 1929. — 60

ILLUSTRATIONS

2.7	Design inserted into a model of the surroundings, *c.* 1929.	60
2.8	Fully detailed model imitating the limestone façade, *c.* 1929.	61
2.9	Close-up of model, *c.* 1929.	61
2.10	Plasticine study models for the *Daily News* Building designed by Raymond Hood.	63
2.11	Plasticine models of the RCA Building, 1932.	64
2.12	Model for a college of engineering at Cornell University by Shreve, Lamb and Harmon, *c.* 1934–8.	65
2.13	Finished model with cardboard façade, *c.* 1934–8.	65
2.14	Hugh Ferriss' drawing of a fictional glass high rise, 1929.	66
2.15	Cardboard model of crystalline design for the Metropolitan Life North Building, *c.* 1929.	67
2.16	Hollow illuminated model.	68
2.17	Vinylite House at the Century of Progress Exhibition in 1933.	70
2.18	The map of Synthetica in *Fortune,* 1940.	71
2.19	Model of the Belgian Pavilion with traditional paper façade.	74
2.20	Model of the Glass Center Pavilion with translucent tower.	75
2.21	Irish Pavilion massing model.	75
2.22, 2.23, 2.24 Pittsburgh House of Glass model, 1939.		76
2.25	First model of MoMA, March 1937.	78
2.26	Model for Fernand Léger's fountain.	78
2.27	Broken model of the Villa Savoye.	79
2.28	New aluminum frame without the façade, early 1938.	79
2.29	Assembly of model.	80
2.30	Model of 100 Park Avenue by Kahn & Jacobs, *c.* 1948–9.	82
2.31	Presentation model of Lever House, 1952–3.	82
2.32	Construction of the Pittsburgh Hilton model, *c.* 1957–8.	84
2.33	Inland Steel Building model, *c.* 1955–8.	85
2.34 and 2.35 Versions of the façade for the Libbey-Owens-Ford Glass Company building, *c.* 1957–9.		86
2.36	Interior model of the Chase Manhattan Bank, *c.* 1955–8.	87
2.37	Manufacturers Trust model, *c.* 1953.	89
2.38	Floor plan model of the Connecticut General Life Insurance Building, *c.* 1953–7.	90
2.39	Conrad working on a sectional model of the Reynolds Metals Building, *c.* 1955–8.	91
2.40	Exterior view of the Reynolds Metals Building model, *c.* 1955–8.	91
2.41	Section of the chapel for the Air Force Academy in Colorado Springs, *c.* 1954–7.	92
3.1	Liebman House, copy of a floor plan by Edward Durell Stone's office, *c.* 1937.	100
3.2	Theodore Conrad sitting at the drawing table in his basement workshop, *c.* 1934.	100
3.3	Blueprint of the House of Tomorrow, *c.* 1937–8.	101
3.4	"Conrad. This print is for you. Landscaping is ok as shown" is marked on this drawing in red crayon.	102
3.5	Conrad's floor plan for the original model of MoMA, *c.* 1937.	103
3.6	Conrad's contour drawing for Edward Durell Stone's Liebman House, *c.* 1937.	103
3.7	Conrad's drawing of the base for *Collier's* Weekend House.	104
3.8	Conrad's drawing of the internal structure of MoMA, *c.* 1937.	104

ILLUSTRATIONS

3.9	Conrad's drawing of pieces and the internal structure for MoMA, *c.* 1937.	105
3.10	Site drawing for the topography of the Bermuda Naval Base model in Conrad's workshop, 1940s.	106
3.11	Conrad reviewing the assembly of the Equitable Life model with the help of a construction drawing, *c.* 1957–8.	106
3.12	Conrad's model drawing of Liebman House, *c.* 1937.	107
3.13	Copy of a drawing by Philip Goodwin and Edward Durell Stone indicating the marble veining for the MoMA model's rear elevation, *c.* 1937.	108
3.14	Copy of a preliminary landscape plan for Liebman House by Michael Rapuano, *c.* 1937.	109
4.1	A 45° mirror is used to photograph inaccessible parts of a model.	114
4.2 and 4.3	Two different kinds of lighting for "glass" windows in photos.	115
4.4	Photo shoot with a magazine model.	116
4.5	Model of the Hartford Bushnell Memorial Hall presented as an object not a building.	117
4.6	Photo taken with a normal camera lens that could not represent a pedestrian's perspective accurately.	118
4.7	Using a pin-hole instead of a lens to obtain an image replicating a pedestrian's perspective.	118
4.8	Chiaroscuro photo for Norman Bel Geddes' Shell Oil model.	120
4.9	Composite photograph: montage of an aerial photo of London and a model photo of Bush House.	121
4.10	Retouched model photo of the United Masonic Temple, *c.* 1929.	121
4.11	Checkman's guide to making model photo montages.	122
4.12	Model of Corbett's George Washington National Masonic Monument photographed in front of a painted perspectival landscape.	123
4.13	Tower of the Metropolitan Life North Building, photographed in front of Manhattan, *c.* 1929.	124
4.14	Simon Breines' comparison between rendering and building.	125
4.15	Photo of Metropolitan Life North Building massing model inserted into a drawn background, repeating the shadows on the model.	127
4.16	The model photo was then translated back into a drawing.	127
4.17 and 4.18	Documentary model photos published in architectural magazines before the 1930s.	129
4.19	Eye-level photo of Fordyce and Hamby's *Collier's* House, 1937.	131
4.20	Original spread of *Collier's* May 6, 1939 issue.	132
4.21	Exterior eye-level view of the House of Glass, 1939.	132
4.22	Fully furnished interior shot of the House of Glass, 1939.	133
4.23	Color model photos in an article in *Woman's Home Companion*.	135
4.24	Close-up of the Speyer house model, *c.* 1948.	136
4.25	Model of a house with a shed roof in a fall setting.	137
4.26 and 4.27	Similar views of two different models of Lever House, *c.* 1949.	139
4.28	Ezra Stoller's photo of a model of the General Life headquarters with extra props and an airbrushed sky for the background, *c.* 1957.	140
4.29	Night shot of Pepsi-Cola Building, *c.* 1956–7.	140

ILLUSTRATIONS

4.30 Airbrushed arcades of Gallery of Modern Art model, *c.* 1958–9.   141

4.31 and 4.32 Night and interior shot of the model of the American Pavilion at the Brussels Expo 1958, *c.* 1956–7.   142

4.33 Cover of the *Architectural Forum*, May 1949, showing the Heinz Research Laboratory model.   143

5.1 Judges of the A. W. Brown Scholarship competition in 1931 with entries.   146

5.2 Model of the winning design for the Metropolitan Life North Building, *c.* 1929.   148

5.3 First press conference with plaster model of Rockefeller Center, March 1931.   149

5.4 Signing the papers on top the model of the Continental Baking Company, December 2, 1937.   150

5.5 Brazilian delegation looking at a model at the Empire State Building on January 30, 1937.   150

5.6 Model of the fairgrounds at night.   151

5.7 Copy of a model of the central mall of the New York World's Fair used as a conversation piece at the dinner table.   151

5.8 Plan and elevation for a model display of the New York World's Fair.   152

5.9 *Democracity* at the Theme Building representing an illuminated city at night, 1939.   153

5.10 *City of Light*, 1939.   154

5.11 Large-scale part of the *Futurama*, 1939.   155

5.12 Model of the Villa Savoye in the International Style exhibition at MoMA, 1932.   157

5.13 Model of Garden House No. 1404, *c.* 1937–8.   158

5.14 Display of the Bissel House model in a storefront.   159

5.15 Conrad's Sun House model for Macy's Forward House exhibition, 1933.   159

5.16 "Tomorrow's World" at the American Institute of Architects, 1948.   161

5.17 Speyer House and car models in "Tomorrow's World," 1948.   161

5.18 Large model photo as a teaser in *Collier's* for Stone's exhibition house at Rockefeller Center.   162

5.19 Gordon Bunshaft presenting an early massing model to a committee of General Life, *c.* fall 1953.   164

5.20 Large-scale floor plan model in a meeting between architects and client inside a mock-up of the Connecticut General Life Building, *c.* 1954.   165

5.21 Model in front of a photo mural, 1955.   166

5.22 Model of the cadet area in front of a photo mural in the exhibition, 1955.   167

5.23 Lever House model in the exhibition "Architectural Work by Skidmore, Owings and Merrill" at MoMA, fall 1950.   168

5.24 Ludwig Mies van der Rohe and Philip Johnson in front of a photo mural of Tugendhat house at MoMA.   168

5.25 Model of the American Embassy in New Delhi inside a mock-up of the building's terracotta screens in the exhibition "Buildings for Business and Government" at MoMA, 1957.   169

5.26 and 5.27 Air Force Academy model as seen from two different directions.   170

5.28 Model of the Seagram Building in front of the construction site on Park Avenue.   171

5.29 Installation shot of "America Builds" with façade mock-ups and model in mock-up of Lever House, 1957.   172

Acknowledgments

This book is based on the doctoral dissertation that I prepared between November 2012 and March 2016 with the support of the Swiss National Science Foundation during my employment in the research project "Architectures of Display," led by Prof. Dr. Martino Stierli at the University of Zurich. I would like to thank Martino Stierli and Barry Bergdoll for their support.

During this time, I had the great pleasure of working with many insightful and generous people without whom I could not have written this book. First and foremost, my deepest gratitude goes to the Conrad family—the late Ruth Conrad, Doris Conrad Brown, Lenny Brown, and Hans-Jörg Meister—who not only invited me into their home but encouraged me to document and study Theodore Conrad's archive. I would also like to thank Wayne Checkman for allowing me access to the collection of his father Louis Checkman's work, and for answering all my photography-related questions. I am grateful for Doris' and Wayne's enthusiasm and patience when it came to finding a permanent home for both collections, which have since gone to the Avery Architectural & Fine Arts Library. This was successful only due to the tremendous efforts of former chief archivist at the Avery, Janet Parks.

Among Conrad's contemporaries who have helped clarify my thoughts, a small selection who invested considerable personal time have to be specially commended: Architects Thomas Killian, Ernest Jacks, George Cooper Rudolph, Gordon Wildermuth, and Hicks Stone contributed their memories of Conrad and individual projects. Jersey City preservationist Colin Egan recalled his collaboration with Conrad during their joint work in preserving Jersey City's historic sites in the 1980s. Former editor of *Progressive Architecture*, John Morris Dixon, talked with me about the use of model photos in architectural magazines. Donald Presa, a conservator and former neighbor of the Conrads, shared his memories of life in Jersey City. Erica Stoller discussed her father Ezra Stoller's model photos and Bob Perrone, grandson of model maker Rene Paul Chambellan, shared information regarding his grandfather's work in modeling clay for Rockefeller Center. Model-makers Paul Bonfilio and Dale Flick graciously shared their knowledge of modeling techniques.

I would like to express my deep gratitude to Oliver Elser for introducing me to architectural models and for his constant support throughout the years. I am also extremely grateful to Ines Fankhänel and Nico Hocke for the excellent reproductions of model drawings in the book.

Lastly, I would like to thank the many colleagues, friends, and family who have listened, helped, and commented on my work and who, in their various ways, have shaped my thinking: Adam Jasper, Andreas Rätze, Andres Lepik, Barry Bergdoll, Claudio Leoni, Davide Deriu, Eeva-Liisa Pelkonen, Edward Bottoms, Emma Jones, Franziska Stein, Gabrielle Schaad, Gail Feigenbaum, Gary Van Zante, Gerlinde Verhaeghe, Helena Doudová, Ines Fankhänel, Jia Yi Gu, Johannes Fankhänel, Johannes Müntinga, Kevin Graf Schumacher, Kim Förster, Lidia Gasperoni, Louis Duva, Mark Morris, Martin Hartung, Martin Prade, Martino Stierli, Matthew Wells, Matthias Graf von

ACKNOWLEDGMENTS

Ballestrem, Max Hallinan, Melchior Fischli, Michelle Millar Fisher, Myriam Fischer, Nadine Helm, Niall Hobhouse, Nico Hocke, Paul Galloway, Philip Shelley, Philipp Sturm, Oliver Elser, Olivia Horsfall Turner, Ralf Liptau, Reinhard Wendler, Sabine Frommel, Sarine Waltenspül, Simona Valeriani, Stanislaus von Moos, Stefan Gruhne, Stefaan Vervoort, Stéphanie Quantin, Tobias Becker, Tom Weaver, and Wallis Miller.

I would like to thank James Thompson and Alexander Highfield of Bloomsbury for their support and encouragement in turning the manuscript into a book.

This book is published with the support of the Graham Foundation for Advanced Studies in the Fine Arts.

Full list of supporters:
Alexander Architectural Archive, Architecture and Planning Library at the University of Texas Libraries, Nancy Sparrow, Curatorial Assistant
Bob Perrone
Carol and Renée, C&R Organizing
Carol Willis, founder Skyscraper Museum
Carnegie Museum of Art, The Heinz Architectural Center, Tracy Myers, Curator of Architecture
Cigna Corporate Research, Cigna Archives, Sarah Polirer, Manager Corporate Research
Christina Cogdell, Associate Professor of Design & Art History, University of California at Davis
Christopher Alexander, Curator of Architecture and Design at the Getty Research Institute, Department of Architecture and Contemporary Art
Colin Egan, preservationist, Director of Loew's in Jersey City
Columbia University Libraries, Avery Architectural & Fine Arts Library, Janet Parks, Curator of Drawings and Archives, Jason Escalante, Drawings Assistant, and Nicole Richard, Drawings & Archives Assistant, Margaret Smithglass, Head, Exhibitions and Digital Asset Management
Dennis Holloway, architect
Canadian Centre for Architecture, Roberta Prevost and Martien de Vletter
Century Association Archives Foundation, Timothy DeWerff, Executive Director
Cooper Hewitt, Smithsonian Design Museum, Elizabeth Broman, Reference Librarian
Corinne Bélier, Conservatrice et Chef de Patrimoine, Cité de l'Architecture, Paris
Cornell University Library, Division of Rare and Manuscript Collections, Marcie Farwell, Collection Assistant
Dale Flick, model maker in Jersey City
Donald Albrecht, Curator of Architecture and Design at the Museum of the City of New York
Donald Presa, conservator
Erica Stoller, Esto Photographics Inc.
Ernest Jacks, architect
Giorgia Bottinelli, Curator of Historic Art, Norwich Castle Museum & Art Gallery
Gordon Wildermuth, architect
Hagley Museum and Library, Elisabeth Fite
Harry Ransom Center, Art, Performing Arts Collections, Chelsea Weathers, Research Associate
Hicks Stone, architect
Imperial War Museum, Alan Wakefield, Section Head—Photographs

ACKNOWLEDGMENTS

Irmgard Bishop, former secretary of Theodore Conrad
Jahn architects, Stephanie Pelzer, Executive Graphics & Communications
Jeffrey L. Meikle, Stiles Professor in American Studies and Professor of Art History, The University of Texas at Austin
Jill and George Cooper Rudolph, architects
John Morris Dixon, former editor of Progressive Architecture
JPMorgan Chase Art Collection, Lisa K. Erf, director
Lawrence W. Speck, The W. L. Moody, Jr. Centennial Professor in Architecture, The University of Texas at Austin
Leon Moed, architect
Leszek Stefanski, model maker
Mark Wasiuta, Adjunct Assistant Professsor of Architecture, Planning and Preservation, Columbia University, Graduate School of Architecture, Planning and Preservation
Medmenham Collection, Michael Mockford, Curator and Archivist
Metropolitan Life Archive, Daniel May
National Archives and Records Administration, Cartographic Section, Peter Brauer, Archivist
National Building Museum, Nancy Bateman, Registrar
Nicholas Adams, Professor of Art on the Mary Conover Mellon Chair, Vassar College
Nicholas Olsberg, art dealer
Oberlin College Archives, Ken Grossi, College Archivist
Paul Bonfilio, model maker
Paul D. Stoller, architect
Pei Cobb Freed & Partners Architects LLP, Emma Cobb
Philadelphia Museum of Art, Matthew Affron and Anna Vallye
Pratt Institute Library, Paul Schlotthauer, Librarian and Archivist
Raymond Gomez, architect
Reynolds Development, Susan McLane, Secretary to Mr. Randolph N. Reynolds
Rockefeller Archive Center, Nancy Adgent
Rockefeller Center Archive, Christine Roussel, Archivist
Rutgers University, Katie Anderson and Erica Gorder, Associate University Archivist
Smithsonian Institution, Archives of American Art, Marisa Bourgoin and Erin Kinhart, Archivist
Smithsonian Institution Archives, Mary Markey
Smithsonian National Air and Space Museum, Elizabeth Borja, Reference Service Archivist
SOM Chicago, Karen Widi, Manager of Library, Records & Information Services
SOM New York, Wendy Chang, Records Manager
Susan Lorence, art dealer
Syracuse University, Marcel Breuer Digital Archive, Teresa Harris and Barbara Ann Opar
The American Institute of Architects, Nancy Hadley, Manager, Archives and Records
The Art Institute of Chicago, The Ryerson & Burnham Libraries, Lori Hanna Boyer, Daniel Dorough and Nathaniel Parks, Assistant Archivist
The Getty Research Institute, Sarah Sherman, Reference Librarian
The Metropolitan Museum of Art, Linda Seckelson, Senior Reader Services Librarian
Archives & Special Collections at the Thomas J. Dodd Research Center, University of Connecticut Libraries, Laura Smith, Archivist

ACKNOWLEDGMENTS

The Museum of Modern Art, Mary Kate Cleary, Collection Specialist, Michelle Elligott, Senior Museum Archivist, Paul Galloway, Study Center Supervisor for the Department of Architecture and Design, Michelle Harvey, The Rona Roob Museum Archivist, Pamela Popeson, Preparator, Architecture & Design, Bret Taboada, Assistant to the Chief Curator of Architecture and Design

The Museum of the City of New York, Susan Johnson, Curatorial Associate, Christine Ritok, Assistant Curator of Furniture & Decorative Arts and Lindsay Turley, Manuscripts and Reference Archivist

The New-York Historical Society, Margi Hofer, Mariam Hofer, Reference Librarian and Scott Wixon

The New York Public Library, Manuscripts and Archives Division, Tal Nadan, Reference Archivist

The Queens Museum of Art, Hitomi Iwasaki, Director of Exhibitions/Curator

Thomas Killian, architect

Union Carbide Information Center, Tomm Sprick

University of Arkansas Libraries, Arkansas Architectural Archives, Catherine Wallack, Architectural Records Archivist

University of Pennsylvania, Architectural Archives, William Whitaker, Curator and Collections Manager

University of Toledo, Barbara Floyd

Wayne Archive, Kristen Lynn Chinery

Wayne Checkman

Wim de Wit, Adjunct Curator of Architecture and Design at the Cantor Arts Center at Stanford University

Yale University Library, Manuscripts and Archives, Claryn Spies

Introduction

The intersection of Park Avenue and 53rd Street in Manhattan could be considered the nexus of the Modernist universe. In the summer of 2013 I was standing at this junction, with the Seagram Building at my back, and looking, for the first time, at Lever House. Both Park Avenue and 53rd Street have been center-stage in the urban redevelopment of Midtown from a residential neighborhood into a business district throughout the better part of the twentieth century. To the south there is Grand Central station, with one of the first glass skyscrapers built after the war by Kahn & Jacobs just below at 100 Park Avenue, and one of the most blatant gestures of Modernism's disrespect to its forefathers right on top, in the shape of the former Pan Am building by the modern "supergroup" of Emery Roth & Sons, Pietro Belluschi, and Walter Gropius. Two blocks to the west from Lever House, between 5th and 6th Avenues, we find the Museum of Modern Art (MoMA), the first institution dedicated to the new style; and a few steps further down the road there is the large chasm of skyscrapers built by such modern icons as Wallace Harrison and Eero Saarinen on the Avenue of the Americas, including the broadcast offices and publishing houses of CBS, WarnerMedia, and McGraw-Hill. If Lever House was the cradle of modern postwar architecture in America, then 6th Avenue was its final resting place, where the opaque all-glass façades of the office slabs act as its tombstones. I had come not to mourn the dead but to learn something new about a building I knew intimately. As I was standing there on the corner across from Lever House I recognized all its familiar features, the slender *pilotis* that lift up the one-story platform on top of which sits the elegant turquoise squeaky-clean slate that the British soap manufacturer Lever Brothers erected to advertise their cleaning products. Yet I had never before experienced the building, with its famous perpendicular angle toward Park Avenue, to be so toweringly imposing. The reason for this new perspective was that I had known Lever House only as a model, albeit a spectacular one. The model had been part of an exhibition at the German Architecture Museum (DAM) in Frankfurt in 2012 where I worked on a show called *The Architectural Model: Tool, Fetish, Small Utopia*, a survey of twentieth-century model making (Figure 0.1). Part of my duties as a curatorial assistant was to research the models on loan from MoMA. This book contains the story of what I found.

The model of Lever House was made between 1952 and 1953 as the final presentation model while the building itself was already under construction. It entered MoMA in the same year as a stand-in for the real building, and was the twenty-sixth model in its collection. It was one of at least four models built by model maker Theodore Conrad for the project and was the most refined version of the structure, including a meticulously scored Plexiglas façade with aluminum inlays to

FIGURE 0.1 Lever House model in the exhibition *The Architectural Model: Tool, Fetish, Small Utopia*, DAM German Architecture Museum, 2012. Copyright © Uwe Dettmar / DAM.

FIGURE 0.2 Theodore Conrad with final Lever House model, *c.* 1953. Copyright holder unknown but see "Scale Model Expert. Want a Skyscraper? This Man Will Build It in Four Months" (1954).

represent the groundbreaking curtain wall that would inscribe Lever House into the canon of modern architecture the very instant it opened (Figure 0.2). The model was one of, if not in fact *the* first to employ spectacular new modeling techniques and materials which made it—without deference to the building it represented—a modern icon in and of itself. It had been on an extensive European publicity tour once before, in the 1950s, when it traveled to shows in Berlin and Moscow, and to the Brussels World Fair to advertise American postwar culture. As part of my effort to learn more about its maker, who, despite being listed in MoMA's database, remained elusive, I contacted Conrad's wife, Ruth Conrad, and his daughter Doris Conrad Brown. A few weeks later, I received the answers to my questions in the form of a binder full of newspaper clippings and photos documenting his life's work. Conrad was, by no means, an unknown figure. In fact, for several decades, he was the most prolific and well-known model maker in the United States whose work was covered in newspapers, architectural and lifestyle magazines, and in movies. Reporters checked in regularly about his work for several decades, documenting the projects he worked on as well as his ideas about creating small-scale objects. Conrad himself actively supported the preservation of his legacy by Xeroxing published accounts and distributing folders to family, friends, and colleagues. It was one of these binders that made its way to Frankfurt in 2011. Most notable among the coverage, Jane Jacobs reported on Conrad's work, and that of several other New York-based modelers, in a feature on postwar model making for the *Architectural Forum* in 1958 she called "The Miniature Boom."[1] Her article was a brief account of the developments in professional modeling in the late 1950s: an increased demand for detailed models by architects and clients; the use of new materials in models; and new, mechanized techniques for processing them. By creating these elaborate and expensive objects, she wrote, a growing number of architectural modelers were able to influence the design and presentation of the new International Style architecture that experienced its commercial heyday in the 1950s and 1960s. Today, her description of the postwar miniature boom has outlived the short life expectancy of the *Forum's* pages and entered a scholarly discourse that extends far beyond her initial observations as a label for the peak of architectural model making after World War II. Her remarks have since made their mark numerous times in the work of historians and journalists alike and the "miniature boom" has become a catch-all term for mid-century architectural models, despite the fact that little is known about its origins.[2]

The Dean of Models

Ted Conrad has probably built more New York real estate than anyone else—in miniature, that is.[3]
JOHN HAVAS, 1956

Over the course of a professional career that spanned more than five decades and 3,000 models, Theodore Conrad was a prolific designer, inventor, and model maker who was involved not just in making small-scale objects but in the larger debates about good design and craftsmanship of his time. His practice linked him to many key figures of mid-century Modernism in New York and across the country, which, in later years, earned him the title "dean of models."[4] He was an outspoken supporter of modern, International Style architecture which roughly paralleled his professional life as a model maker. The son of German immigrants, Conrad was born on May 19, 1910, in Jersey City, New Jersey, where he lived and worked most of his life. After studying architecture at the Pratt Institute in Brooklyn between 1928 and 1931, he quickly turned to model making as a profession and became one of the first independent professional architectural model-makers in the United States when he opened his studio in Jersey City in 1931 (Figure 0.3). Throughout the respective turmoil of the 1930s' Great Depression and World War II, the economic boom of the postwar years, and the oil crises in the 1970s, Conrad managed to maintain his workshop until his death in 1994. He first gained wider acclaim when he won first prize in the

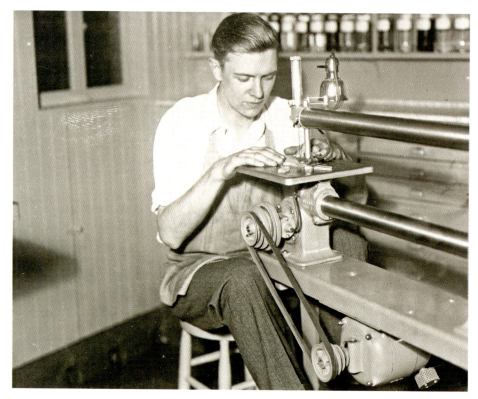

FIGURE 0.3 Theodore Conrad in his first workshop, *c.* 1934. Copyright © Doris Conrad Brown, Theodore Conrad papers, 1937–91, Avery Architectural and Fine Arts Library, Columbia University.

1934 Delta Power Tools competition for the nation's best small basement shop. Early on, he established important alliances with successful architects based in New York, among them Harvey Wiley Corbett, Wallace Harrison, and Philip Goodwin, as well as wealthy and well-connected clients such as Nelson Rockefeller. His early commissions included models for the 1939 New York World's Fair, Rockefeller Center, and MoMA. After the war-time slump in construction work, Conrad's career took off when he started to work for large International Style offices such as Skidmore, Owings & Merrill (SOM) or Edward Durell Stone, eventually becoming the premier model maker in the United States engaged in some of the most high-profile and widely publicized building projects of his time, as reporter Anna Quindlen documented in 1981: "Nelson A. Rockefeller sent visitors to see the view from his window. Doris Duke argued over doorways. Jacqueline Kennedy Onassis first saw what President Kennedy's grave would look like from a Conrad model."[5] After three decades in a business he helped invent, in 1962 Conrad became the only model maker to ever receive the American Institute of Architect's Craftsmanship Medal for his lifetime achievement with architectural models and his "creative collaboration" in the development of architecture.[6]

The exceptional level of acclaim during his lifetime, diligently recorded by others and safely filed away by Conrad himself, is an anomaly in the history of model making, which our team at the

INTRODUCTION

DAM realized quickly as we prepared the 2012 exhibition. Though plenty of miniatures have survived the hazardous conditions of architectural offices, the lack of storage space in modeling studios, or the often fateful journey to the client, only rarely did the information on their creators. Even today, archives often routinely label models with the dates of the building and the name of the architect as if models could be easily equated with full-scale structures and as if a modelmaker's work, the construction of a small-scale object, was merely reproductive. Conrad's collection was given to the Avery Architectural and Fine Arts Library at Columbia University in 2015 following years of effort from Conrad's family, the Avery's chief archivist Janet Parks, and myself to save and preserve as much of it as possible, and it remains the only known source documenting a mid-century architectural model maker's work with a wide-ranging scope of information: from model pieces, drawings, and model photos to business files, letters to clients, invoices, and information regarding employees. About thirty models have been preserved in addition, many of which were given to collections throughout the United States.[7] Today, Conrad's archive has become an authoritative source for the study of model making in the twentieth century and it forms the backbone of the research that went into writing this book.

Before the collection went to the Avery, a major initial undertaking included documenting and cataloguing Conrad's oeuvre in the basement that had been part of his former studio in Jersey City, and piecing together the scattered information to identify his most important projects. To cross-reference these findings, my research extended out to encompass the collections of his collaborators, including architects, corporations, and photographers. From the work of his closest professional ally, the Jersey City-based model photographer Louis Checkman with whom he shared a decades-long personal and professional relationship, to the archives of architects such as Wallace Harrison, Harvey Wiley Corbett, Edward Durell Stone, Gordon Bunshaft, and Norman Bel Geddes, and to such comprehensive collections as the New York World's Fair Corporation's or the records of the former Connecticut General Life Insurance Company, I retraced his footsteps all across the United States. In all these archives, my work was almost archeological groundwork that required me to sift through large numbers of files and collect relevant information ranging from planning processes of individual projects to a more general use of models. Throughout all these repositories there was one unifying thread: the main difficulty as regards model research, which is concomitantly a major challenge in architectural history since the application of photography for the reproduction of art, given that as models are fragile objects, images are often their only trace. For understanding the history of physical objects, photography is both a blessing and a curse: a blessing because it records things otherwise lost; and a curse because photos do not record modeling materials and their construction beyond doubt, leaving much room for interpretation. It is therefore impossible to separate talking about models from talking about their photographic representation. To make up for the lack of reliable information on the objects first hand, written sources such as letters, contracts, or invoices add an invaluable insight, often counterbalancing the shortcomings of photos through detailed records of prices, materials, and structural decisions. Model drawings form another medium that has been looked at only rarely, as they are of an even more elusive nature and are almost always lost during the model making process. It is extraordinarily fortuitous that several sets have survived in Conrad's archive. Another obstacle, and one that might well have contributed to the dearth of information in most institutional collections, is that model makers, much more than photographers and draftsmen, were (and still are) barely credited in architectural publications. Interviews and oral histories of Conrad's contemporaries have helped to clarify individual contributions, including the many conversations I have had over several years with Ruth Conrad and Doris Conrad Brown, as well as with architects Ernest Jacks (formerly Edward Durell Stone's office), Thomas Killian, George Cooper Rudolph, Gordon Wildermuth (all formerly SOM), and Hicks Stone (Edward Durell Stone's son). I consulted Ezra Stoller's daughter Erica Stoller and Louis Checkman's son Wayne Checkman, both of whom contributed their intimate knowledge of architectural and model photography. Besides the interviews I conducted myself, I used, to great advantage, the Chicago Art Institute's *Chicago Architects Oral History Project*, especially the interviews conducted by Pauline Saliga, Betty Blum, and Sharon Zane, which added vital information regarding former partners and employees at SOM and in Mies van der Rohe's Chicago office. Aside from the evidence that can be traced across these archives, the surge in model making that Jane Jacobs summarized so poignantly is most easily quantifiable by assessing the number of model photos in magazines. A statistical overview of publications such as the *Architectural Forum* supports her report of an increase in the use of models after World War II. Archives of newspapers such as the *New York Times* provide a broader picture of the publishing standards for announcing new structures to a non-professional audience, and, as a relatively obscure but no less valuable source, women's and lifestyle magazines such as *Ladies' Home Journal*, *Life*, *Collier's*, *McCall's* and *Woman's Home Companion* were at the forefront of presenting spectacularly realistic model photos to their readers. As for the more professional outlets, Jacobs' article is only one out of a surprising number covering architectural models. The author and model maker LeRoy Grumbine was possibly the most prolific American writer on the subject, with an total output of four articles dating from the 1920s.[8] Among other early key texts are Harvey Wiley Corbett's introduction to model making, "Architectural Models of Cardboard" (1922), published in *Pencil Points*, and the July 1939 model issue of the same magazine that, among others, presented the New York World's Fair planning models.[9] Modeling manuals in book form are equally as insightful when it comes to understanding the broader material developments and the evolution of assembled models. Manuals such as Edward W. Hobbs' *Pictorial House Modelling* (1926) appeared as of the 1920s, some of which became enormously influential among architects, not least Rolf Janke's *Architectural Models* (1962).[10]

Objects in Their Own Right

In contrast with the sole authorship that many archival holdings seem to suggest through their lack of documentation, architecture is, as practiced in its most common form, not a profession carried out by mythical Howard Roarks, but one that is based on the labor of many differently educated and skilled professionals. The development of a building and its final form are usually also shaped by the input of many non-professionals who can have considerable influence over what is built: from corporate boards of directors to individual clients who need to be filled in on all the incidental little decisions made and the often costly features architects try to spend their money on. Architectural models, when seen in this context, are always made to either solve a problem or to communicate an idea. At the same time, they share equal concerns with aesthetic and representative tasks that may extend well beyond their initial utility. Their evolving

INTRODUCTION

materials, the technology used to make them and, ultimately, their final appearance are crucial in achieving the right solution for the right partner in the creation of a building. Innovation, therefore, lies not just in the design practices inside the architect's office but is an interplay of all actors involved in a project.

The novelty of Lever House, for both model and building, was based precisely on this interplay of professions and their innovative use of technology and materials. For the building, it was the thin, non-load-bearing glass curtain wall, the air-conditioned climate, the automatic window cleaner, and the siting of the tower in the urban fabric of the uniform limestone blocks of Manhattan that made it a novelty. The model mirrored the design's most obvious feature, the glass façade, through the use of Plexiglas but was otherwise constructed in stark contrast to the building. Its wall of acrylic glass was load-bearing and the entire structure was held together by an internal "elevator shaft." This did not keep the model from representing the building and its most important features in a way that both the architects and the clients could follow. By inventing a new technique for scoring and cutting Plexiglas, Conrad made it possible to realistically depict the glass in models which had proved hitherto to be one of the major obstacles to building tall glass towers, as clients were unwilling to take a gamble on designs that seemed unfeasible even at a small scale. When looking for the driving forces of the model boom, it seems necessary not only to look at models made as part of the immediate design process—as the representatives of a Roarkian interpretation of architectural invention—but also to include all those that were made as part of the wider dissemination, discussion, and approval of ideas in presentations, in photos, and in exhibitions which have contributed widely to modern architecture as we know it today.

As the example of Lever House illustrates, models, despite their close connection to the structures they represent, are never just scaled-down copies of buildings—they are objects with their own history, for which individual decisions about construction, material, scale, detailing, and presentation are made. As one of several media used as stand-ins for architecture, they are not impervious to outside influences and their use is often significantly affected by the fads and fashions circulating at any time in the architectural professions. In distinction to all other "flat," two-dimensional architectural media such as sketches, drawings, or photos, however, the average architectural model has several unique characteristics: it is three-dimensional, it has a distinct and tangible material quality, it has to be built physically, and it is bound to a specific place. Oscillating between the two opposing poles of design and presentation, models take on many other secondary roles, ranging from a preview of a building or a promise that an as-yet unattainable feat of engineering *will* succeed in the future, to a work of deception, as Leon Battista Alberti famously pointed out in *Ten Books on Architecture*, instigating a centuries-old preference for austerity in model making that is still prevalent among architects today.[11] They can also represent an ideal or sentimental state that does not exist in reality or they can be a fetish, a spectacle and an event to be observed.[12] The adoration of the object, which Alberti was so cautious to avoid at all costs, can be based on many aspects, including the design it refers to, its making, or its materials. Linked to their wide dissemination, models at mid-century were often regarded as representative of a "new" and unprecedented future. Other than one person's fetish or the parallel reality of the ideal model, their spectacular nature was closely linked to their translation in media directed at a mass audience which ultimately did as much for the success and acceptance of buildings such as Lever House as did their novel design features.

The Postwar Modeling Boom

In recent years, the model has seen an astounding renaissance that, arguably, has propelled it to become the defining tool in the creation of architecture today, albeit not in the form that this book details, but through its digital cousin, the BIM model, which aims to connect all building trades, contractors, developers, and architects and allows them to store and exchange a seemingly infinite wealth of information. This digital turn has been to the detriment of other architectural modes of representation, among them traditional analog techniques. How many architecture students today are masters in ink washes or watercolors rather than SketchUp or AutoCAD? The postwar modeling boom, in its own way, was a similarly seismic shift of architecture's slow-moving plates as the one we are witnessing today. Models challenged the primacy of older and more dominant media, especially the established order of Beaux-Arts drawings that was the basis of American architecture schools well into the first half of the twentieth century. Their heyday lasted from, roughly, the 1920s until the 1970s, when drawings took back center stage in the postmodern mutiny against Modernism. Models did not disappear at this point but around the time of the drawing's resurrection, the highly detailed and assembled presentation models made by Conrad and his contemporaries slowly receded into the niche of developer's models. By the end of the 1960s, as the perception of Modernism in architecture and realism in model making changed—from being the pinnacle of innovation in the 1930s to being a deceptive tool of second-rate architects, and a representative of the world of real-estate agents at large—these models themselves were considered as fake and abandoned in favor of more abstract signature models made by architects.[13] More recently, models as physical artifacts have seen another revival in the form of 3-D-printed small-scale objects that came about with new technological developments in stereolithography with the help of malleable substances that can turn out objects more quickly than ever before. Thus for architectural media, it seems that there are no linear developments, no deaths or extinctions, only waves or shifts that foreground one or several media for limited amounts of time based on the problems they are meant to solve. In offering their unique characteristics, they shape the way architects can think about a problem, and influence the outcome they create with them.

According to current scholarly belief, models experienced a long period of decline in architectural practices throughout the nineteenth century, a decline which makes the postwar modeling boom seem even more astounding in comparison.[14] Yet the revival of models in the twentieth century was not an isolated phenomenon that sprang up randomly in the long decade after the end of World War II. It had its roots in a medial shift during the 1920s and 1930s away from drawing and rendering toward three-dimensional representations, and photographic translations of these three-dimensional objects. Based on newly available historical evidence, there are at least three evolutionary strands that displayed significant changes between the onset of the turn in the 1920s and its peak in the 1950s: the development of the new, independent profession of the model maker as part of a growing split within the network of architectural professions; the technical and material innovations made by model makers and architects with regard to modeling; and an increased focus on realism in all architectural media which was initially based on the physical properties of models, but extended into drawings, photography, and exhibitions through a complex system of translation and adaptation. Beginning in the 1920s, individuals such as Conrad began to

INTRODUCTION

turn model making into an independent profession. Their forays were based on a solid architectural education in combination with a high level of craftsmanship that was not part of the architect's academic education at the time. What set them apart were their distinct skills and a new, independent workflow that in the 1950s led to studios operating like manufacturers with an almost Fordist logic behind them. From former in-house modeling practices to standalone workshops, these craftsmen became specialized professionals that depended heavily on power tools to be able to hold their own in a highly competitive market. At the same time, architects relied increasingly on independent modeling studios as they could not keep up with the more specialized knowledge and the financial burden of machinery. The new demand for models could be met only by the establishment of sophisticated and large-scale external workshops that could provide high-end objects within tight deadlines, supported by the electrification and seriality of the modeling craft. Materials underwent an equally radical development that was based less on wartime achievements, as often cited in the literature, and more on the interplay between innovative design elements in modern architecture and the availability of newly developed and advertised materials that came onto the market in the 1930s, most notably acrylic glass. Architectural models as physical objects changed significantly between the 1920s and 1950s, moving away from folded three-dimensional drawings on cardboard or sculpted volumes in plaster toward detailed and assembled structures. Large public events such as the New York World's Fair played a pivotal role in popularizing and disseminating novelties in building materials to a wide audience, not least to architects and model makers. Models made specifically for presentation purposes were at the forefront of innovation regarding the imitation of modern building materials. At the same time, materials that had entered model making for their representational qualities were transferred into the design process where they affected the development of modern architecture more fundamentally as they broadened the spectrum of was what possible to depict at early stages of invention. The translation of these new ideas through different architectural media and their subsequent uses in mass media meant a process of transformation of the idea according to each medium's capabilities. The 1939 New York World's Fair was not just a showcase for the new material and aesthetic world of a modern age in Kodachrome colors, but also the moment a wide audience first became acquainted with architectural models as a medium, which happened concomitantly with the modeling craze that swept across America in the 1930s. Its lasting effect on prospective clients, both in large corporations as well as on single family home-owners, sensitized them to the merits of models and led them to actively demand their use after the war. This general shift toward a three-dimensional representation of architectural ideas was facilitated by two relatively new auxiliary tools: the model drawing; and the association between photography and photo models. The introduction of the former—elaborate model drawings—was a direct consequence of the changing modeling practices from simple cardboard models to assembled miniature buildings. With the growing importance of material imitation in models, model photos created their own aesthetics as part of the modern agenda toward realism, led by lifestyle magazines in the 1940s, which became defining for the portrayal of architecture during the postwar boom through their transfer back into purely architectural publications and presentations. Mass media, both architectural and lifestyle magazines as well as exhibitions, encouraged and facilitated the widespread application of realistic models, and exhibitions translated the realistic photos back into a three-dimensional space, using models in combination with other media, especially photo murals.

Taken together, all these factors contributed to a three-dimensional shift that occurred some time in the middle of the twentieth century. As a historical period formerly assumed to be confined to the two decades after the war, this research shows that the postwar uptick in modeling—the miniature boom—had started two decades prior, in the 1930s and 1940s, when all the necessary developments first occurred that were constitutive of the boom later on. The noticeable fatigue toward modeling that set in as of the early 1970s was due to several changes. The first generation of independent model makers (including Conrad), who had peaked at the same time as their models in the 1950s, was beginning to retire by the 1970s. The tightknit group of architects, photographers, and model makers who jointly created the model boom was disappearing. At the same time, modernist architecture and the buildings represented by these models had exhausted their potential for innovation and many younger architects who were later brought together under the label of Postmodernism turned toward a more abstract use of models. This is best exemplified by the architects affiliated with the New York Institute for Architecture and Urban Studies and the infamous exhibition *Idea as Model* (1976). With the advent of Postmodernism, architecture itself changed, turning away from glass and steel International Style office buildings toward a more historically conscious and eclectic practice. More economic turmoil, in the shape of the oil crises of the 1970s, brought the building industry to a standstill once more and models again became a medium of personal expression for architects, who took to modeling themselves. Simultaneously, the renunciation of realism and models as appropriate for the design and display of architecture was part of a medial shift that favored abstraction and renderings. The profession of the architectural model maker, however, did not cease to exist completely but instead adapted to the changed scene. The materials introduced in the 1930s remain to this day a staple of the professional architectural modeler's workshop but have simply been adapted to more abstract modeling practices.

Editing Out

A history of model making centered on the life of only one modeler could be regarded as a bold statement within the myriad architectural monographs available. In presenting Conrad's work, however, it is not my aim to establish yet another canon of "great model makers," but rather to treat it as exemplary for wider practices in postwar model making and the profession of architecture in the twentieth century which, hopefully, will become clearer as further research into his contemporaries complements the picture. History-writing, much like model making, is about editing out unnecessary detail to get to the essence of a story. The same way that Theodore Conrad could see the entire island of Manhattan and many of the buildings he helped create in miniature version when he looked out of the picture window of his living room on the bluffs overlooking the Hudson Valley, making sense of his legacy from the distance of more than half a century can be an overwhelming sight: Everything seems at once visible and yet obscured by the sheer magnitude of details. In searching for the most outstanding projects and threads, and the stories that link them together into a coherent narrative that can help us understand what caused the miniature boom in modeling that Jane Jacobs sketched out, I followed the trails of many questions and ultimately let the objects respond to the ones they could answer; or, to use model making terms, I let the models be the solution to my problem.

INTRODUCTION

When looking at such a history of physical objects, it sometimes seems to me that, since Walter Benjamin's writings first appeared a century ago, we have become so used to looking at architecture through media that flatten it in order to represent it—from photos to magazines to books and all the way to their digital counterparts on ArchDaily or today's ubiquitous Instagram feeds—that it can be hard at times to remind ourselves that the building and the object are material in the real world. The model, as the prime three-dimensional working method, occupies an exceptional role among these media because architecture, despite its reproducibility, is still something physical: It is, first and foremost, to be experienced in real, three-dimensional space, and ultimately no medium can fully express the range of experiences the real world has to offer. The same seems applicable to history-writing and the historical evidence we are faced with—they always fall short of the real events, people, and stories that unfolded in all their complicated and opaque real-life messiness. However, by studying the way that technological advances in model making were used to edit out aspects of the physical world at large, we can aim to understand what was important to those inventing and using them. There is the famous—and surely apocryphal—story of the invention of the hammer to solve the problem of putting a nail into the wall: As soon as you have it, everything else starts looking like a nail; once invented, the tool takes on a life of its own. Technology, following this interpretation, is not neutral. It is a stand-in for and a mirror of human thought, and a document of our interpretation of the world. In offering my own version based on the story of the postwar miniature boom, its protagonists and its objects, what I found is that in the small and minuscule world of the miniature, there lay answers for the world of architecture at large.

1

Architectural Model Making as a Profession

From Ghostwriters to Co-authors

The architect in tackling a building problem today must be more than a designer; he must have knowledge of architecture, construction, business values, laws, etc. In a large enterprise, an architect naturally becomes a part of a group cooperating and working as a unit, guided by the strongest minds in the group, whether architects', owners' or builders'. The architect of course should build himself into a position where he is, if possible, a directing mind in this group.[1]

ANDREW REINHARD, 1932

The emergence of a new network of architectural professions in the twentieth century had been in the making for hundreds of years. An early predecessor of the architect's dissolving professional boundaries, the medieval cathedral workshop was a major landmark in a changing field that separated architects, knowledgeable patrons, and the building trades.[2] This division of labor in architecture has—contrary to a Marxist understanding of it as a collaboration between specialized but often lesser qualified workers who fulfil a single task on an assembly line—always been based on highly skilled individuals who spend years in training to perfect their craft.[3] Each an expert in their respective field, they come in at specific times during the inception and execution of architecture, translating one architectural medium into another. Since the Gothic cathedral, these architectural networks were the foundation for the execution of architectural ideas. From the 1850s, the division of labor began to permeate the growing architectural offices, ateliers, and partnerships as the profession of the architect itself split rapidly into more specific careers.[4] Now, it included not only the construction of a building but also its design and public presentation. Since the establishment of the Beaux-Arts system in architecture schools in the mid-nineteenth century, American architects had been primarily educated as draftsmen. With the introduction of the blueprint in the late 1800s, copies of drawings were obtained more easily, leading to a declining need for low-wage draftsmen that made higher and specialized education more desirable. Architecture schools offered new degrees in design, management, and engineering that began to subdivide the profession into engineers, designers, draftsmen, and renderers. In the large architectural offices of the nineteenth and early twentieth century, these employees worked on parts of a project, while only the partners and chief designers were involved from beginning to end. What became important was teamwork and "delegation, specialization, and hierarchy."[5] Before the turn of the century, the only way to become a designer was to rise through the ranks from copyist to draftsman and then designer. In 1912, a standard educational requirement was introduced for any individual to call him or herself an Architect.[6] The hurdles to becoming a professional architect were raised even higher when universities increased study times in the 1920s from initially four to five or even six years, resulting in an overall study time of seven to ten years including travels abroad and a mandatory apprenticeship as a draftsman.[7] The increased specialization was reflected in architectural offices. Starting in the 1920s, many larger practices employed in-house renderers and specialists who came in at specific points in each project: Some specialized in the design stage, others focused on detailing, working drawings, or construction supervision. On a broader level, Mary Woods summed up the expanded job description: Architects were now "collaborators, partners, entrepreneurs, merchandisers, educators, employers, and lobbyists."[8] More important for the emergence of the model maker, the intensifying specialization soon crossed the boundaries of the studio and connected independent professions. The first to split was the professional architectural renderer, which became an influential but separate occupation in the late 1800s. In her account of Hugh Ferriss' work, Carol Willis went as far as calling the delineator the "unknown 'ghost-writer' in successful architectural firms," the one who charmed the client with perspectives and won the commission but who no longer had an allegiance to a single office.[9] If the early 1920s were all about rendering, the following decades were largely about model making and photography. The profession of the architectural model maker emerged out of the disastrous collapse of the architectural trades during the years of the Depression. Providing a foundation for the ascent of model making into a separate profession, the material developments of the 1930s and 1940s assured the model maker a more permanent and exclusive position, as the expensive machines used to manufacture acrylic glass and aluminum were prohibitive to non-professionals. The growing importance of models, and the drive to simulate reality necessitated yet another specialization: the model photographer who worked hand in hand with the model maker.

The separation between those thinking and inventing architecture, and those making it, has existed for many years, as Alina Payne pointed out with a nod to Giorgio Vasari: "'[Architecture's] designs are composed only of lines, which so far as the architect is concerned, are nothing else than the beginning and the end of his art, for all the rest, which is carried out with the aid of models of wood formed from the said lines, is merely the work of carvers and masons.'"[10] Until the nineteenth and early twentieth century, the architect's "art" had, by and large, remained the drawing. With the ensuing split of the profession, modes of expression were separated into subcategories to the point that the designer in some cases provided only a series of detailed sketches and supervised the execution of all other drawn work by architecture's ghostwriters. Similar to medieval stonemasons and carpenters who worked in one material only, the new professions each focused on a single architectural medium: the rendering, the working drawing, the model, the photo. To translate an architectural idea from one medium into another, each expert brought their own set of tools and knowledge that influenced the idea. The experience and skills unique to each profession gave them certain leverage over their part in the project. Yet, the derogatory depreciation of "merely the work of carvers and masons" that Vasari displayed for manual labor never fully disappeared as architects became more aware of their increasing reliance on ghostwriters. The model and its makers have been looked at with equal measures of awe and contempt since one of Vasari's predecessors, Leon Battista Alberti, first uttered what would become a standard critique of the model that reverberates until today: "There is a particularly relevant consideration that I feel should be mentioned here: the presentation of models that have been colored and lewdly dressed with the allurement of painting is the mark of no architect . . . Better than that the models are not accurately finished, refined, and highly decorated, but plain and simple, so that they demonstrate the ingenuity of him who conceived the idea, and not the skill of the one who fabricated the model."[11] In short: do not admire the hand that built the model. Architectural historiography, following in the footsteps of Alberti and Vasari, has often neglected or obscured the division of labor in favor of singular authorship.[12] Representative of this phenomenon, the most comprehensive account of model making in the twentieth century, Karen Moon's *Modeling Messages: The Architect and the Model*, takes a similar stance on authorship. Yet, as responsibilities within and outside offices have been shared by many, claims for singular responsibility in architecture are seldom accurate but not without reason, as the persistent focus on how architects used and created models is based, in part, on a general problem of historical research: In many cases, there are no clear records of the collaborative nature of architecture that attribute distinct ideas or input to individuals. Over recent decades, several researchers have ventured away from this historical oversimplification and tried to capture a more complete image of the profession by researching and interviewing employees and colleagues of well-known authors like Ludwig Mies van der Rohe or the firm SOM.[13] Possibly the most inventive study, *Architecture: The Story of Practice*, Dana Cuff's rich ethnographically inspired account of the architectural profession, was based on interviews and case studies conducted during the 1980s in several studios that enabled her to dissect architects as socially constructed beings with their own mores, codes, and behavioral patterns. As for the architect's way of working, she summed up her findings bluntly: "The fundamental point is a simple one: the design of our built environment emerges from collective action."[14] For photographers, the scholarly transition from ghostwriters to co-authors has been accepted more readily in recent decades, not least because photos are often easy to attribute due to their makers' dependence on royalties which are represented visibly by professional stamps on the backs of the prints. Model makers seem to have been less perceptive to questions of authorship, or at least, they were credited much less frequently than photographers. As an example, in 1951, Mary Davis Gillies, editor of *McCall's*, published a collection of modern house designs that were all illustrated through model photos. In the foreword, she explicitly thanked the photographers individually but only mentioned model makers generically.[15]

Until the mid-nineteenth century, American architects came out of various traditional craft professions associated with construction work. They were trained carpenters, masons, and builders with no academic education. After successfully mastering a trade, winning an apprenticeship in an architect's studio was the only way to enter the profession. This changed with the aforementioned split between the artist-architect who came out of the Beaux-Arts schools and engineers that provided technical assistance. At the same time, the ensuing specialization and professionalization further diversified the tools and practices of the new experts. The different sets of tools and the invention of modes of practice set the new professions apart from the architect and over time formed new trades or crafts. Based on trial and error, they turned from amateur to professional. The growing network of trades eroded the definition of architecture as a fixed and finished product and gave rise to a more intricate chain of co-authors who were increasingly dependent on one another. Each an expert in their own field, the process of developing and bringing into existence a building required skills that could no longer be held by one person. Mastery of one's trade, and the ingenuity with which singular solutions unique to the medium were found, were based on exclusive skills that required long and intense training: A perfect watercolor wash could be made only by a trained Beaux-Arts architect, a Plexiglas model could be built only by an architectural model maker, and a perfect foundation could be poured accurately only by a professional concreter. It is through craft and craftsmanship, expertise and excellence in a specific part of architecture, that authority and, thus, authorship was established. The rhetoric of industrialization held by proponents of twentieth-century Modernism removed this idea of craft from the historiography of the progressive movement's machine aesthetic. But craft does not *per se* stand in stark opposition to mechanization and prefabrication. Joining precast parts together, whether in a building or model, requires equally skilled preparation and hands. Inventive work with materials and translations between architectural media is possible only after the techniques of the profession have been mastered. Jane Jacobs realized this in her description of model making and made the distinction between prewar handcraft and postwar machine craft which still used hand work.[16] What changed were the tools. Model makers as craftsmen and -women, while not designers themselves, became unique authors in architecture by translating (drawn) architectural ideas into three dimensions and giving them a material appearance for the first time. In their relation to architects, engineers, and photographers, modelers served as mediators of different interests in design, construction, and communication. Their knowledge of techniques and materials which shaped the models—and thus the way architecture could be depicted—handed them their potential for invention. As the model became a catalyst in the development of architecture and its marketing to clients, it became a decisive signifier for the agency of the model maker.[17]

A New Generation of Model Makers

Until the 1920s, architects were the makers of the majority of models. Possibly the most famous supporter of in-house modeling at the time was Harvey Wiley Corbett. Corbett had a longstanding predilection for working with models, winning a gold medal for his modeling work at the École des Beaux-Arts in the late 1890s.[18] His interest in models was widely known in architectural circles through a number of articles he published in the magazine *Pencil Points* in 1922 under the title "Architectural Models of Cardboard."[19] In these texts he gave an insight into his practice, revealing that he utilized hand tools to make simple models with cardboard and watercolor paper (Figure 1.1). Emphasizing his constant need for models, he wrote: "The value of an accurate model as an aid to study while designing a building is, I believe, beyond question. [. . .] I, for one, cannot visualize a design as clearly as my eyes can see it in a well-made model."[20] Others chimed in. Raymond Hood, another an avid supporter of design models, had been collaborating with sculptor and model maker Rene Paul Chambellan since the early 1920s. Most notably, both their careers accelerated after Hood won the *Chicago Tribune* competition in 1922 with, among others, a model by Chambellan. Chambellan worked exclusively in modeling clay which lent itself to quickly react to design changes. This practice required close collaboration between model maker and architect, which would later be reflected in the proximity of Chambellan's studio to the Associated Architects' office during the design of Rockefeller Center. Professionally made models in materials other than cardboard were generally expensive in the 1920s and commissioned only for important

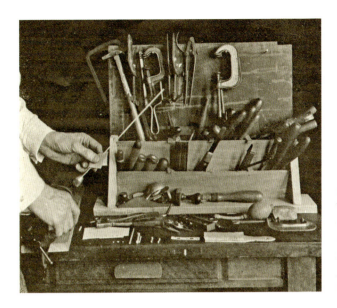

FIGURE 1.1 Hand tools used in Harvey Wiley Corbett's office in the 1920s. Copyright holder unknown but see Corbett, Harvey Wiley. "Architectural Models of Cardboard." *Pencil Points*, April–August 1922, 11–14; 28–32, 37; 14–17; 14–18.

projects. Depending on the material desired, they were made by stucco workers, modelers, carpenters, stage designers, plasterers, or sculptors for whom modeling was part of their daily work. Very few specialized in models alone. Information on how many of these model makers worked before the 1920s is limited, even though some became famous, such as the well-known plasterers of the eighteenth and nineteenth century, Jean-Pierre Fouquet and his son François, who received praise for making a model of the State Capitol at Virginia for Thomas Jefferson.[21] In the United States, modelers were often European immigrants, such as the New York-based sculptors Ricci, Ardolino, and Di Lorenzo or Emile Garet, the creator of a model of the Capitol in Washington, D.C.[22] Other notable twentieth-century immigrants were the mothers of Eero Saarinen and Peter Pran, Catharina Pran, and William McCallum from Scotland.[23] Many of the early modeling businesses provided several closely connected services. The British Twining Models company, a subcontractor of the Northampton-based toy maker Bassett-Lowke, was founded in 1920 by artist and telephone engineer Ernest W. Twining and produced a wide range of mainly wooden miniatures from airplanes to architectural models, including a large model of the city of Durban, an illuminated model of the National Cash Register Works at Dayton, Ohio, and Queen Mary's Dolls' House by Edwin Lutyens (1924).[24] More exclusively serving architects, LeRoy Grumbine operated a workshop in Cleveland, Ohio, and later in Los Angeles, that sold both rendered perspectives and models of cardboard. As one of the first, he called himself a "maker of architectural models and perspectives" and, later, a "modeler of architectural designs."[25]

As the demand for refined models increased in the 1920s, independent model making grew more important. In 1926, the British model expert Edward W. Hobbs remarked that "in recent years a considerable industry had developed for the making of models of cities, factories, large estates and notable buildings."[26] Many of these models, he added, were made by professionals who had spent years in training. For the American scene, Grumbine argued that "in this day of specialization and striving for efficiency, it is more practicable to have models and perspectives made by a specialist than to make them in your own office."[27] Pointing to the lack of specific architectural education tailored to modelers, Grumbine highlighted the need for an architecturally educated craftsman: "The model maker should be familiar with the fundamental principles of architectural design, with drafting-room practice, and with architectural details, so that he can interpret the architect's ideas with the minimum of effort and supervision. He bears a relation to the architect similar to that between pianist and composer."[28] In comparison with in-house or closely associated shops, independent businesses had one weakness: the difficulty of accurately transmitting the architect's ideas to the modeler. What would be needed in the future were architecturally trained craftsmen and women. This is where Conrad and other young architects came in. Among the first trained architects to become model makers was London-based John B. Thorp, who at the turn of the century had started out selling drawings and later offered cardboard and wooden models from his home at 88 Grays Inn Road to architects such as Edwin Lutyens and Gilbert Scott.[29] Two decades later and across the Atlantic, eighteen-year-old Conrad enrolled as a student at the School of Architecture at Pratt Institute in Brooklyn, beginning his studies on September 14, 1928. Pratt itself was a product of the growing professionalization of architecture. It had opened with only twelve students in 1887 as a school for tradesmen, artists, and artisans. By the time Conrad enrolled, it had grown to over 4,000 students split between several schools. The School of Fine Arts offered courses in architecture, fine and applied arts. Day and evening courses covered architectural drawing and design as well as construction. After an entrance exam, forty students were admitted each year with two course options at the School of Architecture: a two-year program in either architectural construction or architectural design. Once accepted, the curriculum for architecture students was rigorous and attendance was required five days a week. Each day consisted of six hours in the classroom and an additional three to four hours of homework. Pratt, as all American academic institutions teaching architecture, followed the French system of the École des Beaux-Arts. All architecture schools were subsumed under the American Beaux-Arts Institute of Design (BAID), an organization that was formed in 1916 in New York City for the education of architects and artists. Most schools used the Institute's curriculum and judgment system, and teaching was based heavily on drawings and renderings of buildings.[30] Students worked in the atelier of a master, a practicing architect, where seniors taught the freshmen. Schoolwork was competitive from an early stage beginning with timed sketches and monthly design problems, and ending with the participation in nationwide competitions for prestigious travel stipends to Europe, organized by the BAID. Most teachers had either studied in Paris themselves or had learned the profession from an architect who had done so. Thus, the aim of every ambitious student in the 1920s was to win the annual scholarship, the Paris Prize, and to experience the French system him- or herself. By the time Conrad entered school, the system seemed to explode at the seams: Whereas in 1922 the BAID had 2,979 competition entries, by 1930 it had more than tripled to 9,500.[31] At Pratt, first-year students learned basic rendering and free drawing, elevations, floor plans, sections of details, and simple designs based on the study of Roman and Greek orders.[32] The history of architecture, especially the Renaissance, was a major subject. For those choosing architectural design, the second year focused on more advanced problems with a heavy emphasis on perspectives, shadows, and washes alongside a study of construction and building materials. One model could be made in lieu of a perspective drawing, but this was not compulsory. Conrad took advantage of the opportunity and handed in a model of a residential building, one of his earliest surviving models. In the second-year construction program, courses focused on methods of construction, building materials such as terracotta and concrete, structural mechanics, heating, and ventilation. Job prospects were different for the two programs: The course in construction was aimed at students who wanted to work as draftsmen and women in builders' offices or pursue detailing and construction work with the ultimate goal of achieving the position of superintendent in that field. Those specializing in design were interested in becoming assistants in architect's offices and eventually working as fully fledged architects. After two years, the subject not yet studied could be added for a third year. A diploma was issued only for those pursuing a teaching degree after completing three years. Conrad followed the suggested three-year program, leaving the school on June 1, 1931. He did not graduate formally according to the school's files, which was not unusual at the time.[33]

In the summer of 1929, while still enrolled at Pratt, Conrad had begun to work as an intern for Harvey Wiley Corbett. Recognizing that he had struck gold, Conrad later retold the story of how he was hired: "Pratt expected its students to find summer jobs in their fields, so my first summer I looked through the telephone book for names of local architects, and clutching an architectural model that I had made in school, I marched into the offices of Harvey Wiley Corbett. Perhaps because she saw me with a model, the receptionist let me in, and I was hired on the spot to make models for the firm. [. . .] It was only later, when I told a teacher at Pratt about my summer job, that I learned who Mr. Corbett was—the dean of the Columbia University School of Architecture. I never would have dared to go in had I known that."[34] Whether or not Conrad was really as naïve in stumbling upon his job as he wanted others to believe, the importance of his early acquaintance with Corbett cannot be underestimated as it set the tracks for his career. As an in-house model maker, he learned the state of the art for his craft by adopting Corbett's modeling techniques. The basic skills needed were manual cardboard and wood working as well as drawing and painting. Conrad was already familiar with the former due to his childhood interest in craftsmanship. As a high-school student he had spent much of his time at an industrial shop course at Dickinson High in Jersey City, attended an art class given by painter and sculptor John Kellogg Woodruff and a carpentry class with Jacob Sieben. As a teenager, Conrad pursued model making further, building a model engine and following publications such as *The Modelmaker*, a magazine geared toward hobbyists. The other key skills, drawing and painting, Conrad was in the process of acquiring at Pratt. His internship in Corbett's office seems to have influenced Conrad's decision to become an architectural model maker greatly, as he realized the need for architectural models and model photos. He also met at least two architects who would become important clients subsequently: Corbett's partner Wallace Harrison and Edward Durell Stone, who was a young draftsman in the office. After the end of his internship, Conrad continued to moonlight for Corbett from his own shop in the basement of his brownstone Griffith Street home in Jersey City.[35] Whereas Corbett still relied on a small toolbox, Conrad soon realized the need for more sophisticated equipment and installed a professionally outfitted and electrified workshop. The new studio opened officially in 1931, the same year he finished school, and with Corbett's designs for Rockefeller Center under way. Smaller and more affordable power tools had become available during the time of the so called "puzzle craze," the DIY movement of the 1930s.[36] In the summer of 1934, after a year of preparation, Conrad entered his shop in a nationwide competition run by the Delta Power Tools Company from Milwaukee, winning a first prize of $75. For the contest, each participant was asked to submit a plan of their studio, including a list of tools and materials. In a detailed account, Conrad described how he converted his small hobby studio only outfitted with hand tools into a large electrified workshop. He went to great lengths to give his shop a professional look. He prepared a list of all equipment, including photos and a floor plan showing around fourteen power tools for processing wood and

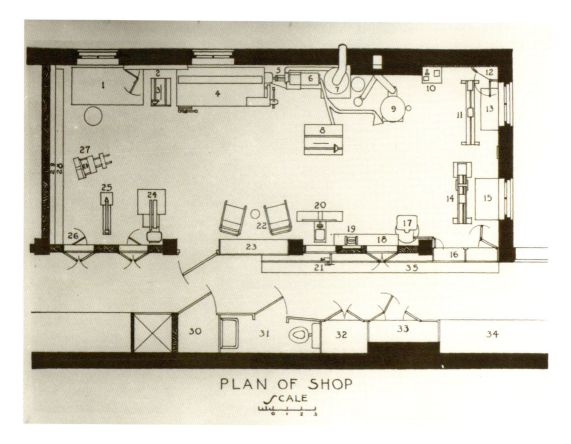

1. Drafting bench
2. Tool cabinet
3. 8" Circular saw
4. Work bench
5. Vacuum pump
6. Sander
7. Saw dust hopper
8. 12" circular saw
9. Furnace
10. Grinder
11. Wood lathe
12. Accessory cabinet
13. Movable shelf
14. Metal lathe
15. Movable shelf
16. Accessory cabinet
17. Drill press
18. Bench
19. Grinder
20. Jointer
21. Swing saw
22. Chairs
23. Bookcase
24. Band saw
25. Scroll saw
26. Wall cabinet
27. Jointer mortiser unit
28. Drawer unit
29. Shelves
30. Clothes closet
31. Water closet
32. Paint closet
33. Miscellaneous cabinet
34. Metal bench

FIGURE 1.2 Floor plan of Conrad's Griffith Street workshop in Jersey City, *c.* 1934. Copyright © Doris Conrad Brown, Theodore Conrad papers, 1937–91, Avery Architectural and Fine Arts Library, Columbia University.

metal including electric saws, drills, and grinders (Figure 1.2). The letter he submitted to Delta Power Tools is the first official record of Conrad calling himself an architectural model maker.[37] His tools, he explained, were vital for his ability to construct models to extremely fine tolerances. This was of utmost importance as his models were built for "conferences or competitions" which required tools to be reliable and accurate (Figures 1.3–1.4). Tight deadlines called for as much

FIGURE 1.3 Wood lathe (left) and metal lathe (right) in Conrad's workshop, *c.* 1934. Copyright © Doris Conrad Brown, Theodore Conrad papers, 1937–91, Avery Architectural and Fine Arts Library, Columbia University.

FIGURE 1.4 Electric sander in Conrad's workshop, *c.* 1934. Copyright © Doris Conrad Brown, Theodore Conrad papers, 1937–91, Avery Architectural and Fine Arts Library, Columbia University.

FIGURE 1.5 Tool cabinet for hand tools in Conrad's workshop, c. 1934. Copyright © Doris Conrad Brown, Theodore Conrad papers, 1937–1991, Avery Architectural and Fine Arts Library, Columbia University.

time-saving as possible, which was facilitated by the electric tools that provided an output of large quantities of identical pieces—the serialization of modeling. Yet hand tools remained important not only in assembling the models, but in making details, carving molds and individual pieces (Figure 1.5). The first prize brought Conrad's work publicity as he began to build up a reputation in the New York metropolitan area. Through his connections, Conrad was able to secure a number of high-profile commissions for his shop, including work on models for MoMA, Edward Durell Stone's modernist house designs, and Rockefeller Center.

The Introduction of Large-Scale Modeling Operations

Many of the early modeling companies had used only hand tools. By the mid-1930s, however, Conrad was not the only owner of a professionally studio equipped with power tools. For many others, however, model making was not their first choice as a profession. The decade before the United States entered World War II saw an enormous increase in architects turning their hand to model making: The financial crisis that followed the stock market crash in late 1929 had left many of them looking for new income streams. At the same time, models had become more established in design and presentation practices, so the demand for professional model makers had risen. Beside private studios like Conrad's that invested on a more long-term basis, large-scale but rather short-lived enterprises such as the Associated Architects for Rockefeller Center or the 1939 New York World's Fair Board of Design demanded pop-up workshops that employed architects and craftsmen for a limited number of years and gave them a thorough education in modeling. Architect and "veteran model maker," Edward Howes, could be seen as an exemplar of how many turned to model making: Trained as an artist, he moved into architecture and model making by working for the New York Architects' Emergency Committee in the 1930s, a New Deal program that gave work to unemployed architects.[38] In 1939, the magazine *Pencil Points* featured architectural model making by presenting the workshops of designers Walter Dorwin Teague, Norman Bel Geddes, and the architecture department at Syracuse University. By now they were all equipped with power tools for wood and metalworking and were able to work in several materials—an innovation that gave them the edge over artisans' and artists' studios that often focused on one or a small number of related materials. In the new shops, different craftsmen could be employed alongside each other, thus widening the possibilities of expression suitable for an array of representational tasks. Arguably the biggest employer and intensifier for the emerging profession of the model maker, and the newly introduced electrified workshops in the New York metropolitan area, was the 1939 New York World's Fair's Board of Design. The need for trained artisans who could draw and translate plans into miniature scales was enormous during the planning and construction stage of the Fair. Job applications for a diverse range of modeling roles far exceeded the demand and show how the scene had advanced in the past decade.[39] The Fair served as a refuge for unemployed artists and visual professionals, including ship model builders, craftsmen in wood, metal, and plastic, precision mechanics, stage designers, landscape architects, lighting specialists, and architects who had lost their jobs during the Depression.[40] Those who had managed to find work also lobbied for commissions by architects designing pavilions for external clients to make ends meet.[41]

There are two different stories about the inception of the 1939 New York World's Fair.[42] The first one—the official one—follows the account of Grover Whalen, the World's Fair Corporation's president. In this story, he and a few businessmen from New York got together in 1934 to follow the example of the Chicago Fair to provide relief from the economic downturn in New York. More interesting for model making, the second story credits Edward Roosevelt, a distant cousin of President Franklin D. Roosevelt, and the Belgian-American engineer Joseph Shagden who pitched the idea for a fair to an editorial writer at the *Herald Tribune* to gain access to George McAneny, the chairman of the Executive Board of the Fair. According to this version, it was Conrad who made the first models representing Shagden's idea.[43] What was more, Shagden supposedly promised to make Conrad model maker for the entire Fair—a pledge that may have caused Conrad to expand his workshop and move to a new location at 52 Franklin Avenue in Jersey City.[44] Shagden's promise, however, never materialized as he was let go in 1937, eventually suing the World's Fair Corporation for plagiarism.[45] Whichever story is true, the World's Fair Corporation was founded in September 1935 and a Board of Design was instituted to develop the physical appearance of the exhibition. It began work in May 1936.[46] Their offices were at the top of the Empire State Building and had a distant view of the fairgrounds in Flushing, Queens. Between May and October 1936, a symmetrical, axial plan was developed. Upon completion of the layout, some pavilions commissions were given to architectural offices directly and competitions were held for others.[47] Over 100 architectural firms worked for the Fair designing, about 375 buildings, including 100 large pavilions, of which one-third were conceptualized by the Board of Design itself.[48] All buildings were scheduled for completion by January 1, 1939 in order to leave enough time for interior designs and exhibits to be installed. As Conrad and Shagden had anticipated, models were of unprecedented importance as tools for design of the overall outline as well as for individual pavilions. On December 9, 1935, model makers Joseph Messineo and Louis Fromm sent a letter to the World's Fair Corporation calling for a centralized approach to model making: "Varied units of the Chicago *Century of Progress* Exposition were modelled by different model makers using different methods and materials of fabrication. Modelling of this development was not coordinated under a single head and it was never possible to make a clear presentation of the whole development as a unit."[49] Such a more unified process was soon taken up by the Board of Design when, on October 8, 1936, the layout of the Fair was finalized and presented in a first massing model at 1/200"=1'-0" scale.[50] A workshop under the leadership of Joseph Messineo was set up in the corner of the drafting room at the Empire State Building to produce models fast and cheaply. This studio worked only on buildings that had been designed by the design department directly. Structures by other exhibitors were done by external architects and their chosen model makers.[51] Half a dozen professional model makers worked for the Fair's model department in 1937, several of them architects by profession.[52] Similar to Conrad's studio, the workshop consisted of a number of electrical machines including an eight-inch bench saw, a jigsaw for wood and metal, a wood-turning lathe, a combination belt, and a disc sander as well as a variety of hand tools.[53] A laboratory was installed on the eightieth floor of the Empire State Building to test materials and illumination on large-scale models.[54] Models were built as soon as a design was approved by the Board of Design and had to give an impression of color and materiality of the buildings as they were intended as a preview for both planners and the general public. By March 1937, in less than six months, an impressive number of 300 model buildings had been created. Responding to Messineo's and Fromm's criticism, officials sought a more unified display of the designs by employing the same model makers for all buildings developed by the Board of Design. In effect, the New York World's Fair model department became the first large-scale modeling factory to equal the size of postwar model enterprises. However, unlike studios after the war, even though the appearance of the models was unified, each modeler remained autonomous and had full control over the entire construction of the projects he or she was working on. Aside from reflecting individual skill sets, this was meant to prevent mistakes in the communication between workers. The importance of model making extended far beyond the World's Fair Corporation's model department, however. A contract between Conrad's former employer, the office of Corbett & MacMurray, and the World's Fair Corporation for the design of the Distribution Building specified the limited services the Corporation offered for pavilions planned by external architects: "The Corporation also shall make all working drawings, prepare the specifications, superintend the work and direct the construction of the House of Distribution Building."[55] No models were included. But as it was important to review them on the World's Fair Corporation's large-scale progress models, they were built at the architect's expense by independent model makers such as Rene Paul Chambellan, the firm Southern & Marshall and Conrad. After the fiasco with Joseph Shagden and the lost commission as the head modeler of the Fair, Conrad's contacts came to his rescue and commissioned models of various other buildings. He built "the first model of the Ball and Trylon" and ten other buildings for Harvey Wiley Corbett, Edward Durell Stone and Wallace Harrison.[56]

Large-scale modeling companies that sprang up in the 1930s, such as the New York World's Fair Corporation's model shop, developed techniques that would become the defining business model for architectural model makers after World War II, when a steady stream of commissions began to pour in. Based on a diverse range of materials and the serialization of modeling tasks, model makers moved toward a division of labor where each craftsman or woman contributed a small part to a larger whole that was overseen by the head model maker. Teamwork became the essence of model making. Better documented than the design models for the New York World's Fair, around 300 models and dioramas exhibited inside the pavilions were built by companies specialized in theatrical model making, especially diorama makers that had existed long before architectural model makers. When not working for expos, companies such as the Marchand Diorama Corporation formed by Henri Marchand, or Ned Burns—who became famous for his history of New York at the Museum of the City of New York—provided dioramas for natural history or anthropological museums.[57] They worked in similar materials and techniques as architectural model makers. But due to the need for a more "theatrical" staging of dioramas, they were more open to using methods of dramatization to enhance their models with light, smoke, or sound. The world's largest manufacturer of that kind, the Diorama Corporation headed by architect Edward Heckler Burdick, had their studios in Long Island City. Two-thirds of the dioramas at the New York World's Fair were built by them, among others Walter Dorwin Teague's *Democracity*, the *National Parks Scene,* and the *City of Light.* Much larger than any model maker's shop, the Diorama Corporation employed 200 specialists, including six architects, two engineers, artists, carpenters, cabinet makers, sculptors, carvers, and electricians. Many of the employees worked in different media. Some had begun model making as a hobby and took it up as a profession only when they lost their jobs during the Depression. As in an architectural model maker's shop, material costs accounted for only up to 5 percent of the overall budget; the rest were labor costs. To reduce these expenses, the Diorama Corporation took a different tack to the practices deployed at the Board of Design model department and operated with a novel, more industrialized system based on a division of labor for different parts of the models. Trees, ships, people, and buildings were made by different individual workers, introducing a practice that would be adopted by architectural model shops after the war. This split of modeling tasks into discrete parts, and the fact that dioramas were more meticulously detailed, called for a more intricate preparation stage in the work process. First, a drawing of the entire scene was made. A small study model would then be built. Only after the mock-up had been approved would work commence on the detailed diorama, with each modeler contributing a small part of the whole. Norman Bel Geddes could be considered the most prominent public figure in diorama making in the 1930s to follow a similar approach.[58] Already established in New York and well connected in the upper echelons of the city's architectural circles, Bel Geddes received the largest diorama commission for the General Motors exhibit *Highways and Horizons*, commonly known as the *Futurama*.[59] Bel Geddes had been a model enthusiast since childhood and had started using them professionally for stage designs in 1915.[60] Unsuccessful in being recognized as an architect, his main aim was to create a perfect environment through large-scale dioramas and photo models such as his *Shell Oil* model or the *Futurama*.[61] At his company, workers were often employed only on a project basis. By 1939, when his office was working on the *Futurama*, he had relocated to Rockefeller Center. For its design and construction Bel Geddes employed about 180 workers, artisans, and artists including the young architect Eero Saarinen.[62] Forty model makers were hired as well as a full-time model photographer.[63] Many of the model makers were selected from General Motors' annual model coach maker competition.[64] The head of the modeling division, much in the fashion of a foreman, was Walter Leuschner, son and successor of a famous German coach maker. To keep control of these large-scale dioramas, Bel Geddes used similar business practices as the Diorama

Corporation based on the division of labor and specialized modelers. Like them, Geddes first had study models made in wood, clay, or cardboard. Then, the *Futurama* was built plate by plate at George Wittbold studios, MGM's old studio at Second Avenue and East 126th Street.[65] Each plate was prepared there and moved to the fairground where finishing touches were added. Throughout the whole process, Bel Geddes himself controlled all parts of the model with the help of detailed progress drawings.

Model Makers for the War Effort

The industrialization of model making has long been credited to developments that happened during World War II. Karen Moon, for instance, stated that mechanization had been encouraged by the war effort because of workshops that were set up in the US for "the fabrication of strategic models."[66] Yet, contrary to persistent scholarly beliefs, World War II was not a productive time for the advancement of techniques or the establishment of progressive studios. Much of this confusion stems from an article by the manager of the Canadian Photographic Survey Ltd., Stephen Waring, who argued that "the decision to use models for strategic and offensive planning led to the creation of large modelmaking workshops, the development of new techniques, and the standardization of practices that have had lasting effects on the industry as a whole."[67] The new techniques mentioned by Waring, clearly with a sales aspect for his own services in mind, were in no way innovative in terms of materials or techniques, aside from one exception: aerial photography as the basis for terrain models, a technique that played only a subordinate role in the postwar modeling boom.[68] In reality, the alleged importance of the war can no longer be considered accurate given that wartime workshops operated by the US government were underequipped and with their reliance on manual labor in no way a paradigm for mechanization.

When the World's Fair opened in 1939, many of the temporarily hired model makers faced an uncertain future. They were soon joined by architects, engineers, and others in the building industry who found themselves jobless as civilian architecture ceased to exist when the war broke out. The Selective Training and Service Act of 1940 required all men between twenty-one and thirty-five, later extended to ages eighteen to forty-five, to register with the draft board; eventually, nine million Americans were drafted to serve in the US Army, Air Force, or Navy, and only those with skills important to the war effort on the home front could avoid the draft. Model makers were among them. By the time war broke out, Conrad had established a flourishing business serving an ever-increasing number of notable clients including Philip Goodwin, Shreve, Lamb & Harmon, Bernard Rudofsky, Shaw, Naess & Murphy, Ely Jacques Kahn, Fordyce & Hamby, Landefeld & Hatch, van der Gracht & Kilham, and French artist Fernand Léger. Nevertheless, Conrad and his four men were drafted in late 1942 and only he was rejected for medical reasons. Having lost his employees and grappling with the insecurity of only short-term exemptions from military service he (unsuccessfully) offered his business for sale in late 1942. Conrad's luck turned when models became part of the war effort. Even though there are no exhaustive sources, it can be assumed that the majority of model making activities during the war concentrated on models for military uses such as targeting and attack plans, troop training, and camouflaging, which often deviated from the traditional tasks of architectural models, employing inferior materials due to rationing. Strategic models of remote or inaccessible battlefields had been used in warfare for centuries. One of the oldest known accounts is a relief model that the Florentine architect Niccolò Tribolo built in 1529 of his home town. It was smuggled out of the city for the pope to use as a planning tool in the siege of Florence.[69] In modern times, the British military was the first to place high value on topographic scale models of enemy territories, facilitated by aerial reconnaissance that provided the basis for these models in form of high-altitude photos taken by fighter aircraft.[70] During World War I, these models were made by a wide variety of model makers, including the toy makers Bassett-Lowke and Ernest Twining.[71] During World War II, photographic intelligence rose to extreme importance for both reconnaissance and targeting, first in Britain and later in the United States. Most of the battle models for the European theater were made in Britain. At the headquarters of the British photointerpretation at the Royal Air Force base at Medmenham in southern England, analyses of enemy territory and weaponry were extracted from images and models of battlefields were built at different scales with larger ones for precision raids of enemy plants and bases.[72] They were used for training soldiers and some were rubberized and could be taken to the field.[73] The initial model section at Medmenham consisted of three professional modelers, two architects, one surveyor, one sculptor, one display artist, and one painter, rising quickly to 140, including many Americans with backgrounds in design, art, architecture, and model making as well as several set designers from Hollywood and New York.[74] Camouflaging industrial sites, plants, and military bases was another important task that resembled civilian architectural modeling more closely, especially in its focus on the realistic depiction of the structure to be concealed. In Britain, artists were gathered by Captain L. M. Glasson for a camouflage section at Adastral House in 1938, where models of British factories could be viewed from a balcony as if looking at them from an airplane.[75] For this purpose, wooden camouflaged models were ordered from independent modelers and were viewed in day- and moonlight.

When the United States entered the war, the value of well-constructed models as educational tools and for camouflage became quickly apparent and a section of professional interpreters of aerial photography was established in 1942.[76] A year before the attack on Pearl Harbor, Conrad had already demonstrated what American modeling would focus on when he constructed a model of a fictitious naval base designed by Edward J. Mathews for *Fortune* magazine. At a very small scale, the model only depicted contours of ships, planes and topography (Figures 1.6–1.7).[77] Another modeling task involved plane and ship models. As part of the training of military personnel, the ability to identify enemy planes and ships became an important asset for which small-scale models were employed. Even though low-cost paper airplanes had been made commercially by the Cincinnati-based firm Burton-Rodgers since 1942, more accurate models were ordered by the US Navy and Air Force from government-owned shops and private modelers under strict secrecy. These shops used magazine and newspaper clippings of military vessels as a guideline. To carry out model making themselves, the American military installed a division called American Camouflage Engineers based at Fort Belvoir, Virginia. Conrad briefly found employment in another government model shop for the Bureau of Aeronautics in Washington, D.C., that made airplane models at 1/72"=1'-0" scale.[78] In the latter, there were five model makers but the few machines available were also used by about forty carpenters, display makers, and machinists. For model makers, this work had the advantage of guaranteed assignments, pay, and exemption from the draft but Conrad soon returned to Jersey City, frustrated with the slow manual work that was caused by a lack of adequate machinery in comparison with his own prewar shop.[79]

FIGURE 1.6 Conrad with his model of the *Fortune Naval Base*, c. 1940. Private collection.

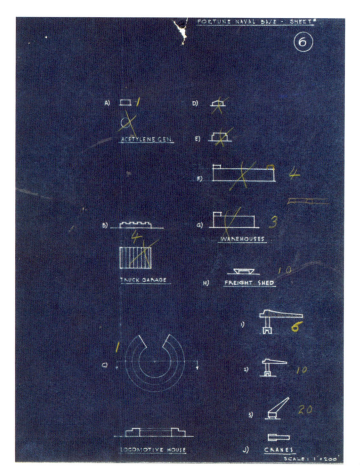

FIGURE 1.7 Blueprint for the *Fortune Naval Base*. Private collection.

After leaving the government workshop, Conrad was one of few who managed to maintain a private business by working on behalf of the Air Force and Navy. In 1942, he was contacted by the army to build models for the "protective obscurement" of the industrial city of Paterson, New Jersey, especially the rail tracks between Bayonne and Paterson and the manufacturer of airplane engines, the Curtis-Wright plant in Woodbridge. Based on an aerial photo, the plan for obscurement consisted of artificial rivers to be built with tar and real water, painted roofs, and decoy buildings.[80] A year later, Conrad received his first direct contract from the Navy, building model planes for pilot training. After posting an ad in the *New York Red Book*, two ensigns inspected his workshop and were astonished by the equipment.[81] Subsequently, similar models were built to train ground troops to recognize enemy planes (Figure 1.8).

As the government-owned model workshops were ill equipped to handle small-scale models, modeling businesses similar to Conrad's were newly established to fulfill the need for military models and small-scale prototyping. Among them was the Camouflage Engineering Corporation run by architect Percival Goodman in New York.[82] Norman Bel Geddes, an enthusiast of miniature war games, received a commission to take fifty model photos of enemy ships for military purposes.[83] One of the major problems of all modeling and architectural endeavors was the lack of trained workers, which caused severe delays for commissions. Frustrated, Conrad wrote to one of his closest collaborators, model photographer Louis Checkman, in 1943: "There just isn't anyone left whose [sic] worth a nickel."[84] Many of the drafted professionals, even though they were skilled in trades relevant for the war effort, experienced a similar lack of equipment and use of their abilities. Louis Checkman had been drafted in 1942 and was categorized as a photo technician. He arrived at Fort Myers Air Base in Florida in 1943, armed with a portfolio of his modeling and photo work including recommendations from Conrad and *Collier's* magazine but there was almost no photo equipment available. Checkman finally got his chance when it was decided, shortly before the end of the war in 1945, to use a model of Fort Myers Army Air Airbase for training pilots (Figure 1.9).[85] Due to a lack of equipment, the model was constructed over two months by Conrad and Checkman in Conrad's shop in Jersey City: Only the base was made by a local carpenter in Fort Myers. Despite these commissions, working for the military was not enough to sustain

FIGURE 1.8 Photo of model airplanes for military training. Copyright © Doris Conrad Brown, Theodore Conrad papers, 1937–91, Avery Architectural and Fine Arts Library, Columbia University.

FIGURE 1.9 Louis Checkman and his model of the Fort Myers airbase, c. 1945. Private collection.

Conrad's or any other modeling business. To find other sources of income, Conrad took on industrial prototyping for Walter Dorwin Teague—an occupation that he thought would have a strong future after the war.

Industrialization and the Division of Labor

In 1952 the British model maker Thomas William Hendrick published his remarkable guidebook *Model Making as a Career*, which laid out the structure of an ideal model making enterprise.[86] Without focusing on a specific branch of model making, Hendrick described the basis on which Conrad's and many other studios operated after the war: a division of labor according to materials and skills needed. Ideally, each firm was to have a general manager who was in charge of client relations, commissions, and estimates as well as a foreman who ran the workshop and oversaw all tasks performed by the workmen. The most important skill for all workers from trades such as pattern-making, joiners, cabinetmakers, or metal workers was the ability to read drawings. Another requirement was that each employee was versatile in working with different materials but a master of at least one. Even though the war has been a serious threat to his existence as an independent model maker, Conrad had prepared yet another entry to a Delta contest in 1944, this time for an ideal postwar workshop that incorporated most of Hendrick's insights. Three years earlier, in 1941, Conrad had moved his studio to the location where it would stay for the rest of his life. Adjacent to what later became his family home, he bought the former Krause diamond shop on 250 Ogden Avenue in Jersey City; the shop had operated on that site between 1914 and 1941.[87] The new studio was on the ground floor, where it replaced the living and dining room. Inscribing the different materials used for modeling into the layout of the shop, he divided it with a glass partition into a wood-working and a metal-working space with the latter serving as a living room (Figure 1.10).

ARCHITECTURAL MODEL MAKING AS A PROFESSION

FIGURE 1.10 Conrad's postwar workshop separated wood and metal working. Copyright © Doris Conrad Brown, Theodore Conrad papers, 1937–91, Avery Architectural and Fine Arts Library, Columbia University.

In the garage, he set up a lumber storage and spray room. His competition entry reflected his recent military work and described the new shop as being furnished to make architectural models, model planes, experimental parts, and furniture using materials as diverse as wood, metals, and plastic. To be more adaptable to different sizes of assignments, the machines could be moved and taken to a loft nearby if the set-up proved too small. Conrad expected to employ larger groups of workers after the war, as can be seen in his purchase of duplicate power tools. The number of tools kept growing to about seventy machines and 120 electric motors, while the spray room rose to new importance for the anticipated work with plastics.[88] None of Conrad's employees after the war was an architect, though he experimented with employing architecture students. This proved unsatisfactory because "they get opinions about the designs they are working on, and want to argue about them or improve them."[89] Even though Conrad's shop had been largely electrified since the mid-1930s, many of the tasks still involved laborious handwork. He had begun to employ a small number of workers when he opened his shop in 1931. Most of them were neighbors, friends, or locals from Jersey City, and their numbers fluctuated based on commissions. In the 1950s, at the heyday of architectural modeling, Conrad's shop multiplied to twenty-six permanent employees—one of the biggest architectural model making businesses in the United States

FIGURE 1.11 Conrad's employees and photographer Louis Checkman (standing on the right). Copyright © Doris Conrad Brown, Theodore Conrad papers, 1937–91, Avery Architectural and Fine Arts Library, Columbia University.

(Figure 1.11). Numbers decreased only in the 1960s. As described by Hendrick, most of his workers were trained craftsmen, carpenters, or furniture makers, who were taught the modeling craft in the shop. Therefore, even in economically difficult times, Conrad was reluctant to let workers go because of the effort expended in training them. In 1953, as his reputation grew, Conrad took on model making apprentices such as the Argentinian Gerard Lefebvre, who studied modeling in plastics with him and Howard Strain, a student at the University of Nebraska.[90] Conrad acted as manager and foreman at the same time, closely supervising each worker's contribution. His job was to solicit commissions and to communicate with clients, plan the work, and brief the workers. All final decisions regarding model construction were made by him. Work in the shop was strictly regulated, not least due the tight deadlines and concerns for utmost accuracy. Conrad used time cards to keep a detailed overview of each worker's contribution to individual projects, a practice in use since the growth of architectural offices in the mid-1800s. Every employee was insured through the Workmen's Compensation Act and paid on an hourly rate. Nobody was allowed to use machines without prior training and the use of materials was closely monitored through material slips. The spray room had its own set of rules, including the operation of an exhaust fan to limit the risk of toxic fumes, fires, or explosions. The working hours of the shop were from 9 a.m. to 12 p.m. and 12:30 to 5 p.m., six days per week. If a job needed to be finished, however, working overtime was a frequent requirement.

Because workers were the most expensive part of the business, model makers constantly sought for ways to minimize costs through newer and faster modeling techniques. After the war, work in model workshops was—even for tasks involving handcraft—industrialized, meaning that workers often performed only one or related serial tasks that they specialized in. This meant that the same employee often worked on different projects simultaneously. For instance, in Conrad's shop, Katherine Minissale took the lead on making trees and plants, working on such diverse models as the Air Force Academy, the John F. Kennedy Memorial, the Ford Foundation Building, and the Chase Manhattan Bank.[91] Constructing trees was a craft based on manual labor. For model buildings, however, as soon as a piece was needed more than six times, it was more economical to produce it with the help of machines, with specially devised mechanical presses, molds, or power tools. The large amount of electrically powered equipment in Conrad's shop was the basis for achieving not only a high degree of accuracy but also for fabricating identical parts in large quantities. Initially, molding and casting was done in-house for various scales of cars, furniture, people, screens, planters, and other pieces. This was a job performed by all workers whenever they had time on their hands. In the 1930s, Conrad's workshop sold handmade and cast pieces such as trees and molds. As the demand for pieces and the workload of the shop rose in the 1950s, Conrad outsourced molding to one of the many companies specializing in miniature reproductions such as the Diorama Studios on West 4th Street in Manhattan or the Microfoam Corporation in Sudbury, Massachusetts. These companies molded pieces to the model maker's design or offered molds to share from other modelers.[92] Industrialization in model making thus meant three separate developments: the division of labor among the craftsmen in the shop; the serialization of repetitive tasks; and the electrification of many of the processes involved in making identical pieces. However, the prefabrication and mechanization never eliminated handwork itself (Figure 1.12). Even though industrialization led to a division of labor that separated individual model makers and their tasks within the workshop and the outsourcing of labor-intensive work to independent companies, postwar model making remained highly dependent on teamwork in assembling the finished model (Figure 1.13).

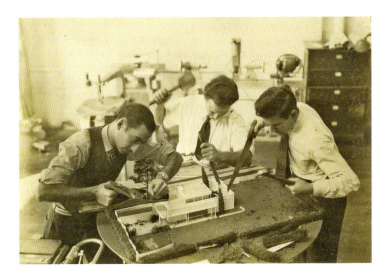

FIGURE 1.12 Self-portrait of Conrad's employees with hand tools. Copyright © Doris Conrad Brown, Theodore Conrad papers, 1937–91, Avery Architectural and Fine Arts Library, Columbia University.

FIGURE 1.13 Conrad and his employees assembling the ground floor of a large model. Copyright © Doris Conrad Brown, Theodore Conrad papers, 1937–91, Avery Architectural and Fine Arts Library, Columbia University.

Competition, Collaboration, and Co-authors

With the introduction of Conrad's apprenticeship program in the 1950s and the establishment of large-scale electrified workshops, the formerly self-taught nature of the architectural model maker officially made way for a new independent profession that taught exclusive skills.[93] After the Depression and the war, some prewar model makers like Conrad had managed to consolidate their businesses whereas others went back to their initial professions: Joseph Messineo, for example, returned to working as an architect in Florida. This did not lead to a stagnation in modeling businesses. On the contrary, they soon multiplied impressively. In her 1958 report, Jane Jacobs counted some two dozen studios that were set up after the war in addition to the thirty-odd existing modelers. Competition for commissions was fierce. Much about these new businesses is still unknown as (with a few notable exceptions) archival sources remain scarce. The same age as Conrad, Raymond Lester had started out making ship and railway models as an artist. He began working for Norman Bel Geddes for the *Futurama* in 1939 and founded his own firm Lester Associates Inc. in Mount Vernon, New York, some time before 1947.[94] Like Conrad, he built military models and prototypes.

Most of his postwar models were made from Plexiglas, including an illuminated model of the Robert Moses Dam at the St. Lawrence River (c. 1954–8) and an eight-foot model of St. Lawrence Valley. In 1960, he received the commission for his *magnum opus*, the 9,000-square foot *Panorama* model of the five boroughs of New York. Inspired by the *Futurama*, the $680,000 model celebrated Moses' lifetime achievement at the 1964 New York World's Fair.[95] Seventy-five employees worked on the 1/100"=1'-0" scale model over three years. His second large coup was a twelve-foot presentation model of the United Nations Building, presented to diplomats at the site of the New York World's Fair in 1947 by Wallace Harrison. Another competitor was the Devon Dennett, a furniture maker from Queens. Dennett had learned furniture making from his mother, the known suffragist and designer Mary Ware Dennett.[96] After the war, he shifted his focus to model making and operated a small shop with three employees and a relatively modest number of thirty machines. His work included an engineering model for the Pan Am Air Terminal by Tippetts, Abbett, McCarthy, and Stratton (Figure 1.14).[97] Like Conrad, Dennett was involved in making models for magazines such as *Ladies' Home Journal* and some of his models were exhibited at the MoMA.

In the late 1940s, Conrad had an exceptional advantage over the many model makers of his generation who were returning from military service. He still operated a fully equipped workshop and was prepared for commissions that started pouring in soon after the end of the war. However, new competition in form of a younger generation of modelers, born in the 1920s and 1930s, started to open workshops. Norman Briskman, who later refurbished Lester's *Panorama* model, opened his studio in 1955 in Monroe Township, New Jersey. Architect Thomas Salmon ran a four-man landscape architecture, graphic design and model making business in Manhattan together with his wife, making models of Wallace Harrison's Time Life Building, the Metropolitan Opera, and the National Zoo in Washington, D.C. (Figure 1.15).[98] Among this younger generation was also Conrad's former student Joseph Santeramo, who became the head of the in-house modeling studio at Johnson & Burgee's office where he worked on the New York AT&T building and the Crystal Cathedral in Anaheim. Another former student, George Gabriel, was hired by I.M. Pei & Partners in 1956 where he established a new model shop that employed up to thirty-five workers.[99] Almost thirty years later, in 1984, Gabriel opened an independent workshop that built a model for the Atlantic City Convention Center and Rail Terminal for Wallace Roberts & Todd. Santeramo and

FIGURE 1.14 Devon Dennett with a model of the Pan American air terminal. No copyright holder known but see Jacobs, Jane. "The Miniature Boom. A Growing Demand for Precision Models Has Propelled the Architectural Modelmaker into the Machine Age." *The Architectural Forum*, May 1958, 106–11, 196.

FIGURE 1.15 Landscape architect and model maker Thomas Salmon using an electrical saw. No copyright holder known but see Jacobs, Jane. "The Miniature Boom. A Growing Demand for Precision Models Has Propelled the Architectural Modelmaker into the Machine Age." *The Architectural Forum*, May 1958, 106–11, 196.

Gabriel were part of a movement in the 1950s and 1960s that drew on practices that had been common in the 1920s: in-house model makers employed by architectural offices. When asked in the "1950 Survey" to classify their employees in nine groups, architectural offices did not mention model makers as they were largely outsourced.[100] A few years later, pioneers in the industry such as SOM, Ludwig Mies van der Rohe, or Eero Saarinen reintroduced modeling to their offices: Mies' model makers included young architects Peter Pran and Edward Duckett, who built design and presentation models; Eero Saarinen employed in-house model maker James Robert Smith and photographer Balthazar Korab; and SOM employed model makers under Harold Gilstein and Richard Hopper in the country's first studio that owned a laser cutter.[101] This was a critical development for the likes of Conrad as the installation of in-house modeling services added to the tough competition. For architectural offices, the installation of model shops meant a considerable investment in tools and labor that saved them the cost of an external modeler and gave them more control over their output. However, the demand for highly detailed presentation models still supplied external shops with work as they had the workers and a greater capacity to meet tight deadlines. It was especially the cutting and bending of Plexiglas that remained the independent modeler's terrain, as machines were economically feasible only if used regularly.

Unlike modeling, model photography never became as separated from traditional photography even though it required a hybrid knowledge of architecture, modeling, and photography alike. Early pioneers were architects, particularly Harvey Wiley Corbett, who were supported by professional commercial photographers such as the New York-based Brown Brothers. As model making became more important, a small number of photographers began to specialize in model photography and photographic realism that was highly dependent on flawless models. Collaborations between photographers and model makers grew to be exceptionally close. Architects often had a preferred photographer for their finished buildings. However, when it came to model photos they often took advantage of established partnerships between modelers and photographers. Conrad worked with numerous photographers over the course of his career. Three of them were especially important inventors in the history of model photography in the United States and as regards Conrad's work: Louis Checkman from Jersey City; Ezra Stoller from New York; and the photo agency Hedrich Blessing from Chicago. Possibly the premier model photographer in the United States, Louis Checkman's extraordinarily close working relationship with Conrad stands out among all these collaborations not just because Checkman's studio was located across the street from Conrad's Ogden Avenue workshop but also because he shared a "stamp" with Conrad, suggesting an even closer, in-house working arrangement. Checkman and his brother Harry, an engineer, had started making models together with Conrad in the 1930s. Entering the professional world around the same time as Conrad, Checkman was a graduate of the New York School of Modern Photography and started out as a commercial photographer in 1930.[102] He worked for architects and magazines. In 1936, he began to work as a freelance model photographer for Conrad.[103] Initially, Conrad and Checkman took workshop photos for their personal use. But as Checkman began taking presentation photos for architects and clients in the 1930s, he also documented Conrad's work as a model maker. During the war, Checkman spent his time in the Air Force, attending photography school at Lowry Field Air Force Base in Denver, Colorado, and operating a photo lab at Fort Myers airbase in Florida.[104] After he was demobbed, his services were much in demand. Working with a 4x5 negative Sinar view camera and 35mm film for slides, Checkman took photos for both design and presentation (Figures 1.16–1.17). Even

FIGURE 1.16 Checkman with view camera. Copyright © Wayne Checkman, Louis Checkman negatives, photographs, and papers, 1955–92, Avery Architectural and Fine Arts Library, Columbia University.

FIGURE 1.17 Checkman photographing a high-rise model after the war. Copyright © Wayne Checkman, Louis Checkman negatives, photographs and papers, 1955–92, Avery Architectural and Fine Arts Library, Columbia University.

though his work was closely linked to Conrad's models, he was engaged by other model makers such as Norman Briskman and by in-house modeling shops in architectural offices. Arguably the biggest success of his career was a photo of the Brussels Pavilion model that was used for a US stamp in 1958 (Figure 1.18). As a model photographer, his trademark were photorealistic images that were almost indistinguishable from photos of the actual building. If the model was not photographed at Conrad's shop, Checkman would bring his equipment, tripods, and lights to the architect's office including the "sky," a large blue fabric roll with airbrushed clouds, and additional model cars and people for the foreground.

Though Checkman's photos were cheaper, important model commissions for one of Conrad's biggest clients, SOM, were handled exclusively by photographer Ezra Stoller as SOM's chief designer Gordon Bunshaft preferred to work with both Conrad and Stoller. Like Checkman, Stoller was not just an architectural photographer and also did portraits as well as industrial and commercial photography. He had studied architecture at New York University with Edward Durell Stone but dropped out before finishing his undergraduate degree.[105] School proved to be a fruitful undertaking nevertheless, as he began to photograph other students' models and artworks with a Linhof camera. After leaving school, Stoller established an independent studio working for magazines and print media, especially *Fortune* and the *Architectural Forum*. Like Checkman, Stoller worked with a view camera for his model photos. Though he preferred working in his own studio he also took commissions at architect's offices or Conrad's studio. Other than Checkman, Stoller rarely photographed a model more than once as he usually handled only finished presentation models. This is of great significance as he was often hired

FIGURE 1.18 Checkman's photo of Conrad's model for the American Pavilion at the Brussels Expo 1958 on a three-cent stamp. Copyright © Doris Conrad Brown, Theodore Conrad papers, 1937–91, Avery Architectural and Fine Arts Library, Columbia University.

to photograph the finished building about one or two years later and the similarities of views of the model and of the actual building demonstrate Stoller's extraordinary competence in anticipating a building's appearance. For his architectural photography, he studied the site closely, in the early years even spending full days watching the light change and picking the right angles and perspectives. Stoller depicted models the same way he would photograph the building with objects in the foreground as a reference for scale and to frame for the image. Conrad's third important model photo collaboration was with the photo agency Hedrich Blessing, which was founded in 1929 and focused largely on architectural photography. Based in Chicago, the family business started out photographing the *Century of Progress* exhibition in that city in 1933 including the models of the Fair. Ken Hedrich, founder and first principal photographer, had learned commercial photography in the studio of Wesley Bowman.[106] Covering many of the new building projects in Chicago and the Midwest as the official photographers of the *Architectural Forum*, they took such famous images as that of Mies van der Rohe holding his model of the Crown Hall. They also worked intensively with local clients such as SOM's Chicago headquarters. Like other photographers, the firm used color film only sparsely. After the war, however, they pioneered its use and it became their principal medium. More important for models, the firm provided specialized composite model photos taken by their staff photographer, Bob Harr.[107] In their collaboration with Conrad, Hedrich Blessing was often engaged for projects in the Midwest if the travel budget did not allow for sending a photographer from New York.

As part of their collaboration, architects usually gave model makers and photographers instructions as to which views they wanted. That said, the photographer was often free to find views of his own that suited both design and image. Similar to practices within the model workshop, the creation of model photos was based on teamwork for which Conrad once went as far as dismantling his studio in order to cater to the needs of an unnamed photographer:

> His job necessitates him to meet people from all walks and dispositions of life—including, on one occasion [sic], a temperamental photographer from a national magazine who insisted that a hole be bored through the roof of the plant so he could obtain a 'down shot' for a photo of a model. After we drilled the hole, he found too much sunlight was coming through, so we had to build a little wooden house on the roof for a shade. The photographer, who was at the studio for six months to take 24 pictures, was finally fired when he demanded his company send him a recording machine so he could play Anton Bruckner's 9th Symphony to fit his mood while he worked.[108]

Model photography relied heavily on the model maker's skills as the large models needed to be disassembled for various views (Figure 1.19). Yet, as architects wanted increasing coverage of their work in printed media, the photographer's fame quickly surpassed the modeler's. Conrad explained the sense of rivalry clearly felt by model makers: "And when you can't tell the model from the real thing [. . .] it's always the photographer who gets the credit, and not the modelmaker."[109]

Model Making and the Architect

No formal school existed when the first generation of professional architectural model makers and photographers went into business. Instead, Conrad and his colleagues studied publications geared toward other niche branches of modeling, such as airplane or ship miniatures, from which they transferred relevant techniques. To keep up to date, shop owners often subscribed to industry news and manufacturers' advertisements that presented the newest materials and machines. Model making was a highly inventive business focused more on an open mind toward materials and techniques, based on trial and error, rather than on codified professional practices. Architects themselves became more aware of the potentials of models as their education slowly changed over the course of the 1930s. In the previous decade, there had been a stylistic schism between the dominant Beaux-Arts style and modern architecture that was hotly debated when the entries to the *Chicago Tribune* competition were published in 1922.[110] Another trigger for change was the Depression, when many felt that the Beaux-Arts system was no longer able to equip students for the tasks of the future. E. Raymond Bossange, dean of the College of Fine Arts at New York University, summarized this criticism in 1933 when he demanded the introduction of new building methods and materials, further specialization of architects in fields such as interior

FIGURE 1.19 Conrad (left) disassembling a model in his studio together with photographer Eric Schaal (center). Copyright © Doris Conrad Brown, Theodore Conrad papers, 1937–91, Avery Architectural and Fine Arts Library, Columbia University.

design or building types, and a more diverse range of media in design: "Pencil, pen, and charcoal drawing, water color, oils and other color media, modeling, and, in addition, materials such as wood, metal, and glass may be used in creating compositions and designs."[111] This was an attack on the Beaux-Arts system with its focus on drawing. Modeling, by and large, had not been a part of any curriculum in the 1920s. It was only slowly introduced in the 1930s when European immigrants from schools such as the Bauhaus came to the United States, bringing with them similar ideas of new materials and methods. Among those introducing modeling courses were the architecture schools of Columbia University, MIT, and Syracuse University respectively, using low-tech practices in cardboard, wood, and plaster. New York University engaged the Austrian Eugene Steinhof to develop a new course based on the Bauhaus' *Vorkurs*. His advice was to use clay and plaster models to teach students a sense of space. But the most radical break with tradition in New York came under the brief stint of Joseph F. Hudnut as dean of the architecture school at Columbia University. Hudnut wanted to create more realistic courses that related to the actual needs of the building industry and society at large. Columbia had been one of the first institutions to start using models as early as 1921 under William Alciphron Boring, who had published a plea for model making in 1922 when he demanded that students should learn two different kinds of modeling: whole house models and details. Details, such as a cornice, were to be made at full-scale and placed in their real location to be studied from the street level.[112] Not surprisingly, Columbia employed Harvey Wiley Corbett and Wallace Harrison as studio critics under Boring's successor, Hudnut. Outside of New York, at the University of Michigan, Eliel Saarinen had started using models with his students that served as photo models in the mid-1920s.[113] Likewise, at the University of Southern California, dean Arthur Clason Weatherhead introduced models in 1930 with a heavy emphasis on three-dimensional visualization.[114] Over the course of the 1930s, changes were slowly implemented by other schools, in some cases after students complained about the dominance of two-dimensional work.[115] By the end of the Thirties, Kenneth Reid, long-time editor of the popular magazine *Pencil Points*, reported that schools were equipping themselves with model making facilities: "Interest among architects in studying their designs in three dimensions, by means of scale models, has grown so in the last few years that many architectural schools now include training in model making as a part of their curricula."[116]

By the 1950s, universities had become the predominant mode of education for architects with large numbers of students pouring in through the funding of the G. I. Bill. Architecture schools started to update their programs to accommodate the student masses by revising their courses, discarding the remnants of Beaux-Arts education and introducing shorter, four-year programs. More advanced and electrified workshops were installed. In 1948, Columbia University contacted Conrad for a tour of his workshop and advice on the purchase of model making tools.[117] As a visiting critic, he reviewed student work and held model making demonstrations. One of the most significant examples of the new embrace of modeling was the Illinois Institute of Technology, where Ludwig Mies van der Rohe had become the head of the architecture school in 1938. Mies was highly influential in introducing the use of models for design problems as Myron Goldsmith remembered: "Even the way of working with models has come out of Mies' way of teaching, where you work on a building with models as a primary way of working rather than sketching and drawing."[118] The model had come to stay in the architects' education.

In addition to the growing interest in modeling in architectural education, there was a wide range of literature available for hobby modelers and the growing architecture student audience. Before the war, English-language modeling books were almost exclusively published in Britain. Some early examples were *Pictorial House Modelling* by model and toy maker Edward W. Hobbs (1926) and *Models of Buildings: How to Make and Use Them* by architect William Harvey (1927). Shorter texts appeared in American architectural magazines such as the *Architectural Forum*, *Pencil Points*, *American Architect,* or *Western Architect* since at least the 1910s. Most of these were geared toward a hobbyist audience and to architects who were open to experimenting with new visual media. In 1945, the British model maker Peter Raymond Wickham published one of the first manuals addressed to aspiring professionals and to "those who may be considering the possibilities of model making, as a postwar career. [Because] in an age of increasing building, engineering and scientific activity, the model maker's work cannot but be needed."[119] As architecture schools began to embrace modeling, many others seemed to believe in Wickham's prediction of a postwar revival of modeling and similar publications soon flooded the amateur modeler's niche market with titles such as *Model Making as a Career* and *The Modern Architectural Model*.[120] The first book about architectural modeling published after the war in the US was Robert Forman's *Make it Yourself: Architectural Models* (1946). Most of these publications still presented prewar techniques and materials such as Thomas Bayley's *Model Making in Cardboard* (1958). One exception, Hendrick's 1957 book *The Modern Architectural Model*, discussed metals and Plexiglas in great detail, more than twenty years after their introduction into commercial modeling. Rather than being consumed by professional model makers—by then their craft-based knowledge was passed on largely through apprenticeships—these publications testify to the increased, widespread interest in modeling from students and architects who used models themselves or engaged the services of professional modelers. Starting in the 1950s, the manuals, like architecture itself, became more international in their scope and even though many were published in Britain or, as in the case of Rolf Janke's widely disseminated student manual *Architectural Models*, in Germany, they frequently used examples made by American professionals.[121]

As architects were increasingly well educated in model making and used models for design purposes, the model maker's importance within the professional network grew. When he set up his model shop in the 1930s, Conrad's first clients were a handful of architects who were connected through personal and professional ties. Harvey Wiley Corbett and Wallace Harrison had been partners since 1927. When Harrison opened his own office, Edward Durell Stone was one of his first employees. Gordon Bunshaft, in turn, started working for Stone in 1937 and it was Stone who gave Bunshaft a recommendation to work for Louis Skidmore around the time the New York office of Skidmore, Owings & Moss opened.[122] Other clients such as Philip Goodwin were early benefactors to Conrad's studio and stayed with him through difficult professional and economic times. Conrad's renown and professional network fanned out with his models for the New York World's Fair and for national magazines in the 1940s bringing in new commissions. In the 1950s, Conrad no longer depended on personal acquaintances. If, before the war, his work was mainly for local New York architects, his services were now requested on a wider geographic level. As architects' work became increasingly international, Conrad started working on projects outside of the United States. At the height of his career, he was building models for such diverse architects as A. James Speyer, C. F. Murphy Associates, SOM, Bernard Rudofsky, Gregory Ain, Louis Kahn and Ann Tyng, R.H. Schickmann and Marcel Breuer, William B. Tabler, Ludwig Mies van der Rohe, Philip Johnson, Raymond & Rado, Minoru Yamasaki, Roche–Dinkeloo, John Carl Warnecke and Hellmuth, Obata + Kassabaum. Aside from the big names, Conrad worked for many smaller firms as well as large-scale developers such as Kahn & Jacobs and William Zeckendorf.

Many of Conrad's long-term clients—such as Wallace Harrison, Edward Durell Stone, and Gordon Bunshaft—were of a generation that, like him, had grown up in the Beaux-Arts system and had traveled to Europe. At the helm of progressive companies, these architects favored the collective sense of teamwork, expertise, and the shared value system of Modernism which had become mainstream by the Fifties rather than the constant competition of decades prior. After the war, their offices received the majority of commissions from the US government and American corporations for headquarters and representative office buildings. In some cases, they established relationships that lasted for decades as in the case of SOM and the H. J. Heinz Company, forming a self-perpetuating network of commissions. In the 1950s, there were several centers of intense building activity in the United States. In the metropolitan areas of Pittsburgh, Chicago, and New York, for example, companies commissioned extensive redesigns for high-rise offices and plants. Equally important, the move to the suburbs kicked off an opposing movement toward low-rise sprawling office campuses that required extensive planning. Each of the architectural firms that Conrad collaborated with followed different design and presentation strategies using models to varying degrees of detail. For model making, elaborate presentation models were a greater challenge than early study or block models as the refined façades of the 1950s often needed to be specially fabricated. Presentations became increasingly important as of the 1930s, when architects became aware of the importance of publicity. Similarly, even though models meant high costs, architects were often willing to pay out of pocket because they could not consider an important presentation without them. As a model could now decide whether or not a design was accepted by the client, architects relied increasingly on model makers and their skills. As with the collaboration between model maker and photographer, this necessitated a close collaboration. Two architects stand out as the most important, innovative, and productive among the long list of Conrad's clients who commissioned many of his finest works: Edward Durell Stone; and Gordon Bunshaft of SOM's New York branch. Upon entering Stone's office at 7 East 67th Street, the first thing a client saw was a large Conrad model set up as the centerpiece in the lobby, the North Carolina State Capitol Building and, in later years, the fifteen-foot-long Kennedy Center.[123] Stone used Conrad's models primarily for meetings with clients but did on occasion work with design models. Having built models as a child in Arkansas, Stone's first professional experience was in 1930 in the same office as Conrad, in Harvey Wiley Corbett's studio.[124] After leaving Corbett, Stone worked as a draftsman for Wallace Harrison on the Rockefeller Center designs, where one of his first major contributions was for the Radio City Music Hall. Here, Stone began to use models as a technical device for experimenting with interior designs and to determine the shape of the iconic golden arches (Figure 1.20).

FIGURE 1.20 Designers standing inside the large-scale model of the Radio City Music Hall auditorium, c. 1931. Copyright © 2020 Rockefeller Group Inc./Rockefeller Center Archives.

ARCHITECTURAL MODEL MAKING AS A PROFESSION

From the outset, Stone collaborated closely with the architectural sculptor Rene Paul Chambellan to study the design of the main auditorium with the help of several models:

From a smaller quarter-inch scale clay model in which we adjusted all curves visually, drawings were made and a second quarter-inch scale was made to check our measurements. From this, a one-inch scale model, a large room some twelve feet square, was constructed. This model was made in the studio of Rene Chambellan and it was our custom to go to his shop and lie on our backs while he corrected the curves to our satisfaction. We determined the location of the radiating organ grilles by pasting on pieces of paper until they looked correct.[125]

After he founded his own office in 1936, Stone hired the young designer Gordon Bunshaft as one of his first employees and they began to work intensively with Conrad.[126] In the early days, Stone's office built private houses such as the Mandel and *Collier's* Houses for which Conrad made the models. When Bunshaft entered the office, he was working on the design for MoMA that Stone designed as the modernist junior partner of the museum's trustee and architect, Philip Goodwin. Bunshaft did not stay long enough to see Conrad's model but it must have been there that he first became aware of his work. Stone, an avid self-publicist and friend of Howard Myers and Henry Luce, the former and current owners of the *Architectural Forum* at that time, needed model photos not just for his clients but to promote his services in printed media. After returning from his forced sabbatical in the Air Force Planning and Design Section during the war, he reopened his office first in Great Neck, New York, before moving to New York City in 1946. Stone's designs were, in a true modernist fashion, first developed as floor plans and later elevations. For his meetings with clients, however, he relied increasingly on more elaborate renderings and models. For an important project, Conrad would come into the office early in the design process to discuss the project. Usually, he would make a small model to get the project approval from the client. Then, he would build a larger model of a more refined design. Sometimes, Stone's office also used simple massing models for the design stage that were built by the architects from balsa wood. On occasion, Conrad was employed to make more elaborate design studies of elevations and three-dimensional effects.[127] The most intense example of a collaboration between Stone's and Conrad's studio was the design for Huntington Hartford's Gallery of Modern Art in New York, at Columbus Circle. Similar to his work on the Radio City Music Hall, a model was the basis of the design due to the building's irregular shape. Stone had worked on the project during a summer vacation in Italy in 1958. Upon his return, he changed the exterior several times with the help of models: The ground floor arches were studied with half-size mock-ups; the front elevation—initially including windows, flags, and a small balcony—was reviewed in a large 1/4"=1'-0" scale model that was constantly updated, photographed, and sent back to Conrad's shop to test different ideas. The model had interior lighting for evening studies and different tops from the eighth floor upward to test the arcades and the design of the restaurant, eventually reaching a $60.000 bill for the model—an enormous sum in 1959.[128] The collaboration also included the photographer Louis Checkman, who took photos of the model's different stages over several months. These would have an important influence on the design of the exterior: "There was, however, one major alteration which we all felt to be beneficial. Originally, the building had a strip of small, square windows at each corner, running full height. When EDS saw the model photographs, he immediately declared that the dark windows—in daylight windows always appear dark from the exterior—were far too much in contrast with the white marble sheathing and must somehow be softened."[129] Since they started collaborating in the early 1930s, Conrad became Stone's favored model maker for more than four decades.[130] Stone's former employee Ernest Jacks went even further and called Conrad an unofficial part of Stone's team (Figure 1.21). Like many others, Stone not only sent his employees to Conrad's shop in Jersey City, but also went himself to inspect models and discuss further assignments. However, the relationship was not always cordial due to frequent disputes over deadlines and fair payment, as Ernest Jacks remembered: "Once, after I had left the office, Mr. Stone wrote to me, 'Conrad arrived as usual breathless and two hours later. He ages me.'"[131] In what was much more of a problem for Conrad, Stone—like many other architectural offices in the mid-1960s—began to make smaller models in-house and to delegate only presentation models to professional modelers.

Models do not seem to have been on the mind of Conrad's second important client, the two founding partners of SOM, Louis Skidmore and Nathaniel Owings, when they started their small office in Chicago in 1936. When Gordon Bunshaft joined their New York branch a year later, one of his first assignments was the Wonder Bread Bakery Pavilion for the 1939 New York World's Fair for which he proposed to build a small study model. Seeing Bunshaft work on the clay model, Skidmore reportedly said "that's not necessary," but was overruled quickly when the client requested a model.[132] It was soon to be followed by large quantities of refined study and presentation models that were increasingly outsourced. Between 1937 and 1938, architect and model maker Walter Severinghaus came into the office at night and worked together with the architects on cardboard presentation models for the World's Fair Board of Design.[133] Picking up this strategy, SOM subsequently disposed of extensive sketches and turned to working with models to develop their designs. After the war, SOM specialized in commercial architecture, mainly inner-city high-rises, suburban low-rise office buildings and manufacturing plants. Their corporate clients were financially equipped to go through extensive planning processes that often included large numbers of models. As many of these companies were governed by boards

FIGURE 1.21 Celebration at Edward Durell Stone's office on the occasion of the publication of his biography in 1962. Conrad can be seen far right. Copyright © Wayne Checkman Special Collections, University of Arkansas Libraries, Edward Durell Stone collection.

of directors, models were frequently used for prolonged presentations and decision-making processes. After his military service, Bunshaft became the most influential designer in the New York office. He was highly critical of the architect's primary tool, the drawing, stating that "architectural drawings are not architecture. They show direction, but not really how the building will be."[134] Even though a model, equally, was not architecture and "the only way to judge architecture is to see the finished building," models and especially model photos must have seemed much closer to reality than a drawing or perspective. As Conrad built almost all models for SOM's New York office, this put him in a powerful position. The design process usually began with a step called "programming," which meant studying the client's needs with the help of elaborate questionnaires. Other than in Stone's or Eero Saarinen's office, the architects did not build study models themselves and there was no model shop at the office. To communicate their designs the architects made model drawings that were sent to Conrad's shop.[135] Close collaboration was necessary to update him constantly on changes. A much larger office than Stone's studio, at SOM every project was led by two senior members: a managing partner and a designing partner. As a collective, SOM followed the traditional route in architecture toward separate specialists to the extreme by encouraging their employees to become specialists in all fields of the building industry. Even though the Chicago and New York offices worked separately—the Chicago office worked intensively with a model maker called Bill Chaffee—exceptions were made for important commissions. Gordon Bunshaft had become the major in-house critic for the Chicago office commenting on such projects as the Inland Steel Building and the Air Force Academy.[136] Serving as the link between the offices, he connected Conrad with SOM's Chicago office. For the Air Force Academy, the Chicago office ordered a model from Jersey City, because as Roger Radford remembered: "at that time, the best model maker was in Jersey City; and he was a model maker whom we used for all our models."[137] Often, several photographers took pictures of the same model depending on its location and whether new photos were needed after the model had been changed. The three major model photographers Stoller, Checkman and Hedrich-Blessing all worked with SOM. Stoller, Bunshaft's preferred photographer, worked mainly with presentation models and took images of all Bunshaft's projects as well as important commissions in Chicago and on the West Coast. Checkman and Hedrich Blessing received more local commissions.

Conrad was often recommended by word of mouth or through displays of his models. Pei & Cobb reportedly commissioned a presentation model of their Mile High Tower in Denver, Colorado, because their developer had seen Conrad's model of Kahn & Jacobs' 100 Park Avenue building displayed in a store window on Madison Avenue.[138] By the early 1950s, Conrad was solidly established as the maker of models for important commissions in the New York metropolitan area. Initially serving a niche in the construction of models for International Style buildings, his reputation exceeded that of many others to such an extent that at times he had to decline business. An assessment of the model makers in the New York area prepared by Leland King for Norman Bel Geddes' office in 1955 reads for Conrad: "Conrad generally is regarded the best model maker in the New York area. [. . .] Conrad's work has extraordinarily fine finish and attention to detail."[139]

Until long after World War II, the American Institute of Architects (AIA) kept its ban on advertising for architects. For model makers, no such rule applied and many businesses sent out letters advertising their capabilities and soliciting work from architects. Architects often invited bids from more than one studio and it was not uncommon that several modelers worked on different models of the same project. For instance, for their Mile High Center, Pei & Cobb employed two New York-based modelers, Thomas Salmon and Conrad, as well as architect Charles Sick of Denver to make models.[140] Salmon constructed a small urban planning model and Conrad built a highly refined 1/8"=1'-0" scale presentation model that traveled extensively throughout the 1950s. A few months after Conrad's model was finished, Sick was chosen to build an even larger 3/16"=1'-0" scale model that was used to promote the building locally. In most cases architects asked for a model maker's bid based on preliminary drawings that were later revised—often dramatically. As detailed presentation models took several weeks to build, it was often necessary to begin construction when a design was still unfinished to have them ready in time for the presentation. Conrad usually went to the architect's office for an initial meeting, to review the drawings and present his ideas on how to build the model. If an agreement was reached, a timeframe and price were set and work commenced as soon as the model drawings were finished. The discrepancy of what could be defined as "working drawings" and what modelers actually needed to be able to build the model often diverged greatly. Architect Ivan Harbour put it very bluntly: "You have to understand a garbled set of instructions and a rather grotty set of sketches [. . .] Also, you have to input on those. You have to come back and say, 'Well, this isn't very good, is it?' That's the real skill."[141] This lack of reliable information often forced model makers to question problematic or unresolved parts. Conrad was well aware of the problem: "How often have I heard rumblings from the shop 'What a lousy set of drawings' only to hear a designer say, 'send over any old thing, Conrad will have to figure something out in order to build the model.'"[142] The problems in communicating designs often forced model makers to pause their work or to proceed without clear information on parts of a design causing serious delays in their delivery and a rapid increase in price. Some, like Conrad seized the opportunity to include their own, often unsolicited, ideas. To ensure that their plans were carried out faithfully, to meet deadlines and to communicate design changes some architects resorted to installing an employee at the model shop who often helped build the model if time demanded.[143] Others, like the sculptor Isamu Noguchi, even stayed at Conrad's Jersey City home to work and collaborate more directly. Beyond hijacking an architect's design, modelers had other, subtle ways of inscribing their signature onto the models: Conrad's work can largely be ascribed to him based on universal solutions he developed for details, the most palpable of which was his design for the walnut bases and Plexiglas covers that were used on all his models. Although less obvious, his plants, precast figurines, landscaping, and roads can also be clearly distinguished. However, the ingenuity of solutions pertaining to the construction of the model rather than the building was the modeler's real achievement, making them authors in their own right, as journalist Gene Flinn pointed out: "Ted lists the task of shaping hundreds of splints of wood into the picket fences among his most tedious jobs. He points out that oftimes seemingly insignificant details, such as the perforations around a miniature garbage can require much time and expense."[144] The rivalry between architect and model maker, even more so than the one between photographer and model maker often involved payment: "On a 78 million dollar project a famous architect has told his client we are not entitled to extras for changes because he feels he has made 'concessions' in simplifying the design. The changes were made a day before we finished the model. I suppose the client feels he should pay for the change himself. Compared to his fee our bill is peanuts."[145] On a deeper level, however, the conflict touched upon Vasari's centuries-old warning against admiring the hand of the model maker. Architects who were traditionally portrayed in images as holding their drawing

FIGURE 1.22 Changed representation of the architectural profession: the architect hands a model to his clients. No copyright holder known but see Burton, Ashford Bugbee. "Paying Plan." *Collier's*, September 18, 1937, 52.

and measuring instruments or reviewing their drawings, now began to be adorned with the outcome of another profession's labor: the model (Figure 1.22).

As they were in a more powerful position through their immediate association with clients and printed media, architects incorporated the model into their self-expression which influenced the public reaction to the model maker. Possibly the most prominent case of a client's depreciation were Conrad's thirty design models for John Carl Warnecke's John F. Kennedy Memorial in Washington, D.C., for which Jackie Kennedy only paid a $7,000 bill after Isamu Noguchi leaked the information to the press and an article appeared in the *New York Times*.[146] By installing modeling studios in their offices in the 1950s and 1960s, architects tried to regain control over the model, demoting the modeler to their employee. At the same time, they confirmed their reliance on the model maker as an integral part of their practice. On a grander scale, the modeler's importance was recognized by the American Institute of Architects when they awarded Conrad the AIA Craftsmanship Medal for his lifetime achievement with architectural models and his creative collaboration in architecture in 1962. Conrad retired in 1982 but kept his shop open until his death in 1994. From the 1970s onward his services were still sought after, albeit on a smaller scale. There were several reasons that led to a decline in model making that were directly linked to the architectural network. The oil crises of the 1970s caused a severe slump in construction that affected architects and all other connected professions. On a more personal level, the height of the postwar boom was closely tied to the generation of architectural professionals who had grown up in the first half of the century and experienced the peak of their careers in the 1950s and 1960s. By the late 1960s, the father figures of the modern movement had all died: Le Corbusier in 1965, Ludwig Mies van der Rohe and Walter Gropius in 1969. Many of Conrad's close professional relationships were coming to an end a decade later as Edward Durell Stone died in 1978, Wallace Harrison three years later, and Gordon Bunshaft retired in the 1980s. International Style architecture, and with it intricate models of glass façades had become increasingly criticized by a

FIGURE 1.23 Stanley Tigerman, Crown Hall model depicted as the Titanic, photo montage, 1978. Copyright © Tigerman McCurry Architects.

younger generation of architects who accused Modernism as a whole for many of the cities' postwar planning failures. Stanley Tigerman's interpretation of Mies' Crown Hall model as the sinking Titanic thus expressed not only a common sentiment regarding Modernism, but its models, too (Figure 1.23). The tight architectural network of Modernism was disappearing because the success of the objects it produced led to a mental fatigue, a stagnation and saturation of the market of architectural ideas. Conrad was well aware of the pitfalls of his success: "I must say, I revolutionized model making so you could see how good a building looked. My complaint now is that the clients look at the model, and nobody studies it, and the architects sell the job, good or bad. I think we've gotten worse architecture along with this wonderful tool."[147]

2

Modeling Materials

Model and Building

Model making is editing. A good model maker is a good editor. By that I mean the good maker must edit thoughtfully. Painstakingly. From occasionally hundreds of drawings, the maker must spot and trim the superfluous, but never ever lose the key kernel, that elusive thing that makes a particular building, however modest, sing.[1]

RICHARD ARMIGER, 2020

Architectural models are unique objects with a history that is separate from their relational dependence on buildings. Yet, for an object to become an *architectural* model, it needs to refer to an existing, built, destroyed, historical, fictional, utopian, or otherwise imagined architecture. This connection is not a one-way street in which the building is the end point. Rather, model and building constantly reference one another, each serving as an original or a representation of the other, depending on the context. In the line of events leading to the construction of a building, a model usually precedes the building and often embodies an architectural idea for the first time in three dimensions. Therefore, the model could be considered an original after which a copy, the building, is made.[2] After a structure is finished, models can turn into alternative or purer versions of the architectural idea and, at times, they remain the only built remnant of a project. As Robert Harbison pointed out, in some instances, models surpass a building's importance as evidenced during the postwar modeling boom when models acted as studies for new building materials or construction methods, becoming small-scale experiments and visions for a new architecture.[3] On the other hand, a model's success is often judged by its ability to represent a building adequately. Building and model are bound together through relations and translations of scale, shape and material. That said, however closely model and building refer to one another, there are fundamental disparities. A model is not built like a building, only smaller, but has its own structural requirements. From the abundance of referential connections, each model edits out only those characteristics that are important for the problem it is meant to solve or represent. Its scale governs its degree of abstraction and detail. Likewise, models' shape and material have a wide range, not least because they are influenced by changing aesthetic norms, material conventions, and individual preferences of architects and model makers. In her book *On Longing*, Susan Stewart described this situation of the model's otherness, even when considered its most popular form, the souvenir, as being similar to islands whose boundaries can never be crossed.[4] Separated from its surroundings through scale, shape, and material, it impossible for the viewer to ever enter the model fully. The first constitutive decision for any model, its scale, refers first and foremost to a relative size binding two objects together—model and building. Traditionally, models were small at the beginning of the twentieth century. Their size and scale have, similar to photographic prints, grown larger over the course of the century, especially during the 1940s and 1950s.[5] Scale directly influences a model's construction and the amount of detail as well as the choice of modeling materials. Not every material can be used at every scale. To retain a truthful relation to the building, utmost accuracy in depicting all parts to scale can go as far as calculating the thickness of a coat of paint.[6] Tom Holert pointed to a key question in the use of scale models when he discussed the Holocaust exhibition at London's Imperial War Museum and one of its main attractions, a large but small-scale model of the Auschwitz concentration camp: which scale and degree of detail are appropriate to bring across a model's message and to avoid minimization or voyeurism?[7] Thus, scale appears, secondly, to be not just a numerical relational measurement between model and building but an aesthetic and contextual category that influences the object's use.[8] Therefore, historical conventions aside, in architecture fixed scales became established for specific kinds of models and their application for design process and presentation.

Architectural models can be categorized according to their function in a project and their physical appearance. Three main types describing models of various of forms are important for this research: working or design models (models "for a building" that are used to study a project and range from simple massing models to highly refined details); presentation or exhibition models (models "of a building" that are generally more refined and made to be presented to a client or audience); and photo models (models that are made solely to be photographed, demanding utmost precision to simulate reality). The former were often built at smaller scales, whereas the latter two grew exponentially larger over the course of the century. All these models can be further categorized: massing models, interior models, illuminated models, and landscape or urban planning models. Each of these categories has a particular place in the progression of a design, but not every category necessarily appears in every project. They mark options rather than steps to follow. For the development of modeling materials, the most important distinction between the above types is the one between design and presentation models as it has a clear connection to the ensuing split of professions within the architectural network. Models that were made during the inception of a scheme are generally less refined, often altered significantly during the design process and of a more fragile nature as low-tech materials lend themselves to depict masses or details quickly. Used to develop ideas or to review decisions, design models were traditionally built by architects, as in the case of Harvey Wiley Corbett, who constructed all-cardboard models in his studio. Presentation and photo models, often including landscaping and props, required a more detailed finish and were built almost exclusively by professional modelers. After the architectural model maker entered the scene in the 1930s, design models, too, were increasingly outsourced particularly due to the material changes in modeling and the growing electrification of workshops. A clear-cut distinction between models for design and presentation proves to be impossible as many models of early stages were also presented to clients or were later turned into exhibition models in museum collections. Likewise, presentation models were often used to reconsider a design.

Modeling materials have a long history. Their expressive characteristics turned into a unique means of expression when the use of models became more widespread and sophisticated in the twentieth century. By the 1920s, several materials had become established: wood, plaster of Paris, and especially cardboard. The radical shift toward the mechanized fabrication of Plexiglas, as well as other plastics and aluminum, that formed the basis for the modeling boom, occurred over the short span of fifteen years, from the mid-1930 to the 1940s. Until recently it has been unclear why the new materials were deemed appropriate for modeling and why they were able to replace all other materials so fundamentally. While the scale and shape of models have received considerably little academic attention in connection with model making, materials and materiality have been viewed largely as regards the historical use and semantics of building materials. The idea that traditional construction materials such as timber have specific characteristics that determine their aesthetic use according to a "truth of material" (*Materialgerechtigkeit*), came out of a nineteenth-century discussion among architects and writers such as Gottfried Semper, John Ruskin, and Adolf Loos.[9] Countering overly decorated historicist architecture and the industrialization of building materials alike, those following the truth of material were against transferring forms from one material onto another. Imitation, the transfer of highly valued into lesser materials, was generally dismissed.[10] Similar reverberations followed predominantly among German philosophers of the Frankfurt School until well into the postwar era, with special regard to synthetic materials.[11] In this context of material aesthetics, the two new modeling materials—Plexiglas and aluminum—are embedded in a long depreciative history of plastics emanating from the 1800s. Synthetic substances such as Bakelite or Ebonite, and bio-derived plastics such as celluloid or vulcanized rubbers, had long been used as inexpensive imitations for more valuable materials such as ivory, tortoiseshell, or mother-of-pearl. They were not used as materials in their own right, though, as a result of the negative connotation of a fundamental lack of definitive qualities and of being malleable without a distinct shape of their own.[12] This negative perception by architects, artists, and the public only changed as of the 1920s with the start of the "Plastic Age," especially in the United States, and the accelerated development of materials in the 1930s.[13] Roland Barthes was one of the first to ideologically clear plastic and to embrace its very lack of a definitive form as its essence.[14] Jean Baudrillard took a similar stance ten years later, in 1968, when he determined that all meaning assigned to materials was simply imposed for ideological reasons.[15] But at that point, plastics and aluminum had long found their way into architecture and model making. For model making, the discussion about materials, aesthetics, and meaning is an important thread because it introduces the term *imitation* that came to play a key role in the development of modeling materials, albeit in a much less ideologically charged way. Model theoretician Albert Smith defined *imitation* as follows: "A representation can be seen as something that stands for something else or it can be seen as an imitation with a change."[16] This *imitation with a change* hints at the complicated relation between model and building, and an emphasis on selected relational aspects between them: massing models highlight the shape and volume of a building; urban planning models show the relation of the building's mass to its surroundings, and presentation models accentuate materials and the exterior of the building. For the latter, the imitation of building materials became a key issue in the twentieth century. Through its close association with the finished building, the presentation model was closely linked to developments in building materials which, since the second half of the nineteenth century, were a driving force behind the development of modern architecture. Most famously, the invention of reinforced concrete and structural steel liberated a building's walls of its load-bearing function and made new, transparent surfaces and open interior arrangements possible—a crucial prerequisite for the International Style architecture from the late 1920s onward. The predilection for glass among the first generation of modernists added another material to the canon of modern building materials. Many of the detailed presentation models attempted to replicate or imitate the new building materials, albeit with different modeling materials, simulating textures, grains, and colors as much as spatial arrangements and masses. Few models have been constructed of a building's actual materials such as Ludwig Mies van der Rohe's model of a glass tower at Berlin's Friedrichstrasse made of glass pieces, or his model for the unbuilt Resor House that used a copper plate for the roof.[17] Difficulties in processing the same material at smaller scales is often the reason to look for substitutes. But another, more fundamental explanation could be seen in the fact that, as Karen Moon pointed out, due to the different scale of model and building "authentic materials can look 'wrong' on a realistic model."[18] From the 1930s onward, it was each material's imitative qualities for imagined building materials that largely determined their use. Some were more successful in imitating modern buildings: Plexiglas represented glass; plaster imitated concrete; aluminum represented steel. Others, such as wood, were limited in their representational qualities due to its grain that could only be used at one scale. Building on this argument, Thomas Raff pointed out that semantic uses of materials often highlight one or a few of a material's qualities while they leave others, that are equally constitutive, aside: glass is only seen as transparent and granite is only seen as hard.[19] To this, Mario Carpo added that it is not a new technical invention, or in this case material, by itself but a strong need for it that ensures its success.[20] It could be assumed then that model makers discovered materials because they were looking for a specific representational quality only to subsequently find others, especially structural merits, that were of use. The drive toward an exact imitation of materials in presentation models and the accurate simulation of a building was strongly linked to a desire for utmost realism in model making, meaning the most life-like representation of a building.[21] Since the 1920s, a model's degree of realism increasingly became one of the major signs of quality, as Edward W. Hobbs wrote: "The ultimate judgment of a model must be based on realism."[22] Tied in with the increasing dependence of architecture and its models on translations into other, two-dimensional media—photography in particular—was a shift during the postwar years in which the lines between model and building became increasingly blurred: "while the models look uncannily lifelike, the real things look uncannily fake."[23] The material qualities of modern architecture, such as transparency and open spaces, were brilliantly represented and anticipated by models, but were increasingly hard to be replicated by the actual buildings that were constrained by the compromising conditions of full-scale construction. Thus, the building itself and architectural photos came to resemble a muddied version of the model's superior representation of materiality.

The quest for perfect imitations during the model's boom years sparked an uncertainty over what constituted an original in architecture: the presentation model's realistic representation of a building or the building's perfect adaptation of what had already been anticipated in the model, and especially the model photos? But even when assuming an overarching importance of the presentation model for the introduction of new materials, the design model retained its central position for the development of architectural ideas not least because it was equally affected by the new materials. The influence which the materials of design models have had on architecture has been acknowledged in previous research.[24] Here, the focal point of the model's materiality was less the imitation of the building's materials than the representation of its mass, shape, volume, and relation to its surroundings. Using the German architect Günter Behnisch's work for the Olympic Park in Munich as an example, Reinhard Wendler showed how his form-finding sand models can still be traced in the shapes of the finished building.[25] Similarly, Barnabas Calder analyzed how Denys Lasdun's work with balsa wood models to develop the wooden imprints in the concrete of the Royal National Theatre in London was able to translate the materials and spatial arrangements still present in the theater adequately.[26] As these examples show, modeling materials influence the final design outcome because they define what is possible to depict. Acknowledging the distinct qualities of materials to depict crucial aspects of the design, Behnisch himself wrote: "Building blocks produce blockish architecture. Clay tends to soft forms, paper and rods produce buildings without accentuated masses etc."[27] Though I do not want to insinuate that a particular material is directly linked to a specific form or shape, as Behnisch does, his argument points to the important fact that not everything can be modeled adequately in every material. Wendler called this the "resistance of the material" or "material pertinacity."[28]

The introduction of materials such as Plexiglas and aluminum added new means of expression, opening up additional representational tasks that previous materials had resisted. They specifically enabled a consideration of aesthetic representations of building materials and fostered structural experimentation at earlier stages during the design process. Rather than being linked to a specific expression of mass or shape, it was the materials' malleability and imitative qualities between transparency and opacity that made them attractive for the design process. Now, one material, Plexiglas, could be used to represent a building's mass and shape, its more detailed relation to the urban context as well as become representative for the building materials in the presentation model later on. For the development of the International Style, which roughly coincided with the postwar boom in architectural modeling, one might ask to what extent the adaptation of these materials for design models influenced the imagination of architects toward a wider application of glass and steel. Here, the modeler's choice of materials can be seen as being of utmost importance in rendering the design model an active artifact that, through the imitative and representational capacities of its materials, influenced the design of the final building because "materials, scoping instruments and new knowledge 'talk back' to the architects, and they are prepared to listen, thus triggering reinterpretations of interim results."[29] Thus, it could be assumed that the design model, through its use of new modeling materials, turned into an original that helped develop the architecture of the International Style.

Material Diversity in the 1920s

> Modelmaking, it appears, is essentially the adaptation of numerous tools and materials to purposes for which they were not originally intended.[30]
>
> ROBERT HOYT, 1939

In 1939, Robert Hoyt was not alone in his belief in the makeshift nature of modeling. Edward Heckler Burdick, president of the Diorama Corporation in Long Island City, would have agreed, mentioning that most of his modeling materials "might be picked up in an average city dumping ground."[31] The inventive nature of model making and the constant quest for more appropriate techniques and materials were the physical expression of the fragmented nature of modeling in the 1920s and 1930s, split between in-house architects turned model makers and external sculptors, carpenters and modelers. Model making skills were handed down through apprenticeships with accomplished masters, many of who favored the use of a particular material. However, without widely disseminated modeling manuals or schools, most of the more advanced solutions and inventions were a mix of general craftsman's skills and conventions for fabricating materials as well as professional secrets specific to each model maker's practice, united only by the use of simple, hand-held tools and relatively cheap materials: "There is no hard and fast rule for the use of a particular material, but the builder should utilise any which is appropriate for the purpose and will yield the desired result. Its choice should be governed by its purpose."[32] Despite the makeshift nature of model making, several standard materials had become established by the 1920s, including clay, plaster, and wood. Cardboard emerged as the most prominent in the United States. Each of them offered slightly different opportunities for reacting to design challenges and they can be divided by the way they were used, either for in-house practices or as part of the architectural network. In the 1920s, the main focus in both design and presentation models—particularly when it came to high-rises in the New York area—was on the exterior appearance of a building's mass, the "building envelope," its façade and its relation to the surroundings. This focus was largely based on the *Building Zone Resolution* adopted by the Board of Estimate and Apportionment of the City of New York in 1916, commonly called the 1916 Zoning Law. Under this regulation, the island of Manhattan was divided into sectors according to usage and height. In each sector, a maximum height for the street wall was introduced, after which "setbacks" were necessary. Unrestricted height was only possible on 25 percent of any given site. Harvey Wiley Corbett was one of the first to take an interest in the effects this regulation had on design. In the April 1923 issue of *Pencil Points* he published a series of images and comments together with architectural delineator Hugh Ferriss on how to apply the Zoning Law to architecture (Figure 2.1).[33]

In contrast to the traditional way of designing a building, beginning with the floor plan and then moving on to sections and elevations, he argued that the Zoning Law made it necessary to first find the maximum "building envelope," meaning the largest possible mass, as most clients wanted as much square footage as possible. Hugh Ferriss showed in renderings how this was done from the "outside," treating the building as a block that was carved out to fit the regulations. Once the maximum envelope was known, the architect went on to refine the floor plan, the external proportions and volumes drawing from the aesthetics of the time. Thus, Corbett and Ferriss argued, this "new" architecture was not based on designing a façade, "one side of a box," but focused on a pyramidal three-dimensional form: "cubes became pyramids."[34] The Zoning Law transformed the architect into a "sculptor in building masses."[35] The newly formulated focus on the building mass, the exterior, and its relation to the surrounding buildings, made the use of models more helpful than drawings since the boxy objects lend themselves much better to experiments and quick changes. They could be studied under changing light and exchanged or replaced by another option without having to alter the surroundings. Thus, the model was deemed a more flexible tool than elevations or perspective renderings. The materials available in the 1920s proved congenial to this new demand for massing models, each emphasizing slightly different aspects of the design and providing alternative ways of experimentation. Cardboard had the strongest

I. THE ENVELOPE AS DEFINED BY LAW.
Assumed a city block 200 x 800 feet. The number and position (but not the volume) of the Dormers, likewise the shape and position (but not the area) of the tower, are optional with the designer. Otherwise this perspective is simply a pictorial representation of the maximum mass allowed by the present laws.

II. THE ENVELOPE MODIFIED BY A PLAN.
Its appearance after having assumed a plan, and having passed this downward through the original envelope.

III. THE MODIFIED ENVELOPE FILLED WITH RECTILINEAR FORMS.
Its appearance after having substituted for the sloping planes, set-backs occurring at every second floor; tentative limitation being placed upon the tower.

IV. THE MASS MODIFIED BY THE STEEL CONSTRUCTION.
Its appearance after conforming the set-backs to the steel grillage and truncating the pinnacles to the highest floor level, which contains a practicable area. The mass is now ready for architectural articulation.

FIGURE 2.1 "Zoning and the Envelope of the Building," published in *Pencil Points*, 1923. No copyright holder known but see Corbett, Harvey Wiley. "Zoning and the Envelope of the Building." *Pencil Points*, April 1923.

advocates during the 1920s and was the favored material for most models made in-house because of its simple but versatile manufacturing techniques that made models a tool that could react quickly to new ideas and changes. Furthermore, the material could be turned into high-quality presentation models that could imitate the predominant stone façades once they were painted. As early as 1914, Scottish-born model maker Berthold Audsley suggested that models should be made largely from cardboard due to its superior characteristics, mainly its durability and accuracy, in comparison with wood and plaster.[36] As a material, model maker LeRoy Grumbine argued further that cardboard was congenial to T-square and triangle—the draftsman's tools and, thus, could be easily used by a trained architect.[37] Cardboard was easy to cut by hand without producing much waste or causing disruption, which made it possible to build models in the drafting room. Cardboards, such as Strathmore illustration board, and thick papers were already a staple in architectural offices and lent themselves for all tasks of modeling, as walls, foundations, and primer for subsequent painting. This meant that models could be constructed from one material only and could vary in scale depending on the thickness of the cardboard chosen. Harvey Wiley Corbett was a widely known advocate of using this method for his in-house practice. Initially, he had started out making large-scale models at 1/8″=1′-0″ scale but abandoned them because it turned out to be sufficient enough to build smaller models at 1/32″=1′-0″ scale with exterior details drawn on them.[38] Painting saved labor and time. In several articles that appeared in *Pencil Points* in 1922, Corbett illustrated his work, presenting how he developed the exterior and mass of a building with the help of massing models.[39] All parts were drawn to scale onto the cardboard (Figure 2.2). To make four walls, Corbett recommended using only one piece of cardboard that was bent over V-shaped grooves to form the corners (Figure 2.3). The interior was left hollow.

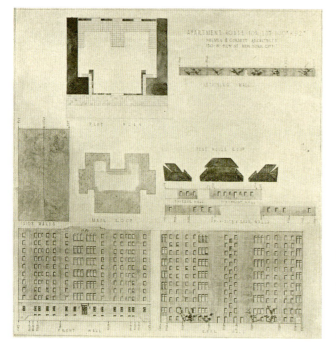

FIGURE 2.2 Drawing of model parts before assembly. No copyright holder known but see Corbett, Harvey Wiley. "Architectural Models of Cardboard." *Pencil Points*, April–August 1922, 11–14; 28–32, 37; 14–17; 14–18.

FIGURE 2.3 Making a cardboard model with a razor blade. No copyright holder known but see Corbett, Harvey Wiley. "Architectural Models of Cardboard." *Pencil Points*, April–August 1922, 11–14; 28–32, 37; 14–17; 14–18.

Though cardboard lent itself well to designing within the constraints of the Zoning Law, it was also a superb material for more refined presentation models. The most well-preserved example of Corbett's use of cardboard for both design and presentation were the models for the Metropolitan Life North Building built by his employee Conrad in 1929. As one of Conrad's first professional modeling jobs, they reflect the standard practice at the time through an unprecedented array of uses and model types. Models were built at various degrees of detail referring to the changing interests during the planning stages. It is likely that Conrad used Corbett's standard scale of 1/32"=1'-0" for most of the models but later moved toward larger models for the finished design. Over the course of the year 1929, the architects studied the requirements of the project, making sketches and models.[40] The most important problem for the design to solve, equaled those deducted from the Zoning Law: the exterior of the building and its arcades as well as the public spaces.[41] When the architects received the commission, the ultimate height was still unspecified and a large number of massing models was built for a building between 30 and 120 stories (Figures 2.4–2.6).[42] The initial massing models all presented what could be regarded as the fourth and last step of Ferriss' Zoning Law drawings after which the "modeling" of the architect began.[43] They were white boxy volumes without façades or details to determine the building's mass, structured only by symmetry or asymmetry. In a next step, selected designs were developed further, with special regard to the façade, and inserted into a model of Madison Square Park. The urban planning model contained all buildings on the northern and eastern edges of the square as well as the park itself. The schemes inserted varied in detail, some were mere white masses, others had complete and detailed façades drawn onto the cardboard (Figure 2.7). Height and designs were eventually discussed in a meeting between the architects and MetLife's board of directors on October 20, 1929, when it was decided that a twenty-eight-story structure would be built on the eastern part of the site.[44] The final design of a tower clad in limestone was further developed with models imitating the material's appearance on the exterior (Figures 2.8–2.9). With a height of thirty inches and a scale of 1/32"=1'-0", they were considerably larger than previous models.[45] Made of the same Strathmore illustration board and painted in watercolors, they simulated the stone façade, the crest of the building as well as its appearance at different building stages, giving an idea of textures and surfaces down to the mullions. Cardboard was able to represent all design purposes at various scales from abstract massing models to highly detailed presentation models depicting the exterior stone façade. Its advantages were easily visible in the

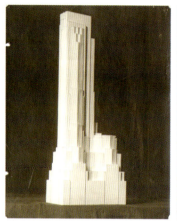 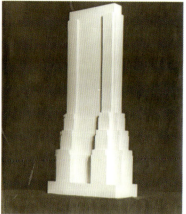 

FIGURES 2.4, 2.5 and 2.6 Massing models of the Metropolitan Life North Building, *c.* 1929. Private collection.

FIGURE 2.7 Design inserted into a model of the surroundings, *c.* 1929. Copyright © Doris Conrad Brown, Theodore Conrad papers, 1937–91, Avery Architectural and Fine Arts Library, Columbia University.

speedy construction of design alternatives of the building envelope as well as interchangeable choices to be inserted into the urban planning model.

Even cardboard proponents like Corbett used other materials. Wood, several formable materials, and an abundance of more idiosyncratic substances such as soap, sealing wax, or Necol, an early plastic, were used for specific modeling tasks.[46] Another material that had been in use long before the 1920s and which continued to be popular was plaster of Paris. Plaster could be used for

FIGURE 2.8 Fully detailed model imitating the limestone façade, *c.* 1929. Private collection.

FIGURE 2.9 Close-up of model, *c.* 1929. Private collection.

casting entire buildings but was preferred for depicting full-scale details and building up a model's contours. It was used for interior models that were built with a hole in the floor to view the inside, but the latter fell out of favor with the advent of cardboard models that could be taken apart.[47] Contributing to the decline in plaster models during the 1920s was the time-consuming process of casting plaster that involved work in a second material: clay. Different kinds of modeling clays, such as Plasticine or wax, were often used to model irregularly shaped objects. In opposition to cardboard, model maker LeRoy Grumbine compared the use of clay to the freehand drawing of a draftsman—a more "intuitive" way of working with the hands but not as accurate.[48] On the other hand, modeling clay, more than cardboard, lent itself to quick changes because it did not dry and could be changed continuously. As a material of which parts were "taken away," it was well suited to the idea of the Zoning Law, a connection that architects were well aware of. Raymond Hood is reported to have said to his employee Walter Kilham and modeler Rene Chambellan, when attempting to work on the model for his *Daily News* Building: "Do you mind [. . .] if I do a little zoning myself?"[49] From the clay working models plaster casts for presentation or further design could be made, which were more durable. In comparison to clay and cardboard, plaster, however, was difficult to work with. Therefore, the casts were made outside the architect's office by experienced sculptors. As a fast-setting material, it had to be poured quickly and in one piece, and it was a challenge to make adjustments other than by carving them with a knife. But plaster's main disadvantage was that it was comparatively heavy and it took about a week for it to set before it could be treated further—not an option for quick-study models or objects that had to be transported to a client. Cost was another downside in comparison with cardboard models, which cost one-tenth to one-third of a plaster model. Unlike with cardboard, plaster and clay meant a clear split of usage with the former being used for presentation and the latter for design. One of the prime examples for clay and plaster's continuing popularity, Rockefeller Center, was planned and exhibited largely with the help of such models. Three architects' offices collaborated on Rockefeller Center—the cardboard enthusiasts Corbett, Harrison & MacMurray, the clay supporters Hood, Godly & Fouilhoux, and the young firm (in every sense) Reinhard & Hofmeister—and formed a joint office called Associated Architects in July 1930.[50] It was Raymond Hood in particular who had extensive experience in using clay and plaster through his long-standing collaboration with modeler Rene Chambellan for projects such as his Chicago Tribune and Daily News Buildings (Figure 2.10).[51]

For Rockefeller Center, a block layout was finalized in a drawing in January 1930 by Reinhard & Hofmeister.[52] The design work for the structures using Hood's method of "zoning" with malleable materials began in July 1930 and was finished by the end of 1931.[53] Large amounts of working models, fifty by the spring of 1931, were made with modeling clay at various scales.[54] Unlike cardboard, which could be used by the architects themselves, clay and plaster required a more elaborate procedure. Each building was a joint effort by a job captain, a designer, assistants, draftsmen and women, and model makers who were part of the permanent office set up.[55] The design of individual buildings followed the standard process of "carving out" the envelope from a block of Plasticine until the final form was reached. When the original design models needed to be more durable or presentable, or when they needed to be replicated, they were cast in plaster. In March 1931, a first overall plaster cast was presented to the public. Another more detailed (yet rough) Plasticine model was prepared before June 1931,[56] showing the architects' progress and an even more refined version was cast in plaster. Interestingly, the Plasticine models for the RCA

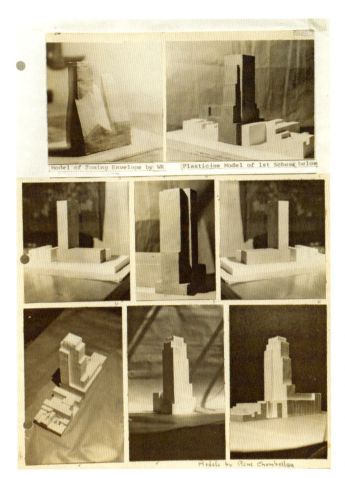

FIGURE 2.10 Plasticine study models for the *Daily News* Building designed by Raymond Hood. Copyright © Walter Kilham: Raymond Hood: Letters about & Enclosures, folder 4, Raymond M. Hood architectural drawings and papers, 1890–1944, Avery Architectural and Fine Arts Library, Columbia University.

building, designed in late 1931, show that the malleability of the material was not pursued to its fullest capacity.[57] Instead of designing with the help of one model that could be changed continually until the final form was found, several models quite similar to Corbett's cardboard models presented steps of refinement that could be compared (Figure 2.11). Ultimately, the materials' disadvantages outweighed their further application as the need for the architect to zone with his own hands became less and less important.

A lighter substance than plaster, wood was the third popular material of the 1920s, though it was rarely used by itself. It was applied mainly as a structural material for the base as well as for entire substructures of model buildings. In a more hybrid approach, details and façades were then drawn on paper and pasted onto the wood. Next to cardboard and plaster, wood was a material of choice for models which could either be made in the architect's office or by a professional modeler. Its great advantage, especially for presentation models, was its durability and structural strength. However, it needed more specialized and electrified equipment than cardboard and the cutting produced fine wood shavings that required a separate room for its handling, thus favoring separate workshops. After opening his own studio, Conrad worked with wooden models on several rather

FIGURE 2.11 Plasticine models of the RCA Building, 1932. Copyright © Walter Kilham: Raymond Hood: Photostats & Paper negatives, folder 13, Raymond M. Hood architectural drawings and papers, 1890–1944, Avery Architectural and Fine Arts Library, Columbia University.

diverse occasions. Upon leaving his joint office with Corbett, Wallace Harrison had formed a new firm with the French engineer J. André Fouilhoux in 1935. One of their early projects—and one of the first known projects for which Conrad used wood as the main component—the Rockefeller Apartments, were developed with design models quite similar to those created for the Metropolitan Life North Building. Instead of cardboard, however, they were made from painted wood. Later on, a façade was painted onto the white primer. Around the same time, Conrad also built more refined wooden presentation models for the College of Engineering at Cornell University (1934–8) for Shreve, Lamb & Harmon.[58] The architects submitted a design for a building in a western location of the campus which was abandoned by the University Plan Committee in 1938 when the complex was moved to the south. For this site, Shreve, Lamb & Harmon submitted yet another unbuilt design. As with the Rockefeller Apartments, the bodies of all models were made entirely from wood (Figure 2.12). Over a wooden base the topography was built up of several layers to depict the hills on the site leaving holes empty for the buildings. The substructures were wooden boxes with protruding cardboard elements attached for detailing. To locate each of the three-dimensional elements on the model, a grid was drawn onto the wood. All detailing was done after the wooden model was inserted into the base and faced with cardboard. As with cardboard models, the stone façade was then painted onto the surface (Figure 2.13). Taking a very different approach, the Cornell model was a detailed and refined presentation model for the client whereas the Rockefeller Apartments model was a massing model giving only the shape of the building envelope. Though a versatile material, one of wood's main disadvantages was that its grain distracted or interfered with the model's scale, making coating and painting a

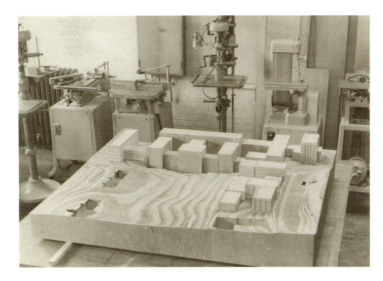

FIGURE 2.12 Model for a college of engineering at Cornell University by Shreve, Lamb and Harmon, *c.* 1934–8. Copyright © Doris Conrad Brown, Theodore Conrad papers, 1937–91, Avery Architectural and Fine Arts Library, Columbia University.

FIGURE 2.13 Finished model with cardboard façade, *c.* 1934–8. Copyright © Doris Conrad Brown, Theodore Conrad papers, 1937–91, Avery Architectural and Fine Arts Library, Columbia University.

necessity even for abstract design stages. This added time which was only a merit if the model's durability was desired for a valuable presentation model. Assembly using several materials would become a standard practice in the coming decades though not in order to conceal the structural modeling material, as in the case of wood, but rather to use the imitative qualities of each material openly.

Whether made from cardboard, clay, plaster, or wood, almost all architectural models of the 1920s focussed on the building's exterior shape and appearance without replicating its internal structure. Design models were often left as undetailed masses openly showing the materials they were made of, or, as in the case of wooden models, concealed them with a coat of paint. For presentation models, the imitation of the façade and its materials was of utmost importance and painting was the most difficult but crucial part of model making. Saving precious time, painting small-scale models eliminated the need to construct details to scale. However, not all materials lent themselves to easy painting. Wood and plaster could not be treated without a primer: The plaster's surface had to be with coated with shellac to make the use of oil paints possible; wood could be painted directly but for detailed façades it was covered with paper and then treated with poster or oil colors. Cardboard models had the great advantage that they could be painted on directly with water colors or Indian ink, either before or after assembling. Common to all, the exterior treatment manipulated the material to represent several different ones in the actual building. There were different degrees of realism that could be achieved through painted and built-up façades based on the model's function. Some only showed a sketched façade with windows and shadows, as in the early Metropolitan Life North Building design models. Others, such as the College of Engineering, replicated a façade through detailed layers. With the advent of the "age of transparency" and transparent surfaces in modern architecture in the 1920s, these practices were already beginning to run into difficulties.[59] In his 1929 book *Metropolis of Tomorrow* Hugh Ferriss envisioned the soon-to-appear use of glass and glass bricks as a material for façades.[60] An illustration of such a scenario included in the book seems rather fictional at first glance but of significance when talking about models (Figure 2.14).

FIGURE 2.14 Hugh Ferriss' drawing of a fictional glass high rise, 1929. Copyright © Ferriss, Metropolis of Tomorrow, 101.

In the rendering, the buildings seem to be transparent, of an ethereal and fragile quality with only a few floor slabs visible through large glass panes. Though no such building existed at the time of the book's publication, the ideas were in the air and already formulated in models. High-rises had influenced the adoption of model making as a result of the Zoning Law and the necessity for a tool to determine the building envelope. At the end of the 1920s, tall buildings were, once again, at the forefront of design, based on ideas for glass curtain walls and yet another shift in model making. It is unknown whether Ferriss knew the rejected design that Harvey Wiley Corbett had clearly favored for his 120-story glass tower for the Metropolitan Life North Building.[61] One of the most daring designs of the 1920s, he had proposed a tower with a crystalline glass curtain wall. Using a similar building envelope as in previous designs for the same building, the shape of the exterior glazing would have been its main feature: above a small, five-story marble base, a spiky, almost expressionist glass tower rose despite a number of setbacks. The model, however, was made from the same materials as the stone-clad designs, cardboard and wood, which were unable to adequately depict the building's intended material expression (Figure 2.15). Over a wooden substructure, the delicate and intricate façade was drawn onto cardboard and bent into the crystalline shape. Above the ground-floor imitation of a marble façade in watercolors, only the thin ink lines on the shaft indicated the mullions between the floor-to-ceiling glass panes of the large bay windows and, thus, hinted at glass as the building material. Unable to represent transparency or the exposed steel frame, the painted cardboard model failed to show the glass'

FIGURE 2.15 Cardboard model of crystalline design for the Metropolitan Life North Building, c. 1929. Copyright © Doris Conrad Brown, Theodore Conrad papers, 1937–91, Avery Architectural and Fine Arts Library, Columbia University.

impact on the exterior of the building. Here, drawings like Ferriss' remained more successful in conveying the new possibilities of transparency and the fragility of glass.

Representing transparent surfaces with the available materials was a problem for which solutions of different degrees of realism existed only on a much smaller level, especially for windows. Model maker Edward W. Hobbs recommended drawing them onto the model in ink, to color them in and to show reliefs with black-lining or shading, a technique that Conrad used for the the Metropolitan Life models: "That is to say, all the lines on one side of the window which represents the part to be depressed below the surface are drawn about twice the thickness of those on the opposite side."[62] Another technique was to build windows as reliefs with different layers of cardboard for frame, sash and window pane. For the glazing, clear materials such as the cheap transparent covers of chocolate boxes or celluloid were used, as was the case for the College of Engineering model for which the windows were so painstakingly executed that it caused the model to miss the deadline.[63] Other solutions included using photos of curtains or materials such as semi-transparent sheet gelatin. Talc and mica were used if there was light on the inside because they could withstand the heat. Sometimes, windows were left open entirely and a piece of string or cotton could be put through them to symbolize the incidence of sunlight.[64] None of these solutions achieved a realistic representation of transparent windows. The available materials resisted ideas of transparency. The opaque outside of the models kept their interiors hidden. Often constructed as hollow boxes, they left room for a technical add-on that both concealed failed attempts at material imitation and highlighted the focus on building masses rather than detail. In his 1926 manual on modeling, Edward W. Hobbs recommended lighting because it "adds a touch of realism" to a model.[65] Berthold Audsley, working for General Electric, followed this advice for a large, seventeen-foot model of a street that was supposed to demonstrate the advantages of electric lighting by using small pea bulbs at the scale of the model.[66] In quite a contrary attempt to conceal the model's details in a nocturnal setting, using only one light bulb, some of the models for the Metropolitan Life North Building took advantage of their hollow core by illuminating the entire model from within—not by replicating lights or lamps but by imitating the effects of lighting (Figure 2.16). Similar to the popular renderings by

FIGURE 2.16 Hollow illuminated model. Private collection.

Hugh Ferriss that had demonstrated how significantly the play of light and shadow could influence the dramatic effects of a building, the models' illumination highlighted their mass. Whereas in Ferriss' drawings the light always seemed to come from an external source, almost like a spotlight, the models seemed to glow from within, making its setbacks clearly visible, highlighting their monumentality.

Imitating Modern Architecture

Plastics had been around for three decades when the New York World's Fair opened in 1939. The first synthetic material, Bakelite, had been patented by the Belgian-American Leo Hendrik Baekeland in 1907. The New Jersey-based Boonton Rubber Company was one of the first to pick it up for their colorful dinnerware sets called Boontonware. The same material was also widely used for the production of shells for radios and cameras. During the Depression and World War II, plastics experienced an enormous leap forward, tripling their annual production in the United States between 1940 and 1945.[67] By the end of the war, the United States had established herself as the largest producer of plastics. Of utmost importance for the surge in the production were such new substances as PVC, synthetic resins, and acrylic glass, all of which were developed in the decade leading up to the war. Widely disseminated by firms such as Rohm & Haas and DuPont at exhibitions and fairs, they not only helped the United States to win the war, but also had a dramatic impact on architectural model making. In 1928, the Union Carbide and Carbon Corporation started to produce PVC, a competitor of linoleum, under the name Vinylite and introduced it to the public at the 1933 Chicago *Century of Progress* exhibition to present the material's versatility for everyday products and a three-room Vinylite House (Figure 2.17).[68] Another substance that would acquire pivotal importance for model making was polymethyl methacrylate, better known as acrylic glass. Almost simultaneously, it was invented and patented by several companies on both sides of the Atlantic. The first was the German Ernst Röhm, who introduced it in 1933. A year later, he was followed by the British Imperial Chemical Industries which had received a patent for the manufacturing process of acrylic glass on August 12, 1932, but only began to market the material under the name Perspex in 1934.[69] Both the American branch of Rohm & Haas and DuPont, the former under the name Plexiglas and the latter calling it Lucite, began production in the United States in 1936.[70] What made the new substances stand out against previous materials was their novel chemical and mechanical properties. They can be divided into two classes, based largely on how they react to heat. Thermosetting materials such as the older plastics Bakelite, celluloid, ebonite, and synthetic and phenolic resins can be formed under heat but once hardened, they are heat resistant. Therefore, their main application was for molds of finished products. Thermoplastic synthetics, on the other hand, such as Styrofoam, Plexiglas, and PVC, warp under the influence of heat without changing their chemical consistency—a process that can be repeated infinitely. To find applications and to advertise the materials to a broader audience, the manufacturers launched PR campaigns and the Society of the Plastics Industry was founded in 1937. A wide range of literature appeared, such as a guidebook by George Scribner, owner of the aforementioned Boonton Molding Company, called *A Brief Description of the Commonly Used Plastics Compiled for the Guidance of Engineers and Buyers*. First published in 1933, in only twenty years it saw nine re-editions.[71] The magazine *Plastics* was founded as another source of information in 1925.[72] Initially containing advertisements and technical information on products, it shifted its focus toward consumers after its rebranding as *Modern Plastics* in 1934 and became an invaluable amplifier as it not only aimed to educate the public but also gave designed examples of how to use plastics, enlisting the help of industrial designers such as Raymond Loewy, Lurelle Guild, Jay Ackerman, Gilbert Rohde, Belle Kogan, and the architect Ely Jacques Kahn.[73] Furthermore, two exhibitions, in 1934 and 1935 respectively, and an Annual Modern Plastics Competition between 1936 and 1941 demonstrated the link between industrial design and the plastics industry. One of the judges for the competitions was Harvey Wiley Corbett.[74] Other companies began to cooperate closely with designers. In 1933, Alan Brown of Bakelite invited designers like Norman Bel Geddes and Donald Deskey to use the product, offering technical support and exclusive features in their advertisements.[75] Rohm & Haas went one step further and held a competition for the application of Plexiglas in cooperation with MoMA that awarded Alexander Calder a first prize for his illuminated Plexiglas sculpture. Around 1939, the campaigns to make plastics more accessible to a non-professional audience reached a peak with large-scale demonstrations of prototypes at the New York World's Fair and coverage in magazines such as *Fortune,* which dedicated its October 1940 issue to the topic, including a fictitious world map of "Synthetica" (Figure 2.18). At the 1939 New York World's Fair, manufacturers tried to upstage one another with spectacular demonstrations such as "live plastic moldings," a translucent Pontiac in front of the General Motors pavilion, or a Ford made

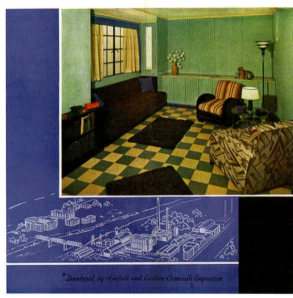

FIGURE 2.17 Vinylite House at the Century of Progress Exhibition in 1933. Private collection.

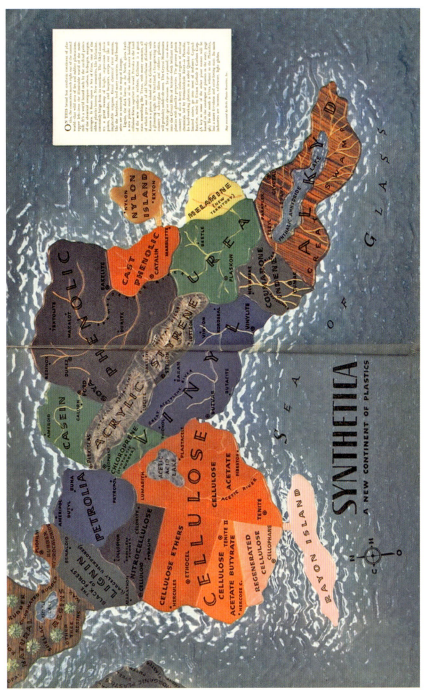

FIGURE 2.18 The map of Synthetica in *Fortune*, 1940. Copyright holder unknown but see *Fortune*, October 1940.

from aminoplast.[76] After the end of the Fair, a permanent display at the PEDAC Galleries at Rockefeller Center and a number of traveling exhibitions continued to propagate the various applications of Plexiglas.[77]

Two other materials came into focus at the beginning of the twentieth century, entering model making at the same time as plastics: linoleum and aluminum. The former had been invented by the British engineer Frederick Walton around 1860 and had been produced commercially in the United States for some time, beginning in 1872 with the Linoleum Manufacturing Company in Staten Island.[78] The more important manufacturer, however, was the Armstrong Cork and Tile Company: Founded in 1860 in Lancaster, Pennsylvania, it started producing linoleum in 1908.[79] A precursor to plastic's triumph in the 1930s, the company ran an advertising campaign in 1917 geared toward popularizing the material for private consumers through magazines such as *McCall's*, *Ladies' Home Journal,* and *Woman's Home Companion*. Made from linseed oil, fabric, cork, resins, and pigments, the material's advantages became quickly apparent: It was elastic and water repellent, and it could be patterned, inlayed, and stamped. Its production was cost, time and labor intensive. Yet, it soon became a household favorite. One of its main advantages for household goods and models alike was that it could represent almost any texture, and was thus able to follow trends, styles, and changing tastes. As the oldest of the new materials, aluminum had been discovered by the Danish chemist Hans Christian Ørsted and was introduced at the 1855 Paris World Expo.[80] As had been the case with plastics, it was initially regarded a precious and expensive metal but was soon used as a substitute for more valuable materials in household appliances.[81] In 1888, the Pittsburgh Reduction Company—which later became America's largest aluminum manufacturer, the Aluminum Company of America—was founded.[82] With the discovery of more cost-efficient manufacturing techniques, the price per pound dropped rapidly from $11.33 in 1885 to $0.57 in 1892.[83] The lower price, as well as a need for new lightweight materials for novel applications such as cars, blimps, engines, and high-voltage cables, increased demand for it during the 1920s.[84] The two World Wars further promoted the material, especially during the 1940s, when aluminum became the standard material for airplane construction. As a building material, aluminum had been in use since the nineteenth century. One of its most famous applications was for the tip of the Washington Monument in 1884. Still, it was presented as a novelty at expositions in the 1930s, and competitions encouraged new applications such the 1931 Aluminaire House. Designed by Albert Frey and A. Lawrence Kocher for the Architectural and Allied Arts Exhibition at the Grand Central Palace, it was presented in the 1932 *International Style* show at MoMA.[85] Widespread applications such as aluminum window frames, however, remained a luxury until the end of World War II when they became widely popular in buildings such as the Manufacturer's Trust or the Lake Shore Drive Apartments by Ludwig Mies van der Rohe.[86]

While Rohm & Haas, DuPont, and Alcoa were still vying for commercial outlets for their products, Plexiglas, linoleum, and aluminum were quickly appropriated for both representative and structural tasks in model making. Conrad and others began using Plexiglas in 1936, the year it was introduced to the American market.[87] It can be assumed that modelers became aware of the material through a mix of personal contacts between model makers, designers, architects, and the manufacturing industries, as well as New York's function as the center of the plastics industry's public dissemination. Based on a constant quest for more suitable substances, the appropriation of new materials was largely due to their superior qualities for imitative tasks. The

1930s marked a transitional period when older modeling materials coexisted with newly appropriated metals and plastics for an ever-increasing number of models. Individual modeling practices, such as Harvey Wiley Corbett's use of cardboard and Raymond Hood's use of clay models, gave way to more generalized applications of materials to certain model types and representational functions. At the same time, architecture itself was beginning to change, requiring novel ways to realistically imitate materials such as glass, steel, aluminum, and chrome as well as new features such as flat roofs, large windows panes and unadorned wall surfaces. In the introduction to the 1932 manifesto accompanying the exhibition *Modern Architecture—International Style* at MoMA, Alfred Barr described the main aspects of the new style and, one could add, model making: "The distinguishing principles of the International Style as laid down by the authors are three: emphasis upon volume—space enclosed by thin planes or surfaces as opposed to the suggestion of mass and solidity; regularity as opposed to the symmetry or other kinds of obvious balance; and, lastly, dependence upon the intrinsic elegance of materials, technical perfection, and fine proportions, as opposed to applied ornament."[88] Given architecture's increasing preoccupation with transparency, Plexiglas offered new opportunities for a realistic imitation of glass. Yet, the material's structural advantages for model making were discovered quickly, too. Just as Thomas Raff explained the adaptation of a material based on a semantic connotation (glass is transparent, granite is hard), new modeling materials were appropriated for their specific physical and imitative qualities. Even though Plexiglas had several advantages, it was its transparency that initially appealed to modelers. Aluminum entered modeling for its ability to represent the reflective surfaces of steel, and linoleum was chosen to imitate opaque claddings for façades. However, once all the materials' properties became known, they triggered a revolution in model making that led to unusual shapes in larger quantities as well as larger and more durable models with more lightweight materials.

Like its earlier plastic sibling celluloid, Plexiglas' applications had been rather limited at first. It was regarded as highly valuable and used for luxury goods such as furniture, glasses, handbags and even musical instruments.[89] Celluloid, developed in 1868, had become more and more outmoded for design objects in the 1920s and 1930s but remained a staple in model making until after World War II, especially for the representation of transparent surfaces. Its advantage over other transparent materials such as glass or mica was that it came in a wide range of thicknesses, was very light, easy to cut and unbreakable. But it had limitations, too: It was only half-transparent and tinted either yellow or blue. Acrylic glass had one great advantage over celluloid: It was entirely translucent and clear. As a thermoplastic material, it was more versatile than any of the earlier plastics. It could be warped when hot but became hard and durable once cool and, like Bakelite, it could be used for injection molding in the mass production of parts. In addition, it could be sawn, milled, and turned. Unlike wood, it had no grain, did not shrink, and could be glued or painted without a primer. It was also light, only about half the weight of glass. All these characteristics must have seemed congenial to resolving difficulties in imitating transparency. The only, albeit prohibitive, obstacle was that new manufacturing techniques had to be invented to facilitate model construction and mass production. One innovation meant that the material was not bonded with other materials with cement but using a liquid that temporarily melted the surface of the individual pieces, a technique similar to welding.[90] Conrad later recounted the event that led to his intensive use of Plexiglas in model making: "The architects thought plastics had to be cut with a spray of water. I proved to them that by regulating the speed of the

FIGURE 2.19 Model of the Belgian Pavilion with traditional paper façade. Copyright © New York World's Fair 1939–40 records, Manuscripts and Archives Division, The New York Public Library.

blade and using the right kind of blade, I could cut it dry. That revolutionized the whole cutting of plastics."[91]

The more important glass became in architecture, the more pivotal was its imitation in model making. Most buildings at the New York World's Fair—the moment when plastics and glass entered the collective consciousness of Americans for the first time—were opaque steel frames with stucco and plaster. A small number of expensive glass curtain walls deviated from these traditional designs, signaling the dawn of a new, modern age. Several were presented with translucent façades in presentation models—not all of which were successful. In comparison with these failed attempts, the benefits of using large sheets of Plexiglas for the imitation of glass became all the more obvious. The model for the Belgian Pavilion was billed as a "modern example of glass and stucco with an imposing entry all in glass." Yet despite its rhetoric, it was built traditionally with painted paper glued to the model and unable to realistically represent the transparent glass façade (Figure 2.19). For the Glass Center Pavilion by Shreve, Lamb & Harmon, which showcased the exhibits by the Corning Glass Works, Owens-Illinois Glass Company, and Pittsburgh Plate Glass Company, the model represented the building's glass façade, blue plate glass, and a glass block tower with a translucent but somewhat milky plastic (Figure 2.20).[92] Once again, the interior remained hidden. More abstract, a model of the Irish Pavilion by architect Michael Scott used a fully transparent material to depict large, load-bearing glass curtain walls (Figure 2.21). As a massing model, it exhibited its most prominent feature—the curtain wall—but otherwise remained without detail, unable to represent the building's structure. More successfully, Louis Skidmore and Nathaniel Owings's Westinghouse model used large, curved sheets of plastic with actual sashes built onto them. But arguably the most successful use of Plexiglas for the New York World's Fair, and in the 1930s in general, was the model for the Pittsburgh House of Glass. It was Conrad's first documented use of Plexiglas yet achieved a level of perfection absent from any other contemporary attempt (Figure 2.22).[93] This was partly necessitated by the model's intended use as a photo model for

FIGURE 2.20 Model of the Glass Center Pavilion with translucent tower. Copyright © New York World's Fair 1939–40 records, Manuscripts and Archives Division, The New York Public Library.

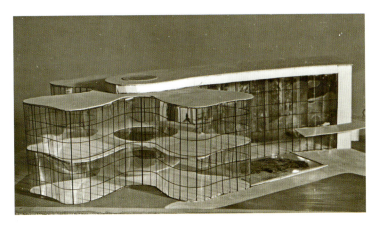

FIGURE 2.21 Irish Pavilion massing model, Copyright © New York World's Fair 1939–40 records, Manuscripts and Archives Division, The New York Public Library.

Collier's, which put an even greater emphasis on the realistic representation of materials. The house, by Landefeld & Hatch, was designed for the "Town of Tomorrow" section of walk-in demonstration homes at the Fair. Intended to promote the use of glass in architecture, it was jointly commissioned by the Pittsburgh Plate Glass Company and the Pittsburgh Corning Company. While the building was under construction, the model was made solely to take photos for *Collier's* May 6, 1939 issue.[94] Its task was to achieve the illusion of a finished building, using as many top-notch details as possible. It was built in early 1939, at 3/8"=1'-0" scale. Not only was it considerably larger than most other presentation models for the Fair, but it could be disassembled. The model is lost today but its materials are well documented: Over a plywood base and substructure, the interior walls were built from veneer. Plexiglas was used for the windows, table tops, chairs, banisters, and interior partitions.[95] The exterior received three air-brushed coats of paint to represent stucco. Inside, the house was fully furnished with sliding partitions, Venetian blinds, and mirrors as

FIGURES 2.22, 2.23 and 2.24 Pittsburgh House of Glass model, 1939. Copyright © Doris Conrad Brown, Wayne Checkman, Theodore Conrad papers, 1937–91, Avery Architectural and Fine Arts Library, Columbia University.

well as miniature furniture and a fully equipped wardrobe. For the windows and larger pieces, Plexiglas sheets were milled. The furniture and other irregular shapes were molded. The floor tiles were assembled of carved linoleum pieces. Wire and bent metal were used for the tube chairs (Figure 2.23). The model photos staged the building's most important feature as a novelty: the transparent surfaces that allowed for a completely unprecedented connection between interior and exterior (Figure 2.24). Other than in any of the previous uses of plastics, the difference between the modeling and building materials was rendered invisible. The open and unaltered use of materials for their unique properties was unprecedented. As a combination of several modeling materials—Plexiglas, wood, metal, linoleum, and paper—the model combined each material's best representative properties.

In comparison with acrylic glass, aluminum and linoleum's use for model making was less spectacular, despite a few notable exceptions. Aluminum had several advantages over more traditional substances such as wood, cardboard, or plaster. Much more malleable, its soft and lightweight properties meant it could be used to model any shape. It could be cut, reused, painted, varnished, and oxidized. It could be glued and did not absorb water, nor did it shrink or break. Due to its scaleless appearance and its availability in fine sheets, the same material could be used in model and building alike or to represent other metals such as steel. Its only, albeit significant, downside was that it took about five times longer to cut than traditional materials and it could not be nailed onto another surface. Possibly the most astonishing use of aluminum before the war was a model presented at the *International Style* exhibition at MoMA. The Lux Apartments, proposed for a site near the Magnificent Mile in Chicago, were designed by the Bowman Brothers in 1930. As early advocates of lightweight steel construction—Irving Bowman had designed a metal-clad building for his thesis project at the Armour Institute of Technology in 1928—the Bowmans had produced metal furniture for the 1933 Chicago *Century of Progress* exhibition.[96] For the *International Style* exhibition, Philip Johnson had requested that all models displayed at the exhibition be of cardboard. The Bowmans' model, however, was made from aluminum to represent a building of glass and thin exterior steel panels—supposedly the first "all-metal apartment house in the world."[97]

Making use of linoleum's ability to represent colors and textures, it was often applied in model making to imitate stones like marble, tiles, and other patterned surfaces. It could also be cut to imitate the shapes of the materials represented, replacing surfaces that had been painted hitherto. Conrad used linoleum on several occasions for the treatment of façades and floors. The most well-known project were the models for MoMA, planned by Philip Goodwin and Edward Durell Stone between 1936 and 1938. The museum had contemplated a new building for a number of years when it bought several lots on West 53rd Street in the fall of 1936.[98] As a visual endpoint to plans for a northern extension of Rockefeller Center and as a prime artwork in the collection of MoMA, the building's exterior came under close scrutiny during the design process. The first conclusive scheme by the architects was formulated in March 1937 for which Conrad made a model (Figure 2.25).[99] The design consisted of a building with a utilities tower clad in dark stone rising twenty-six feet above the penthouse. Another model was made in December 1937 after the tower had been absorbed into the main cube and Thermolux was chosen for indirect lighting on the southern façade. As in the first model, two quite different materials—in this case the marble on the façade and the blue terracotta tiles on the sides—were made from linoleum and attached in little pieces to simulate stones and tiles.[100] Soon after the museum was finished, it became obvious that more space was needed. Goodwin proposed a first annex in the spring of 1943 including an east and west wing with TV studios and an auditorium for which a new part was added to the original model in the summer of 1943 by model maker Kendall Bassett.[101] For the model, the linoleum's representative qualities were so important that Philip Goodwin himself approached Conrad to inquire whether he would sell his spare material to Bassett to make the addition look realistic.

Aside from the new materials' ability to imitate building materials and surfaces, their chemical qualities lend them to broader applications such as prototyping and molding that had far-reaching implications for the assembly of models. For the serialized production of objects, there were different forming techniques available: Injection molding could be used for all thermosetting and thermoplastic materials, die-casting was used for metals, and Plexiglas sheets could be pressed into form. For all casts, a master model of the object had to be made by hand. From this original, negative forms were made that could be used for casting. Norman Bel Geddes was one of the first to work intensively with molding techniques, using plastic and brass for car models from 1933.[102] Conrad, too, had experience with molding curved or streamlined forms, the most

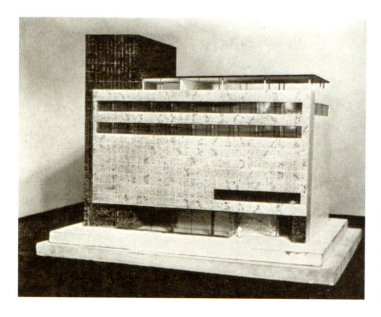

FIGURE 2.25 First model of MoMA, March 1937. No known copyright holder but see *The Architectural Forum*, August 1937, 5, 69. Photographer: Soichi Sunami.

FIGURE 2.26 Model for Fernand Léger's fountain. Copyright © Doris Conrad Brown.

astonishing example being an unrealized model of a sixty-foot-high kinetic fountain for the New York World's Fair by Fernand Léger.[103] A model of the abstract scheme was made by Conrad using bent metal and molded red, blue, and clear plastic pieces (Figure 2.26). Without indicating or imitating a specific material to be used in the real fountain, the polished metal and plastic elements became the main materials and the basis of the fountain's unusual shapes. In the model, two semicircular-shaped metal walls rotated against one another, opening up and enclosing spaces in between. Later on, molds and prefabricated pieces were needed in large quantities for increasingly detailed façades of high-rises as well as for interior and exterior furnishings of presentation models, including human figures, cars, and furniture. Except for the colorful plastic parts of Léger's fountain, painting remained pivotal for the realism of these casts as the plastic materials used were monochrome. Though no model in the 1930s was made entirely with the new materials, modelers had already begun to use them for structural purposes, foreshadowing Plexiglas' career after the war. Instead of acrylic glass, however, the most well-documented prewar case of using new materials for structural tasks was aluminum. Conrad began restoring models for MoMA when many of the exhibits arrived broken for the 1932 *International Style* exhibition.[104] Originally made of wood, the Villa Savoye model had been built in 1929 in France by M. Pissarro.[105] It arrived in New York badly damaged and had to be reconstructed several times due to frequent transportation. In late December 1937, the model was once again falling apart and Conrad suggested building a frame of Duralum, the strongest lightweight aluminum available at the time, with brass columns to house the surviving model pieces and to make future repairs easier (Figures 2.27–2.28).[106] For the frame, the metal parts were riveted and screwed together. It was covered

FIGURE 2.27 Broken model of the Villa Savoye. Copyright © Doris Conrad Brown, Theodore Conrad papers, 1937–91, Avery Architectural and Fine Arts Library, Columbia University.

FIGURE 2.28 New aluminum frame without the façade, early 1938. Copyright © Doris Conrad Brown, Theodore Conrad papers, 1937–91, Avery Architectural and Fine Arts Library, Columbia University.

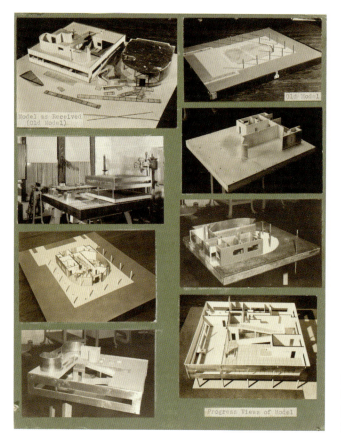

FIGURE 2.29 Assembly of model. Copyright © 2020. Digital image, The Museum of Modern Art, New York/Scala, Florence.

with paper and latex cement to receive a coat of paint (Figure 2.29). Eventually, the colored walls were made of rubber which had the advantage that it did not need repainting and wood panels were painted to match the color of "old" model.[107]

The Postwar Modeling Boom

As much as the 1930s were a mad scramble in search for commercial applications for the newly developed materials, the 1940s brought a prompt solution. With the onset of the war in Europe and even more so after the attack on Pearl Harbor in December 1941, American research into materials intensified and the production of aluminum, copper, magnesium, and steel increased manifold. Plastics were in high demand as shortages of aluminum and steel forced engineers to look for substitutes which oftentimes performed better than the original materials. With its superior unbreakable qualities, Plexiglas became an essential as laminated safety glass, with 90 percent going into aviation for use in cockpit canopies.[108] Most non-military building work came to a standstill when the United States entered the war. All remaining construction efforts shifted largely to the construction of military bases, government research facilities such as the town of Oak Ridge built by SOM for the Manhattan Project, and privately operated plants. The return to civilian building kicked off a golden age for modern architecture in the 1950s, for which the new materials were embraced in a much more all-encompassing way, slowly eclipsing the older modeling materials for all building types from massing models to highly refined presentation models. At the end of the war, the demand for both Plexiglas and aluminum fell rapidly, causing prices to tumble and sparking a search for new markets. Sales numbers rose again quickly as the industry recognized the material's value at a time when public trust in scientific progress was at an all-time high and plastics, aluminum, and steel were regarded as the quintessence of modernity.[109] Among the new customers were architectural model makers. Many models that became significant for their application of new materials represented building projects that were noted equally for their novel building materials, especially aluminum and glass. The steel frame which had long existed in American architecture became fully married to transparent glass façades, making the internal structure of the building visible. Models became a key element for the design of these façades. Previous models could either be built analogous to the actual buildings with load-bearing walls for small house models as in the Pittsburgh House of Glass, be hollow or have wooden nondescript substructures behind their opaque façades as in the case of the models for the Metropolitan Life North Building. This would not be possible for models of large glass skyscrapers, though, as they had to visualize a building's interior *and* structure. At the same time, the miniatures had to be structurally sound as models. Plexiglas fulfilled both requirements: It was transparent and self-supporting. The general use of models for design had not changed significantly since the 1920s. Phyllis Lambert described the design practices involved in creating the Seagram Building, which could serve as an illustration for general processes, as follows: Beginning with a study of building regulations and vertical transportation, models were used to depict a project's preliminary form, its siting, structure, enclosure, plaza, and details.[110] The difference to prewar modeling practices was that material imitation and detail received greater attention not just for presentations but during the inception of a project. After the war, some architectural offices, such as SOM or Ludwig Mies van der Rohe, started to embrace this practice on a much grander scale, using massing models for early design studies, details, and models presenting alternatives and, most importantly, highly refined presentation models. By being able to develop ideas for transparent façades in more accurate models and by simulating glass curtain walls, Plexiglas left a significant imprint on architecture because it helped find aesthetic solutions for the design of a building's exterior and its connection to its surroundings. As such, Plexiglas was extremely well suited to the architecture it represented.

For the acceptance of acrylic glass in model making high-rises were, once more, of great importance. Early attempts at achieving transparency in models of tall buildings such as Raymond Hood's remarkable model for an Apartment Tower in the Country, which was built for the *International Style* exhibition at MoMA in 1932, were not able to marry height, thin windowpanes, and transparency fully. After the war, it was in collaboration with SOM that Conrad developed his signature style of large Plexiglas walls as the basis for entire models. His first postwar high-rise model, one of the early spectacular glass skyscrapers on Park Avenue, was Kahn & Jacobs' 100 Park Avenue office building, erected between 1948 and 1949 (Figure 2.30).[111] Built in wood and celluloid, it was one of the last traditional models that was superseded quickly by Conrad's ingenious models for Lever House (Figure 2.31). The difference could not be bigger: 100 Park

FIGURE 2.30 Model of 100 Park Avenue by Kahn & Jacobs, *c.* 1948–9. Copyright © Doris Conrad Brown, Theodore Conrad papers, 1937–91, Avery Architectural and Fine Arts Library, Columbia University.

FIGURE 2.31 Presentation model of Lever House, 1952–3. Copyright © 2020. Digital image, The Museum of Modern Art, New York/Scala, Florence.

Avenue was built over a wooden substructure with windows of celluloid which gave the model its common opaque look.

The Lever House model, built between 1952 and 1953, on the other hand, included everything that would become established during the postwar modeling boom: large sheets of Plexiglas with inlaid small details and aluminum mullions to represent an elaborate façade, a hollow core with a visible interior, and the accurate imitation of all other building materials. Assembled models were an idea that had been around since at least the 1930s when designers such as Corbett and Bel Geddes were experimenting with models for standardized housing that would show clients and buyers how the system of prefabrication could be applied.[112] The postwar models, however, did not replicate such a structural system of the building at model scale. Only in rare cases did model buildings replicate the construction of the building: Devon Dennett built a model of the Pan Am Terminal at Idlewild Airport that mirrored the building's cantilevered and cable-suspended roof and Conrad's model of the Pittsburgh Hilton used load-bearing Plexiglas tubes to represent the columns of the building (Figure 2.32).[113] Following their own logic of structure, most models, however, were built with a hollow core that was braced with a solid "elevator" shaft on the inside to give them stability (Figure 2.33). Smaller structures could have entirely hollow cores. In opposition to the novelty of modern buildings' non-load-bearing curtain walls, the transparent Plexiglas sheets representing these curtain walls were the main feature of the new high-rise models, both structurally carrying the floors and roof together with the inner shaft, and representing the exterior appearance through inlays and painted details. Even though models were constructed differently, they tried to visually replicate the load-bearing and structural elements of the building like columns that were not necessary for the model's own construction but were now exposed due to the transparent façades. Aluminum and its substitute, aluminum-painted wood stripes, were the second modeling material that came to be used extensively in skyscraper models. Aluminum was used increasingly in buildings and models alike: While in 1949, only 5 percent of all window frames were made from aluminum, in 1953 that number had risen to 25 percent.[114] As the shiny surfaces of mullions and aluminum sheathing became one of the main features of modern design, models needed to replicate them closely. Façades were no longer painted onto the surface but often assembled from separate pieces. Conrad was one of the first to devise a technique to make intricate metal inlays in Plexiglas by scoring the aluminum with the same machines used on acrylic.[115] This meant that the external appearance of a model was built in and could not be changed easily or washed off after assembly. Besides being used to replicate window frames, aluminum could be pressed into forms and assembled from individual pieces for façades, as in Conrad's model for the Alcoa Building in Pittsburgh by Harrison & Abramovitz. These assembled models were highly dependent on mechanized and electrified workshops for cutting, scoring, and casting. The time-efficient serial production of the same piece, a mullion, a panel of exterior cladding, or any other part of the model, was a key factor in a model's accuracy and success, as prices for models were rising exponentially due to higher material costs and longer construction times. The division of labor within the shops facilitated speedy workflows as tasks could be finished in parallel. The assembly of the parts and the finish of the model, however, still depended on painstaking handcraft that required the combined efforts of all modelers involved.

As the internal structure and the façade became increasingly important, large-scale models were needed to represent material and layout choices for both architects and clients. For the

FIGURE 2.32 Construction of the Pittsburgh Hilton model, *c.* 1957–8. Copyright © Doris Conrad Brown, Theodore Conrad papers, 1937–91, Avery Architectural and Fine Arts Library, Columbia University.

MODELING MATERIALS

FIGURE 2.33 Inland Steel Building model, c. 1955–8. Copyright © Ezra Stoller/Esto.

latter, the choice of exterior materials was often more than a simple question of taste: Many clients were manufacturers of building materials, such as the Chicago-based Inland Steel Corporation, who wanted to showcase their products with the help of their new headquarters. They expected utmost realism and material imitation in models to be able to judge the appearance of their buildings. For the design of Inland Steel's new steel-clad office building in Chicago's Loop, a preliminary design by Walter Netsch was presented in an abstract model built by W.M.H. Chaffee Model Builders Inc. in early 1954. After seeing the small-scale object, the clients were concerned that it would be too unconventional because the model was of Plexiglas and they had expected to see metal on the façade.[116] The negative effect that the model and its misunderstood abstraction had on the clients were remembered clearly by Gordon Bunshaft, who attended the meeting: "At the first meeting, the Chicago office had made a little plastic model of it. Pure plastic, just a little toy. There was no metal or anything. Just scratch lines for floors, and they liked it. I had to present it. [. . .] The second meeting they started showing the design, the metalwork. [. . .] Leigh Block said, 'God, what a relief! I thought you meant to make it all glass!'"[117] Only the second, assembled and much larger model could satisfy the client in representing the building's steel cladding and mullions. To facilitate experimentation with building materials, larger numbers of models became a common phenomenon, often depicting alternatives. The comparison of façade designs with the help of models and model photos was used by architects to test variations in three dimensions and to allow the client to make a fully-informed decision, as in the case of SOM's building for the Libbey-Owens-Ford Glass Company in Toledo. Here, two versions of a façade were built and photographed from the same angle to make the effects of the two designs clear (Figures 2.34–2.35). Rather than photographing one model and adjusting it to show a

FIGURES 2.34 and 2.35 Versions of the façade for the Libbey-Owens-Ford Glass Company building, c. 1957–9. Copyright © Ezra Stoller/Esto.

different design, the emphasis lay on a three-dimensional comparison that could be studied simultaneously.

Even though the intricately assembled façades were the most important innovation in model making, painting, formerly associated with the external treatment of cardboard and wood models, remained an important component in the imitation and simulation of materials other than glass and metals. Rooms for spray-painting had been established in larger workshops such as Bel Geddes' and Conrad's in the 1930s, and painting Plexiglas became one of the principal tasks. Spray-painted Plexiglas could resemble any other material and texture either by applying paint to the flat surface of a sheet or by painting a carved piece that already reproduced the texture of the intended material. As the materials for a building's façade came under close scrutiny, clients did not just want to see the assembled layout of the exterior but its materials and colors, too. For the Chase Manhattan Bank, designed by SOM for a site in Lower Manhattan, four different schemes were developed in late 1955 and early 1956 and reviewed by the client with the help of models.[118] The use of three different materials was to be determined: aluminum, steel and granite.[119] Over a Plexiglas corpus, the façades were assembled with inlaid aluminum to represent the mullions. The other two materials, granite and steel, were painted as opaque color patches onto the Plexiglas. Through the reproduction of colors, textures, and materials, it became possible to simulate the actual appearance of the interior of the building. A large model of the Chase Manhattan Building's entrance and plaza (Figure 2.36) was used to determine the materials for the lobby, as Conrad remembered: "Plans for the Chase building called for the use of a dark marble in the main lobby. [. . .] The place looked like a cellar. Once we made a realistic scale model, it was immediately

FIGURE 2.36 Interior model of the Chase Manhattan Bank, c. 1955–8. Copyright © Doris Conrad Brown, Theodore Conrad papers, 1937–91, Avery Architectural and Fine Arts Library, Columbia University.

plain. So, plans were altered to specify the very light marble finally installed."[120] As such, the refined imitation of building materials contributed to both the design of a structure and the communication and decision making with clients.

Even though Plexiglas had been introduced because of its transparency, its ability to represent modern steel construction and open interior spaces and its part in the assembly of intricate façades, it was soon applied more universally because of its superior structural properties. As model makers were trying to reduce the number of different materials in models, Plexiglas became the overall solution for the majority of modeling tasks. Almost immediately, the material was applied to more abstract massing models that would previously have been built from cardboard or wood. Early design models, as in the case of the Chase Manhattan Bank, were often left abstract and in the color of the modeling material. In larger urban planning models, painting once more became the main treatment on façades to save time. Now, the material's hailed transparency was less of an advantage. To make Plexiglas opaque, massing models were spray-painted with a dark gray color from the inside while cellophane strips were glued to the outside to represent windows.[121] In addition, as Plexiglas had become established as the core modeling material, the shifting interest by some of the former advocates of glass façades like Gordon Bunshaft toward concrete in the early 1960s did not spark another radical shift in the use of materials. Rather, the large, transparent and intricately inlaid façades imitating glass and metal were substituted with painted surfaces representing concrete—made with the same material. Simultaneously, paper, cardboard, and plaster had largely disappeared from the professional modeler's palette. They had not vanished completely, though: some in-house practices in architectural offices still utilized older modeling materials and low-tech approaches, as was the case of Mies van der Rohe's cardboard siting models for the Seagram Building, built by Edward Duckett in his studio at 219 East 44th Street.[122] Wood remained a staple of the professional model maker's studio for both bases and finely carved pieces. At times, it was used as a substitute for aluminum window sashes and mullions. Due to the architects' increased dependence on detailed models for the accurate depiction of materials, Plexiglas became indispensable as it was the only structurally sound material that could replicate large glass panes. Simultaneously, since Plexiglas was reserved for the professional modeler's studio because of the expensive equipment and the specialized knowledge required to cut and assemble it, modelers became more influential as they entered a project during the initial design phase. Their ability to imitate the materials and structure of a building became a crucial aspect of both design and presentation.

From Miniature Buildings to the Idea as Model

These new applications emerged at the same time as a heightened demand for models. Outside their importance for the inception of a scheme, architects' increased requirements for models could be regarded as a consequence of their new representational properties that made an integral part of the (potentially lucrative) sale of a project. Presentation models had become extremely elaborate, combining several formerly separate models in one, namely the urban planning model, interior, and presentation model that had traditionally depicted only the exterior of a building. More functions followed quickly. Aided by the new transparency of the buildings and increasing electrification, the interior rose to an unprecedented prominence. Floor plan models and sections capitalized on the unprecedented views into the miniatures and adapted them for planning purposes. In 1957, Thomas William Hendrick noted that, contrary to prewar models of cardboard or wood, the interior of models was now visible through the large windows represented by sheets of transparent plastics.[123] This change forced architects and model makers to attend to a neglected part of the model: interior design and decoration. Fully furnished models were not only used to woo the client but subsequently also became an essential tool for studying the internal structure of the building and its relation to the exterior. One of the earliest examples in Conrad's work was a series of presentation models for SOM's design for the Manufacturers Trust, built in 1953. Other than models of high-rises, the final presentation model of the Manufacturers Trust was a hybrid made from several modeling materials. Its main corpus and roof were of painted wood on a Plexiglas ground plate. The curtain wall was made from large sheets of Plexiglas with aluminum-colored wooden inlays and was back-painted where the façade was meant to be opaque. But the detailing was not confined to the outside: The model also included a colorful interior complete with a mural on the first floor, the building's signature vault door on 5th Avenue, furnished offices, and small images on the walls that could be seen through the windows (Figure 2.37). In order to expose and highlight the interior and to replicate the actual building more closely, interior lighting made with seventy-six feet of thin neon tubes, hidden in the model's ceiling. To prevent glare from the window panes and to allow for completely visible interiors, illumination became a standard in presentation models in the late 1950s and 1960s for companies such as SOM. For model makers, the addition of lighting technology triggered further electrification that turned presentation models into independently functioning small-scale structures. As the models' lighting system threatened to overheat and melt the Plexiglas, add-ons such as built-in air conditioning and dust filters became vital.[124] Often, hardware was not readily available for purchase at such small scales and had to be devised from scratch or be appropriated from other equipment of a similar size. For a 1957 presentation model of the Pepsi-Cola building in New York, instead of using

FIGURE 2.37 Manufacturers Trust model, *c.* 1953. Copyright © Ezra Stoller/Esto.

expensive tiny light bulbs, Conrad devised a system of neon tubes that were secreted in the ceiling but shone through perforations to imitate 12,000 tiny light bulbs.[125] To prevent overheating, he devised a switch that turned the lights off automatically after thirty seconds to let the Plexiglas cool. However, the addition of electrical control systems also proved to be a threat to models. In the case of the Pepsi-Cola model, the timer broke after six months: The lights went on at night and the model burnt down. Such technical appliances, especially interior illumination, added to the realism of the models but produced further problems. Electrical systems such as ventilation, transformers, or fans were often too large to be incorporated in the models and had to be hidden in a base or pedestal, making the models more stationary. These elaborate objects were not feasible for use during the design process, but (as noted above), meant that the design of the interior gained importance given that it was now visible from the outside. Used as a sales tool, elaborate models with interiors aimed to overwhelm the client by presenting a vision of the future that was so realistic, you could even see pictures on the wall. In project design terms, visible interiors meant that models could help plan a building's layout now too. Models of layouts and interior sections *had* been used before the war for projects such as Rockefeller Center, but became increasingly important for large-scale office schemes in the 1950s. It became possible to review the design of lobbies, main public spaces, and office layouts, their lighting and materials. Enabling a more participatory design process—bearing in mind the growing involvement of boards of directors and corporate clients who wanted to be kept informed about every step of the planning—floor-plan models were large-scale objects that represented each floor without full walls or ceilings to depict the potential arrangement of partitions and furniture in relation to architectural features such as elevators and stairs. Deployed after the main features of a design were decided, these large models showed every desk on every floor. Furniture could be moved around to study circulation and spatial layouts in meetings with the client and the models could also be presented to the company's employees. As part of an extremely long planning process of over four years and the most intense collaboration between SOM and a client at the time, the design process for the Connecticut General Life Insurance Company's new headquarters is one of the most elaborate examples for the use of floor-plan models.[126] Contradictory to SOM's designs for high-rises, for this building, the architects largely neglected the façade in favor of interior layouts. For each department, floor-plan models were used.[127] The company's own planning department first came up with an abstract layout with the help of paper templates for desks and chairs. These were then translated into models by Conrad and rearranged in consultation with the client until the organization of furniture was found to be satisfactory (Figure 2.38).

The most radical expression of these new planning tools, melding together interiors and façades, was a new type of model that Conrad devised for several of SOM's projects: corner sections. In conjunction with model photos, these objects were the most efficient representation of a project's interior and exterior, adapting the elaborately furnished presentation models for the design process without having to build several costly models. Though highly detailed and realistic in the parts that were built, they often comprised only a few bays on a corner that were open to view and the camera lens on all other sides, and could be re-adjusted when necessary. As a working tool, corner sections such as the one for the Reynolds Metals Company in Richmond, Virginia, represented all technical features, materials, and furniture in the building (Figures 2.39–2.40). In this case, Conrad built a large sectional model of only four bays. Interior lighting was simulated with the help of spotlights directed at the ceiling. The louvers, one of the main features introduced for the structure, could be adjusted by means of a mechanism to test the impact of sunlight on the interior. Building a corner section instead of an entire model saved time and money and could be used to review features that would have been difficult to test in a

FIGURE 2.38 Floor plan model of the Connecticut General Life Insurance Building, *c.* 1953–7. Copyright © Doris Conrad Brown, Theodore Conrad papers, 1937–91, Avery Architectural and Fine Arts Library, Columbia University.

MODELING MATERIALS 91

FIGURE 2.39 Conrad working on a sectional model of the Reynolds Metals Building, *c.* 1955–8. Copyright © Doris Conrad Brown, Theodore Conrad papers, 1937–91, Avery Architectural and Fine Arts Library, Columbia University.

FIGURE 2.40 Exterior view of the Reynolds Metals Building model, *c.* 1955–8. Copyright © Doris Conrad Brown, Theodore Conrad papers, 1937–91, Avery Architectural and Fine Arts Library, Columbia University.

larger model. They took the model's capacity to expose and focus on the important problems of a project to extremes: A corner section of the Beinecke Library in New Haven served the sole purpose of showing the building's exterior when illuminated from within. Originally Peruvian onyx was considered for the building's façade and an earlier 1/8″=1′-0″ scale presentation model used the actual stone shaved down to scale. It was discovered only later that onyx could not be cut in sheets large enough for the actual building. After a two-year search, Vermont marble was proposed as a substitute.[128] Instead of building yet another expensive presentation model, a large-scale corner section tested light and translucence with the help of a light bulb installed on the inside. Aside from representing materials and the connection between interior and exterior, sections also explained a building's technical features or structure, as in the model of Walter Netsch's Air Force Academy chapel for Colorado Springs (Figure 2.41). Here, only a section could explain the intricately folded roof of the church as it would have been visible in neither the finished building nor a model of it. As a working tool, these sections were the most extreme and fruitful translation of the achievements made with presentation models in the imitation of materials and the realistic representation of architecture.

For the brief duration of two decades, between 1950 and 1970, Plexiglas was the main modeling material used in architectural models made by professional modelers in the United States. The shift from cardboard, paper, plaster, and wood to plastics and aluminum had taken place over the short span of thirteen years, roughly between 1936, the year of the introduction of Plexiglas to the American market, and 1949, the year the final Lever House presentation model

FIGURE 2.41 Section of the chapel for the Air Force Academy in Colorado Springs, *c.* 1954–7. Copyright © Doris Conrad Brown, Theodore Conrad papers, 1937–91, Avery Architectural and Fine Arts Library, Columbia University.

was built as one of the first to use large Plexiglas sheets. Karen Moon called this development the "transformation from soft to hard," from clay and plaster to cardboard to Plexiglas and aluminum, and equated the material development in modeling making with the "transition from the organic curves of the Beaux-Arts, Art Nouveau, and Art Deco to the crisp geometry of the Modern Movement."[129] The link between models and developments in the architecture they represent seems obvious and there is a certain overlap in the application of Plexiglas at a time when structural developments in architecture opened up new possibilities for large, sealed-off window panes in the first curtain-wall skyscrapers after the war. At the same time, however, the need for "soft" modeling materials—such as various molded plastics and metals that were used for irregular shapes and mass production—never disappeared. The development of new materials was strongly linked to their superior solutions for representational and structural problems that had nothing to do with architectural styles. Rather, the material shift followed the changing interest away from depicting simple masses, or building envelopes, to more realistic and detailed models. This affected presentation models first but was soon adopted for design models as well. Moon, thinking about the eventual demise of Plexiglas models, eventually pointed to the underlying question of whether a limitation in modeling materials would also limit the architectural ideas that could be presented through them.[130] For Conrad and his colleagues, it could be argued that it was less the all-encompassing victory of Plexiglas than the types of models that became obsolete when the focus in model making shifted away from highly detailed to more conceptual models at the end of the 1960s, as exemplified in the *Idea as Model* exhibition at the Institute for Architecture and Urban Studies in New York in 1976.[131] Many of them retained Plexiglas as a material for their abstract objects and transparency remained a significant feature in modeling. However, as the exhibition showed, material imitation and realism was no longer of concern for progressive architects: "from the 1970s, the more experimental and innovative the architect, the greater, it seems, his or her distaste for realism."[132]

3

Model Drawings

The Three-Dimensional Shift

When locating models within a broader framework of architectural media, it becomes possible to determine some of the reasons for the model's triumph over other means of expression during the postwar modeling boom. This also means looking for what Alberto Pérez-Gómez called "the space 'between dimensions' [which] is a fertile ground for discovery."[1] Media, here, can be understood as any means of communicating or transmitting an idea. The most common architectural media—the classic devices of visualizing and representing an architectural idea—are sketches, drawings, renderings, models, photography, film and, of course, the building itself. These, in turn, can be used in mass media such as magazines, books, exhibitions, or online. The translation and interpretation of architectural ideas through media is a major theme among the processes of architectural design and presentation that are, as Albena Yaneva pointed out, not always linear.[2] Starting with an initial idea for a building, there is a chain of possible visualizations that can be achieved with the help of architectural media. These vary in the way and the moment at which they are used—they are options and potentials rather than strictly regulated steps in the creation of architecture.[3] Their use is based as much on professional conventions and contemporary practices as it is on individual tastes and fashions. Together, these architectural media form a "complex system" of planning tools for architectural reflection about form and design that Andres Lepik described as crucial in his study of Renaissance models: "Planning methods, their execution and ideas of forms create a complex system of mutual, causal dependencies in architecture. The idea of a proposed building influences its design methods the same way as, inversely, the available planning methods have an impact on both ideas of forms as well as on the execution of a building."[4] Architectural media have received a considerable amount of scholarly attention in recent decades, especially as regards photography and drawing as well as considering new, born-digital media. Most famously, Beatriz Colomina's research, based heavily on the study of architectural photography and printed matter, could be considered a cornerstone for defining architecture as a "series of overlapping systems of representation" through media.[5] Media such as photos or exhibitions, she argues, have gained a greater importance than the actual building as they are more widely disseminated and consumed.[6] It was the mass media that created modern architecture by distributing photos of new buildings—the success and essence of modern architecture was measured by its visibility.[7] For the building, this meant demoting it to just one among many other media referring back to an original architectural idea: "The building should be understood in the same terms as drawings, photographs, writing, films, and advertisements; not only because these are the media in which more often we encounter it, but because the building is a mechanism of representation in its own right."[8] While acknowledging the power of architectural and mass media, others have resisted the idea of raising all architectural media to the level of "architecture," most poignantly Kester Rattenbury in her essay collection *This is Not Architecture. Media Constructions*.[9] Regardless of their status, architectural media are influential and substantial parts in the creation and representation of architecture. What many earlier studies have in common is that they confine themselves to looking at the making of architecture through media *after* a structure already exists. For research into mid-century models, however, this does not suffice. The perspective needs to shift toward architectural media's influence during the inception of a project and their subsequent cross-overs into more widely disseminated mass media, even long after a structure is under construction. Robin Evans, who was following a similar trajectory in his research on architectural drawings, pointed to the profound influence media have on the making of buildings and to the fact that architects always depend on means of representation other than the real structure, mainly drawings, sketches or models to work in: "I was soon struck by what seemed at the time the peculiar disadvantage under which architects labour, never working directly with the object of their thought, always working at it through some intervening medium, almost always the drawing."[10] Drawing on both Evans' and Colomina's observations, there appears to be a divergence in the relationship of media and architecture. First, the creation of architecture is heavily influenced by the architectural media that architects and their network use for invention. And second, the mass media circulating specific kinds of architectural media influence the way that same architecture is later perceived by a wider audience. For the former, especially with the ensuing architectural network in the twentieth century, architectural media gained a new prominence as both a means of communication, of representing architectural ideas and of recording decisions. Because of the specialization of professions in one particular medium, such as renderers or model makers, secondary auxiliary media that had no representative values (such as the model drawing) became a new and necessary tool for communication between these professions that needed to be unambiguous and easy to understand. For the latter, the application of architectural media in mass media was bound much more by conventions of display so that changes could only be implemented slowly.

In her study of early twentieth century models in Germany, Wallis Miller connected the use of different architectural media with the nineteenth century's longstanding battle over architecture's status among the fine arts, between *Baukunst* (the art of building), architecture, and building. Her underlying question goes to the core of what studies of architectural media are often trying to ascertain: which medium could be considered the original in architecture; the building, the photo or the drawing?[11] Even though this debate was never resolved, the drawing's longstanding predominance, which Evans had thought of as the basis for all architecture, was broken in the twentieth century when the model emerged as a prime architectural medium.[12] Rattenbury, in her essay collection on architectural media, identified four key shifts in the representation of architecture: perspective, photography, film, and e-technology.[13] Focusing entirely on new technological developments in two-dimensional media and the representation of built architecture, models are not even mentioned because their introduction as an architectural medium was based on the design phase and not on finished architecture.[14] Their application in mass media was left out entirely. In addition to Rattenbury's four shifts, others such as Alberto Pérez-Gómez and Louise Pelletier have noted that there have been many more small-scale shifts over time.[15] For research into mid-century Modernism, it seems necessary to add the model to the list of turning points, as part of a move toward three-dimensionality.[16] This was evidenced by the resurgence of models based on new requirements resulting from the New York Zoning Law to display and develop architectural ideas three-dimensionally. The new realism and the truthful representation of building materials was enabled by new materials that upgraded the model as a medium. A decade later, the success of model photography translated the model back into the more easily consumable two-dimensional realm.[17] The following modeling boom in the 1950s meant an undisputed victory of the model over other architectural media, especially the drawing and the rendering and its representations in mass media. As such, the postwar surge of models could be understood as a medial shift in architecture.

To explain these shifts in influence between architectural media, Mario Carpo pointed to the fact that each medium possesses unique representational qualities that at times may become foregrounded against others.[18] While this rings true particularly for the application of media for public dissemination, more often, different kinds of representations tend to coexist and influence one another. This was theorized by Arthur Drexler, who argued that different media take on specific tasks during the work on an architectural project, signifying what is important to look at or consider at particular moments.[19] Moreover, individual tool choices point to the fact that design is dependent on the idiosyncratic and personal methods of architects.[20] When it comes to determining the causes of the three-dimensional shift, this poses the question of what was important to depict in architectural media from the 1920s through 1950s and how it changed over time. More specifically, we might ask how the material changes of the model as a medium affected its use over the course of time. And, lastly, it is vital to consider the influence of contemporary media on one another and the adaptation of their techniques by newer media.

Translations and Gaps

Despite the fact that one architectural medium might have been foregrounded at specific moments in history, none have ever managed to eclipse all others fully. Some architects and writers, such as Robert Harbison, have argued that certain buildings can be represented appropriately in only one medium.[21] Similarly, Adolf Loos claimed that "what has been conceived in one art does not reveal itself in another," highlighting the specificity of each architectural medium to its content.[22] Even though there seems to be a considerable truth to such claims, especially as regards adequate material representations, most architectural projects utilize more than one medium, each of which has its unique physical and representational qualities. Used in a iterative process, all media become subject to translations and interpretations that influence and alter the rendering of an architectural idea.[23] The term "translation" was famously appropriated for architecture to describe a transfer between media by Robin Evans in his seminal text "Translations from Drawing to Building."[24] Comparing the transmittal of ideas to translations between languages, Evans summed up the essence of translation as a process: "The assumption that there is a uniform space through which meaning may glide without modulation is more than just a naïve delusion."[25] Meaning—and thus, an idea—is influenced by its translation between different architectural media. Using the inherent unlikeness of drawing and building, Evans was the first to reveal poignantly the need not to look at each medium independently, but rather to see them in their referential relation to one another.[26]

As such, looking at translations between architectural media means looking at how Colomina's "overlapping systems of representation" interact and influence each other, as well as the depiction of the idea. In the same way that models have not been considered a shift in architectural media, they have not been introduced into the discussion about translations between them. In fact, they have been left out of most discussions about architectural media by default. To begin looking at them means focusing attention at two main translations that can be assumed as the most important for model making in the twentieth century and that were connected to the postwar modeling boom: first, an initial translation went from drawing to model. Second, the translation of model to model photo contributed largely to the model's stunning success from the 1930s onward. Subsequently, they were adapted for mass media through exhibitions and printed magazines. In her account of architecture as media, Colomina acknowledged the limitations of individual means of expression such as photography or drawing which cannot represent a building in full. There are always boundaries between the two.[27] In crossing these barriers, translations alter architectural ideas and adapt them to the new medium's system of representation. The model, in opposition to all two-dimensional architectural media, occupies a unique place in among these translations as it converts an idea into three dimensions, often for the first time during a project. The "space between these dimensions" or, as Robin Evans called it, the "blind spots,"[28] become the main focus of problem solving but also of invention, making the model a unique part of architectural creativity. The model makers, as those who translate one medium, the drawing, into another, the model, inhabit this gap and can be considered authors in their own right through their expertise in their field. As Stan Allen pointed out for the architect who is placed between drawing and building, the modeler inhabits several worlds, those of drawing, modeling and building.[29] On the level of the three-dimensional object, the translations include considerations regarding structure, materiality, and representation. On a grander level, these translations have the potential to achieve new understandings of an idea or the world more generally.[30] To bridge the gaps, liminal or auxiliary tools such as the model drawing, the photo model as well as written and oral descriptions help guide the work. Not independent architectural media *per se*, their sole purpose is to facilitate the translation. Through their properties, however, they influence it heavily.

Drawing Models

"Here we work directly from plans," he said. "If we were in some handy spot in town, the architects would come in and watch us building a model and say 'Do this. Do that,' instead of putting their changes down on paper, where they belong."[31]

THEODORE CONRAD, 1956

Architectural drawings and renderings were the first and foremost mode of representation in the 1920s. By the 1950s they were, especially in architectural magazines, largely eclipsed by architectural and model photography. As the architect's primary mode of expression, their representational qualities were clearly distinct from the building they represented and had "intrinsic limitations of reference," as Evans pointed out: ". . . the properties of drawing—its peculiar power in relation to its putative subject, the building—are hardly recognized at all. Recognition of the drawing's power as a medium turns out, unexpectedly, to be recognition of the drawing's distinctness from and unlikeness to the thing that is represented, rather than its likeness to it, which is neither as paradoxical nor as dissociative as it may seem."[32] Adolf Loos, one of the intellectual forefathers of the medial and stylistic shifts of the twentieth century, was well aware of this problem when he concluded that the drawing should be a means of communication rather than representation and that the only reason for architects to use drawings is the division of labor.[33] Among the purely communicative drawings, one sticks out as the basis for the model's very existence—the model drawing. As an entirely new medium it was introduced, possibly in the 1920s or 1930s, to facilitate the communication between architects and model makers. At the same scale as the model, it translates the necessary information from the architect's working drawings. In the model drawing, the gaps or "blind spots" of the translation from the architect's working drawing to the model are addressed: decisions about its details, material representation, construction, and the way it is assembled and disassembled. As an auxiliary tool, these drawings are often destroyed during the model's construction. They are neither a medium in and of itself nor are they intended for public presentation. Therefore, only very few model drawings have survived the hazardous working conditions of modeling studios. Among them, and one of the earliest sets preserved by Conrad, are the drawings for Liebman House in Mount Kisco; an unbuilt design in an affluent town in Westchester County, New York. Aline Meyer Liebman was a wealthy art collector and painter who, together with her husband Charles J. Liebman, commissioned the design by Edward Durell Stone in 1937. Mrs. Liebman was one of the founders of MoMA and the couple was heavily involved in the modern art scene in New York. Both had been patrons of the famous 1932 *International Style* exhibition and supported modern architecture. The 1930s Depression was a difficult time for architects, and hit young graduates without a full Rolodex of clients particularly hard. Architectural and lifestyle magazines tried to alleviate some of the pressures by giving talented designers exposure through commissions for fictitious schemes for suburban houses of which readers could buy floor plans for as little as one dollar. Liebman House was of a comparable size and program yet developed for a private client. The surviving set of model drawings includes twelve sheets of varying planning stages and purposes. The earliest is a copy of a floor plan from Stone's office (Figure 3.1). It shows the layout of the house and its adjoining facilities without much detail except for labels indicating the function of each room. Since Stone was not the only contender for the job—the Liebmans had reportedly considered several other architects to design the house, among them Raymond Hood, Harry Allen Jacobs, and even Le Corbusier—the drawing was probably meant to give the clients a basic idea of what the house would look like so as to secure the commission to build a model. Its presence in the archive suggests that it might have also been the basis for model maker Conrad's cost estimate for Stone.

Modern architectural drawings were first mentioned by Leon Battista Alberti in his book *De Re Aedificatoria* in the mid-fifteenth century as part of the growing split between the more academically minded profession of the architect and the building trades.[34] Since the architect was no longer continually present at the building site, he needed a way of communicating his ideas to the workmen. It was only in the nineteenth century, however, that the architectural drawing rose to become the most important tool for communication when descriptive geometry made it possible to translate three-dimensional objects into precise two-dimensional drawings through standardized representations and scales.[35] To communicate ideas, copies were made laboriously by hand until in the 1880s blueprints became more widely used, requiring fewer in-house copyists at architectural offices.[36] The advent of mass-reproduced drawings not only contributed directly to

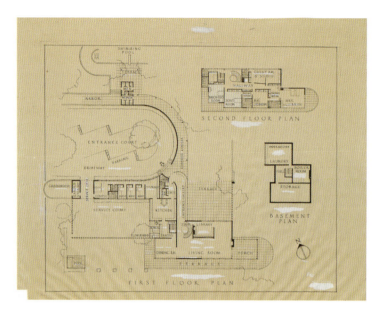

FIGURE 3.1 Liebman House, copy of a floor plan by Edward Durell Stone's office, c. 1937. Private collection.

FIGURE 3.2 Theodore Conrad sitting at the drawing table in his basement workshop, c. 1934. Copyright © Doris Conrad Brown, Theodore Conrad papers, 1937–91, Avery Architectural and Fine Arts Library, Columbia University.

the split of the architectural profession, but was also a prerequisite for the collaboration between independent professions as they made communication outside the architect's office possible. Drawing—and the ability to translate drawings into three dimensions—were quickly recognized as essential for the profession of the model maker, as Robert Forman noted in 1946: "The model maker should learn to draw to scale and be able to read scale drawings."[37] Especially for young architects like Conrad who were struggling to find employment, familiarity with drawing techniques facilitated their transition into model making (Figure 3.2).

Between architect and model maker, drawings were more than just a form of communication. They became a contract that indicated the architect's specifications and the modeler's contribution. During the twentieth century, a multitude of specialized drawings—from sketches to elaborate working drawings—emerged that formed the basis of different models: For a quick massing model, the model maker needed only an architect's rough sketch with measurements whereas for a highly elaborate model, more detailed drawings were necessary.[38] However, models were almost always based on a well-prepared variety of drawings. The detailed presentation model, the most common and elaborate translation during the postwar boom years, depended on a standard set of drawings including floor plans, elevations, sections, landscaping, site plans, and details that were prepared by the architect. When Conrad started his practice, these drawings were either provided as blueprints of detailed working drawings for the building or as more simplified model drawings that omitted measurements and other unnecessary information. Original drawings usually remained in the architect's office. However, architects often deviated from this practice according to their office's policy, workload, and the schedule of the project: whereas Wallace Harrison provided Conrad with blueprints of model drawings made in the architect's office (Figures 3.3–3.4), Edward Durell Stone often sent detailed working drawings and blueprints for Conrad to make the model drawings himself. For Liebman House, since plans were still in an early stage, it is likely that no blueprints of working drawings existed at the time the model was designed and, hence, Conrad made his estimates with the help of the floor plan produced by Stone's office. After the initial discussion with the clients, the architect altered the scheme to include their wishes and another drawing at the scale of 1/8"=1'-0" was used for planning the model. Two versions of the same drawing survive as copies and indicate the thickness and color of the walls in the model. They are less presentable and polished than the previous drawing—the hallmarks of a working tool.

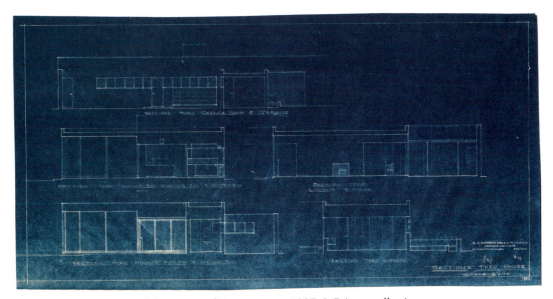

FIGURE 3.3 Blueprint of the House of Tomorrow, *c.* 1937–8. Private collection.

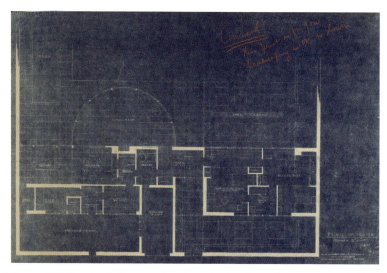

FIGURE 3.4 "Conrad. This print is for you. Landscaping is ok as shown" is marked on this drawing in red crayon. Private collection.

If the drawing provided by the architect was not to the same scale as the model, dividers were used to produce a new set of drawings. This was done by taking a fixed line on the original drawing with the dividers and multiplying it with the ratio of the model's scale. A tool that made this transfer easier was the proportional compass which could be fixed for the translation from one scale into another. Even though copies of drawings formed the basis for the communication between architects and model makers, the latter preferred to work from scale drawings rather than blueprints because copies never aligned perfectly with the originals and were considered inaccurate.[39] Therefore, modelers made a separate set of accurate model drawings. To Bel Geddes, the accuracy of these drawings was of such pivotal importance that each had to be approved by him personally before modeling could begin. Equally, in the New York World's Fair model shop each model maker made his or her own drawings and assembled the model on top of it to avoid mistakes in the collaboration between different modelers.[40] Another reason for the need for a separate set of model drawings, was that papers and drawing utensils influenced their use significantly.[41] Blueprints and other kinds of copies reproduced drawings on heavy, opaque paper. In opposition, model drawings were made with tracing paper and pencils which made transferring contours easier. Model drawings deviated from the architect's drawings and blueprints significantly as they only contained information necessary to build the model, including scale, size, materials and model construction (Figure 3.5). They rarely indicated the dimensions of the model numerically as they were in the same scale as the model and the model maker could directly transfer the dimensions from the drawing with dividers. Unlike working drawings, they often included the building's surroundings and labels for spatial descriptions. Thus, the architect's drawings were meant to give the modeler an overview over the final appearance, important design features, and the building's furnishing. Based on them, the model maker needed to prepare more specific drawings that did not correspond with the building but explained the making of the object. These technical drawings outlined its base, substructure, and assembly as well as topography

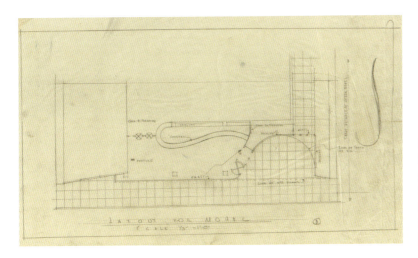

FIGURE 3.5 Conrad's floor plan for the original model of MoMA, *c.* 1937. Copyright © 2020. Digital image, The Museum of Modern Art, New York/Scala, Florence.

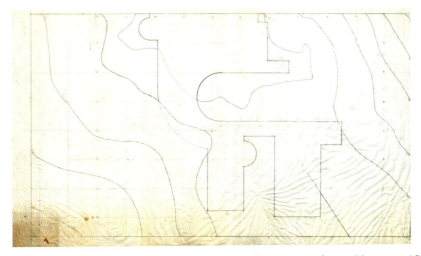

FIGURE 3.6 Conrad's contour drawing for Edward Durell Stone's Liebman House, *c.* 1937. Private collection.

(Figures 3.6, 3.7–3.8). They were necessary since in the model, whether built from cardboard, wood or Plexiglas, materials and structure were different from the actual building. A brick wall was not built with small bricks but with one large sheet of material and the bricks were later relayed through surface treatment.

Models were often built in sections so as to make it possible to disassemble them for future changes and repairs, or to enable others to continue the construction in case the model maker was unable finish it (Figure 3.9).[42] Allowing small tolerances for materials to expand due to changing climatic conditions was another reason for separate parts. The basis for a model's site drawings were often aerial photos and topographical maps that were provided through the architect's office or by photographic agencies such as Fairchild Aerial Surveys. Still, establishing an accurate topographical map including vegetation could mean a considerable effort by the

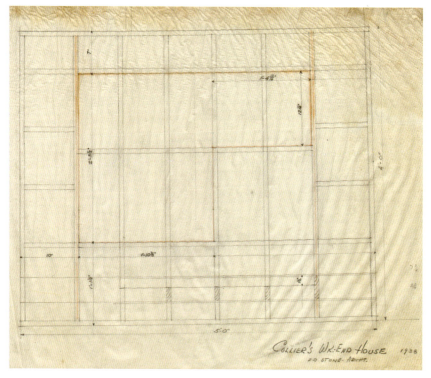

FIGURE 3.7 Conrad's drawing of the base for *Collier's* Weekend House. Private collection.

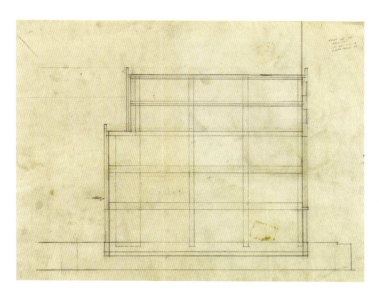

FIGURE 3.8 Conrad's drawing of the internal structure of MoMA, *c.* 1937. Copyright © 2020. Digital image, The Museum of Modern Art, New York/Scala, Florence.

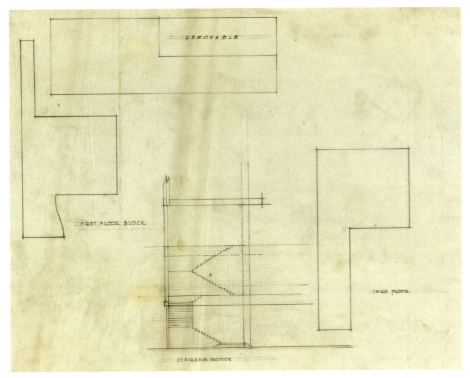

FIGURE 3.9 Conrad's drawing of pieces and the internal structure for MoMA, *c.* 1937. Copyright © 2020. Digital image, The Museum of Modern Art, New York/Scala, Florence.

modeler. Drawn onto thin paper, a site drawing was used to transfer the lines marking the terrain's contours onto the model with the help of a sharp wheel (Figure 3.10). For the average model project, a wooden base was built over which the landscape was modeled either in plaster or wood. The contour lines were then either carved into the plaster or were built up with wood on top of the drawing to ensure utmost accuracy. Drawings for the base and internal structure functioned as construction manuals and showed sections through the model indicating the location of screws, dowels and bracing elements. Inhabiting the gap between the architect's drawing and the model maker's model, these drawings were a result of the developments in modeling materials in the 1920s and 1930s that started out with the peculiar likeness of model drawing and modeling material: cardboard. Initially, untreated cardboard enabled quick sketches to be made for massing models for early design phases. Soon, however, painted façades took more time to be executed as they became elaborate model drawings folded into three dimensions. In his 1926 modeling manual, Edward W. Hobbs explained what was needed for an accurate scale model of cardboard: drawings of the four elevations and a floor plan.[43] To transfer the drawing into a model, the outlines of the façade were drawn onto the cardboard, inked in with waterproof Indian ink and then bent into shape. Whereas these early cardboard models were essentially three-dimensional renderings, the development of models toward miniature buildings of various materials that displayed their internal structure called for a more complicated translation of architectural ideas. As models became

FIGURE 3.10 Site drawing for the topography of the Bermuda Naval Base model in Conrad's workshop, 1940s. Copyright © Doris Conrad Brown, Theodore Conrad papers, 1937–91, Avery Architectural and Fine Arts Library, Columbia University.

FIGURE 3.11 Conrad reviewing the assembly of the Equitable Life model with the help of a construction drawing, c. 1957–8. Copyright holder unknown but see Equitable Agency Items, November 3, 1958, 12.

assembled from individual parts, the model drawings were no longer the material basis of the models. Instead of showing the finished exterior of a building they demonstrated how its parts were put together. The elevations that had formerly become the model's exterior turned into detailed instructions for assembly and painting (Figure 3.11). They translated the two-dimensional drawings into an object without being a part of it themselves. After an updated copy of Liebman House arrived from Stone's office, a drawing on tracing paper that was made in Conrad's workshop was the first to inhabit exactly this gap (Figure 3.12). It contains instructions for materials to use for parts of the model and is of an exploratory nature. It breaks down the model into different sections with two alternate designs for the second floor. A small sketch shows a section of the model's interior as a wooden box. More drawings were prepared as part of the model making process for Liebman House to explain the making of the object. One was made at full model scale indicating the sections of the model. Another detailed drawing explores two alternative solutions for the second-floor bedroom for Mrs. Liebman. They indicate structural concerns and contain notes for the assembly of the pieces.

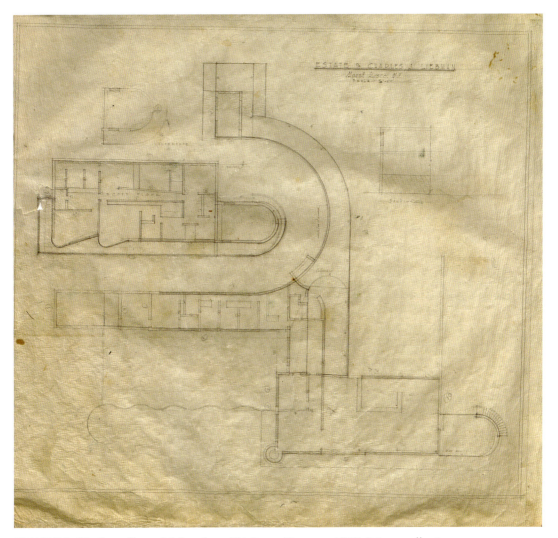

FIGURE 3.12 Conrad's model drawing of Liebman House, *c.* 1937. Private collection.

The main communication between architect and model maker was through drawings, and the modeler's creative input and interpretation often came into play when working drawings were still unfinished. As model makers made most of the technical drawings themselves, they were the ones who decided the specifics of the construction that were made to resemble the appearance indicated in the architect's drawings. The realization of technical add-ons (such as hidden interior lighting) to enhance the object's realism depended on the technical model drawings as much as the assembly of the transparent façades. Model drawings also envisioned an object's use, especially for photo models, by designating the built-in openings for the camera and, thus, the views of interest for photos. After initial model drawings were completed, architects often sent changes or additions. As the work progressed, further details were given to the model maker in drawings that indicated materials to be mimicked (Figure 3.13). Thanks to an article in *Pencil Points*

FIGURE 3.13 Copy of a drawing by the Philip Goodwin and Edward Durell Stone indicating the marble veining for the MoMA model's rear elevation, c. 1937. Copyright © 2020. Digital image, The Museum of Modern Art, New York/Scala, Florence.

from 1939, one such list of materials is available for the model of Liebman House.[44] It was made using wood for the base and structural parts of the house, plaster and aluminum for the sheathing of the walls, celluloid for the windows, rubber for the floor, and various plant materials and wires for the landscape.

In 1937, the drawings for the Liebman House model were a relatively novel yet indispensable tool that aided the translation of Stone's drawings into Conrad's three-dimensional model. Yet as a tool, the model drawings had their limits. They were pinned up or laid out in the workshop for constant reference, often used up during the model building process as templates that the model stood on or were destroyed by paints or fluids. They were not regarded as originals for either building or model, which led to them being discarded after the model was finished or updated drawings arrived. Furthermore, not all information could be relayed through drawings: Written annotations on the blueprints were done in red crayon; building materials were marked in writing and exact colors were provided through paint chips and descriptions. Landscaping, one of the most important aspects of large models, often had a set of separate drawings provided by the landscape architect that included written instructions for the season, colors, and the state of vegetation (Figure 3.14). Eventually, all these systems of notation were no substitute for the need for constant communication between model maker and architect to ensure that the architect's drawings were translated faithfully. In the case of Liebman House, it is unclear whether the model was ever presented to the clients or whether the Liebmans only saw the photos taken by model

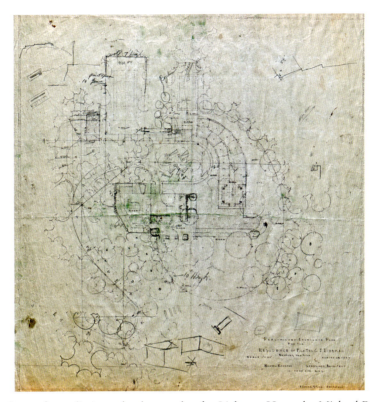

FIGURE 3.14 Copy of a preliminary landscape plan for Liebman House by Michael Rapuano, *c.* 1937. Private collection.

photographer Louis Checkman. His images indicate a certain familiarity with the design and geographic features of the property, which seems to suggest that they were the primary way of showing the clients a preview of the building. Some of the surviving prints are mounted onto canvas, which further points to their use in a private presentation. Ultimately, neither model nor model photos seem to have been successful in convincing the Liebmans. The model is long lost and the house was never built. The model drawings remain as one of the last documents of the translations in the conception of Liebman House.

4

Model Photography

Realism

It is for the camera as a mediator to present the model's most favorable view.[1] In any event, the model and its workmanship determine the way it is photographed.[2]

JOACHIM GIEBELHAUSEN, 1964

The most significant translation of the model leading up to the postwar modeling boom was model photography with its subsequent uses in magazines, advertisements, books, and presentations to clients. In spite of its importance, however, model photography has been talked about very little.[3] One of very few historical accounts of it from the 1920s was published by LeRoy Grumbine.[4] Early modeling manuals such as his mentioned the topic only in passing and usually referred their amateur audience to the help of professionals.[5] After the end of World War II, more comprehensive instructions appeared in specialist guides, especially from the 1960s onward, such as Joachim Giebelhausen's guide to architectural photography or Rolf Janke's widely read manual *Architectural Models*.[6] Model photography reduces a three-dimensional object back into two dimensions. As both a means of communication and interpretation, it was heavily influenced by its roots in the tradition of architectural photography but largely dependent on the advancements of the objects it translated: the model's physical qualities, its material, size, scale, and details as well as its surroundings and landscaping. The choice of materials in particular, depending on the model's development toward the representation of reality and the imitation of building materials, became a pivotal criterion with the introduction of model photography, as it influenced the photo's desired effects. According to the image's intended use, there were different strategies for transforming the model, oscillating between the illusion of a real building and the plain documentation of an object. Lighting, the frame of the image, and backdrops further influenced the way a model could be transformed. Documentary photography depicted and recorded the model as an object, meaning that is was viewed from above or with the edges of the ground plate visible, mostly in front of a white or black background. These photos often gave no indication of scale and the model was clearly identifiable as such. Their aim was to keep a visual note of an object for comparison, storage, or illustration, or because it might be altered or lost during the design process. They were used as working tools for the architects to make design choices but were published, too. Arguably the more important strategy for photos during the postwar modeling boom, the term "realism" has received a considerable interest in research into model photography not least through Davide Deriu's account of twentieth-century model photos in which he postulated realism and documentary photography as the two poles of modernist practices.[7] Mark Morris' account of the same time attests architects a desire "to present their models as if they were buildings."[8] Increased realism, meaning the simulation of reality, was made possible only by new modeling materials and construction techniques. For this, highly refined models were needed as Jane Jacobs illustrated: "A complete and meticulous model of a large building—one that can stand close-up photography without shrieking 'model'—can hardly cost less than $2,000."[9] "Not shrieking model," or what model photographer Louis Checkman called an "air of realism,"[10] meant that the model was not depicted as an object but as a building; as if it were built in full scale. To achieve realism, the model had to be detailed to allow for close-ups, so that its edges could be obscured. Its real size and materiality were concealed by low or "human" vantage points introducing a simulated size with props such as figurines or cars. Lighting, shadows, and backgrounds enhanced the simulation. A demand for these more accurate miniatures for photography, for "real architectural models" and not "toys" existed at least since the 1930s: "A real architectural model, when photographed with the proper background or made into a composite photograph with the actual foreground and background of the building site, must look like the real building."[11] As the model was often built before the building, realistic model photos anticipated the building's most important views and materials. Yet, the ultimate point of reference remained the finished building. To simulate reality, there were several options available to the photographer: the primary translation of model into photo by staging the model during the photo shooting using elaborate built backgrounds and photo models; and a secondary translation through editing after an image was taken with the help of photo montages and retouches. Often, these methods were used in combination. The above strategies—that is, documentary photography versus the simulation of reality—addressed the translation of model into photo in fundamentally opposite ways. Filling in the gaps between the two were several auxiliary techniques of photography that were used in connection with the model's own physical qualities in order to create the different kinds of images. In conjunction with realism in model making, photographic simulations of reality became a powerful translation that attracted further uses in mass media.

In the translation of model to photo, the object's unique ability to produce more than one image from different angles seems to be its most crucial difference to architectural drawings. Davide Deriu attributed this advantage to the "agency of the camera" that "can draw out the model's photogenic aspects."[12] Adding to this, it could also be said that it was not just the camera that had agency but the object itself, as it presented the camera with multiple, yet limited, built-in options for images. Given that it was made purely to be photographed, the photo model inhabits a similarly liminal space as the model drawing.[13] It is not meant as an object in or of itself. Rather, in a very Benjaminian sense it existed only to be translated and thus catered more to the needs and logic of its photographic representation than to the truthful representation of the architectural idea as a model. False openings or blank exterior treatments prove this especially in photo models of interiors in which walls and roofs could be taken apart to provide strategically important views but which were not part of the built structure. Interior models also illustrate that it is not just the camera that shows a model's best aspects but rather the model itself that determines its translation into a photo. Together, model and photo staged the architectural idea and translated it into a new two-dimensional image. Therefore, I would suggest revising Deriu's statement on the impact of photography on modeling: "While photography helped to revive the role of the model, at the same time it destroyed its aura as a unique, original object and paved the way for its progressive de-materialization."[14] While photography clearly accelerated the development of the modeling boom, it did not destroy the model as a unique object. Instead, by offering such a close look at it, photography forced models to be made to a new degree of perfection in material representation. In order to assess model photography and photo models, it becomes necessary to return once more to the model's materiality to review its influences on the images. Subsequently, we also need to ask how the photos' underlying visual codes were translated for their audiences to bring across the model's message in their use in magazines and exhibitions. In an article about the Palais Stoclet, Sigfried Giedion described the effect that such photos had in print: "The most notable thing about this (very photogenic) house of Hoffmann when one looks at it in magazines [. . .] is the moment of doubt as to whether what one is seeing is a built thing or a model."[15] The "moment of doubt" was the crucial achievement in the realistic translation of models into photos that defined model photography during the boom years. The editors in the popular press further altered and selected them according to their own agenda between architectural news items and entertainment or commercial purposes. Because of their widespread dissemination, the role of magazines and exhibitions as active forces facilitating the modeling boom cannot be overestimated. As clients, magazines were agents in the production of models and, depending on their own development, their changing requirements left a metaphorical mark on both models and photos.

Camera and Model

At first glance, photography's value for research into model making seems to be auxiliary, merely recording objects otherwise lost. But in the hands of architects, model makers, and photographers, the camera became not only a mediator but also a powerful instrument for staging models. Based on the changes in the materiality of the objects, model photos gained enormous authority in the 1930s and 1940s until they largely supplanted drawings and renderings in architectural and lifestyle magazines. Model photos had been in use since the invention of photography in the 1800s.[16] Their extensive application, however, is a phenomenon that first developed during the interwar period of the twentieth century for which Davide Deriu suggested two main causes: an increased use of models; and a greater need for representing architecture in mass media, especially architectural magazines.[17] Constantly referencing each other, model and architectural photography share many aspects in the way images are produced, such as framing, lighting, perspective, depth, focus, color, composition, and vantage points. They are, however, divided by the techniques by which the photos are created. Most importantly, the scale and material of models and buildings call for different approaches. Model photos are perspectival images in which the model is fixed, as seen from a particular standpoint. Its measurements and scale become harder to identify unless made otherwise visible in the image. The three-dimensional quality of walking around a model, and being able to change the angle when looking at it, is lost. But it is not just the camera that influences the final outcome. Model photography also depends largely on the model itself, its materiality, construction, and built-in image creating capacity, openings, or dismountable parts. Not all models will yield the same kind of photo. As such, model photography is the interplay between camera and model which draws out "the model's most favorable view" in realistic model images.

As in architectural photography, the main difficulty in creating realistic model images was to avoid perspective distortion—vertical lines in the model had to appear vertical in the image. This could be achieved only by using large-view cameras that could tilt and shift to balance out overly large (building) or overly small (model) objects by adjusting the way the image was projected onto the film.[18] With this type of camera, small objects that had to be photographed at close range retained a reasonable depth of focus and it was possible to achieve a parallel projection.[19] The height of the camera and the type of lens used influenced the outcome greatly. Although bird's-eye-view shots were frequently used by designers to survey an area and to study the relation of buildings, models were increasingly photographed with low vantage points, mimicking the pedestrian's eye level. Bird's-eye-view shots could be achieved by placing the model upright against the wall, ideally with a 45° shadow. Eye-level shots were more difficult to obtain. In a 1/8"=1'-0" scale model, eye level meant that the camera had to be placed at a height exactly three-quarters of an inch above ground (assuming an average height of a person to be six feet). Even a slight deviation would be visible. The type of lens also influenced the representation of space in the image. A wide-angled lens could make spaces look larger and a telephoto lens melded foreground and background together, a good option for photographing a model in front of an urban background. In most cases, a photo could be taken from the edge of the model. Often, larger models could be taken apart to position the camera as close to the desired object as possible. Trees and other accessories could be taken out to allow for further close-ups. If a view was still inaccessible, the picture could be taken with the help of a mirror (Figure 4.1). For utmost realism, the model was best depicted without its edges visible. Often, the position of the building in the landscape determined the composition and the frame of the image. For large models, this was achieved by spotlighting the most important part and fading the rest into the darker surroundings. Smaller models posed greater difficulties as they lacked enough background to conceal the edges. In this case, additional plants and accessories could be used to obscure the boundaries of the object.

The material changes in model making affected model photos greatly. White plaster and cardboard posed fewer problems than colored or large-scale models as the former were often less

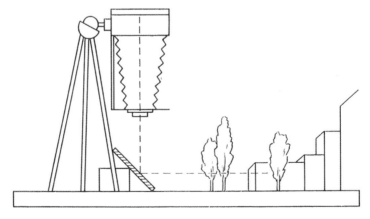

FIGURE 4.1 A 45° mirror is used to photograph inaccessible parts of a model. Copyright holder unknown but see Rössing, Architekturfotografie, 91.

detailed, but their painted façades already included shadows which made elaborate lighting unnecessary. The utmost accuracy was important for models that were photographed: The slightest mistake would destroy the illusion by giving away the model's material and its making. As realism became more pronounced from the 1930s onward, photos had to balance a desire to hide the model's true nature as a small-scale object, and an increased need to exhibit building materials such as transparent glass and reflective metals. Transparency in windows, for example, was made visible by using a polarizer to avoid reflections. Yet it was often exactly the mirroring effect that helped to articulate the window's material glass (Figures 4.2–4.3).[20] To enhance the

FIGURES 4.2 and 4.3 Two different kinds of lighting for "glass" windows in photos. Copyright holder unknown but see Giebelhausen, Architekturfotografie, 137, 142, 143, 147, 151, 156.

illusion of three-dimensional space in model images, the effects of light and shadow were adopted to give large assembled models depth.

Natural light *was* used but often, models were photographed in the model maker's shop, the architect's office or the photographer's studio, where they needed to be illuminated. With artificial lighting, the aim for realistic images was to have only one source of light (the sun) and one shadow. Indirect lighting to make the surroundings brighter was done with lamps directed at the ceiling. If areas in the model were too dark, they could be brightened with white cardboard placed next to the model to reflect the light. For massing models or models without details, hard shadows could be created with light from a low light source. Interior lighting was used in models from the 1920s to create a similar effect of strong lights and shadows for night shots. Smaller models could be set up on a tripod and then turned under the same incidence of light to take several images, but many of Conrad's models were too large to be rotated so the photographer and lighting had to move around them (Figure 4.4). Color entered model photos in the mid-1930s when lifestyle magazines started to print limited numbers of color pages, made possible through the introduction of new and improved color films.[21] It was not until after the war, however, that color model photos became more widely used.

FIGURE 4.4 Photo shoot with a magazine model. Copyright © Wayne Checkman, Louis Checkman negatives, photographs and papers, 1955–92, Avery Architectural and Fine Arts Library, Columbia University.

Models, Photos, and Drawings

> What we do want to know and show the client is, what the building will look like when seen as most people will see it, from the street and at no great distance.[22]
>
> HARVEY WILEY CORBETT, 1922

Even though drawings remained the main mode of representation for architecture, the use of model photos for both design and presentation increased during the 1920s. Early model photography was heavily influenced by drawings, architectural renderings, and architectural photography. Their techniques of representation were adopted to fit model photos into contemporary modes of expression. Models provided an opportunity for a variety of different angles, lighting, and framing which—in the eyes of their makers—gave them a great advantage over renderings that could present only one angle of a proposed project at a time. The translation of models into photos was not invented by Harvey Wiley Corbett but his ubiquitous use of them can be regarded as groundbreaking. A model photo, he argued, was the best option for achieving a life-like imitation of a real building as it facilitated the task of imagining the building for both client and architect. In several articles for *Pencil Points* in 1922, he explained how to "freeze" a pedestrian's perspective by holding a model to one's eye or by the photographer bending down to its height. To achieve realism, it was important to choose the right angle and distance between camera lens and building (Figures 4.5, 4.6–4.7): "Now if we examine the three photographs with the purpose of studying the design by means of them, we will find from the pin-hole picture that the tower and portico will count much more effectively than one would have been led to believe from an examination of the photograph on this page. Furthermore, the pin-hole picture gives an impression of the mass of the building rising before one and above one while the other photographs lack this impressiveness and realism and make the building look rather like a toy."[23]

In the 1920s, one of the first and foremost tasks of realistic photography was to obscure the model's materiality, in the same way as painting a façade concealed its material—cardboard.

FIGURE 4.5 Model of the Hartford Bushnell Memorial Hall presented as an object not a building. Copyright holder unknown but see Corbett, Harvey Wiley. "Architectural Models of Cardboard." *Pencil Points*, April–August 1922, 11–14; 28–32, 37; 14–17; 14–18.

FIGURE 4.6 Photo taken with a normal camera lens that could not represent a pedestrian's perspective accurately. Copyright holder unknown but see Corbett, Harvey Wiley. "Architectural Models of Cardboard." *Pencil Points*, April–August 1922, 11–14; 28–32, 37; 14–17; 14–18.

FIGURE 4.7 Using a pin-hole instead of a lens to obtain an image replicating a pedestrian's perspective. No known copyright holder but see Corbett, Harvey Wiley. "Architectural Models of Cardboard." *Pencil Points*, April–August 1922, 11–14; 28–32, 37; 14–17; 14–18.

Hiding the object was pivotal because the existing modeling materials would have revealed that the model was not a real building. Often, a lack of definition and blur, especially when it came to close-ups of small-scale models prevented too close a look at the model. In 1929, seven years after Corbett's articles, the photos of the models for the Metropolitan Life North Building still followed his guidelines for using low vantage points. However, there were visual strategies other than the depiction of a finished building based on other model types, mainly massing models. Chiaroscuro model photography was the most prominent non-realistic depiction of models that could be loosely associated with "New Photography": Based on the German *Neue Sachlichkeit*, it presented buildings as objects with strong lights and shadows by omitting details.[24] Corbett's early design massing models for the Metropolitan Life North Building, made of white cardboard, as well as the design models for Rockefeller Center followed this strategy and were highlighted with hard shadows to define the building's envelope. In some photos, the edges of the volumes were retraced on the print to make them even more prominent. Similar experiments with the representation of a building's mass through light and shadow were a major focus of architectural renderings and stage design in the 1920s, and were transferred onto architectural projects when the focus in early design stages shifted to the building envelope after the adoption of the New York Zoning Law. A pioneer in chiaroscuro rendering and one of America's most well-established delineators, Hugh Ferriss, used similar techniques to convey a structure's mass in his drawings.[25] Ferriss introduced his new style, chiaroscuro black-and-white renderings, in the early 1920s. His highly seductive charcoal drawings were a dramatic interpretation of a building's shape rather than a detailed overview. What he was more interested in than accuracy was the "essence" of a building, its most important features. Therefore, he rejected the use of exact perspectives, on-site sketches or photos. His approach was soon favored for important commissions by a number of progressively minded architects, among them model advocates Harvey Wiley Corbett and Raymond Hood. The value they placed on Ferriss' drawings was not least exposed by the fact that they occasionally honored the promotional effect of his drawings with a bonus if a project was built.[26] One of the first to transfer chiaroscuro rendering techniques into model photos was stage designer Norman Bel Geddes whose main interest in models was to create highly illusionistic environments. A pioneer in model making and a strong self-promoter, Bel Geddes used model photos constantly and in 1950 retroactively marketed his photo techniques under the name "Norman Bel Geddes Process of Model Photography."[27] His basic techniques were summarized by Christina Cogdell: "These techniques included highly realistic model making, variable scaling for variable distance, representing temporal and atmospheric conditions, simulating motion, positioning the audience to have an aerial view, and correlating camera/viewer distance and angle to match the scale and narrative of the model."[28] For him, the physical models were merely a basis onto which special effects were projected. Even though originally working for theater productions, Geddes quickly realized that dramatic lighting was of the same pivotal importance for architectural model images as it was to the drawings and models of stage settings (Figure 4.8). Around the same time the Metropolitan North Life Building was designed, his first architectural project to be photographed with dramatic lighting was the Toledo Scale Factory that showed aerial views as well as close-ups.[29] To plan large-scale models and dioramas, Geddes' workshop went as far as preparing massing models to test light effects. In all these images, the intention was not to depict the models as accurately as possible but to achieve effects by obscuring their physical qualities. This was further enhanced by Geddes' use of gauze in front of the lens to blur the image.[30] Architects, model makers, and photographers adopted similar chiaroscuro techniques for model photography, especially massing models of high-rises such as the Metropolitan Life North Building and Rockefeller Center. Well suited to drawing out the setbacks of these models, the technique proved highly effective for night shots where all details could be concealed.

Rather than create sharp contrasts in chiaroscuro images, Corbett and others simultaneously developed more life-like images once a design had progressed beyond simple massing models.

FIGURE 4.8 Chiaroscuro photo for Norman Bel Geddes' Shell Oil model. Copyright © Harry Ransom Center, The University of Texas at Austin.

This was closely connected to representing a building's urban context. Prior to the twentieth century, models were only rarely depicted with surroundings.[31] Now, some had their immediate surroundings built, but in order to insert a model into an even larger context there were other options for processing model photos further. The techniques presented in Corbett's 1922 *Pencil Points* article remained largely unchanged until after World War II. Corbett had presented two options of making a photo montage: through composite photos, meaning a montage of a model photo and an image of a real background as for his Bush House in London (Figure 4.9); and through alterations to the print with the help of drawings, as for his design for the George Washington National Masonic Monument in the US' capital city (Figure 4.10). Corbett regarded the former technique—montages or what he called "composite photographs"—as an effective way of designing as well as presenting an idea to a client.[32] In a 1967 article on the topic, photographer Louis Checkman explained how the technique was used: A photo of the real site was taken, measuring the distance between the camera and the building and the height of the lens to the ground (Figure 4.11).[33] The same was done with the model but converted to the model's scale. It was important for both images to have the same lighting and the same focal length if they were to achieve a uniform perspectival impression. The site image was then projected onto a print of the model photo and its size adjusted to the model's image. After developing the site photo, the model photo's sky was cut out and the site photo glued onto the model image. From this montage, a negative was made which could be used for prints. A similar effect could be achieved if the surroundings were drawn onto the print. Particularly in montages when two images were pasted together, retouches were frequently added to the photos. In the 1920s, surroundings were drawn onto the print in ink matching the image's lighting, tone, and perspective. Montage and retouches were often used in combination to achieve a seamless connection between model photo and photographed or drawn surroundings. Corbett applied this technique on several occasions, most

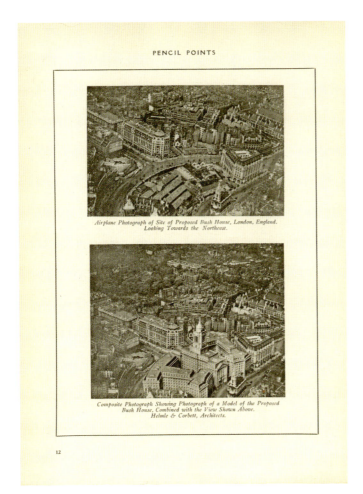

FIGURE 4.9 Composite photograph: montage of an aerial photo of London and a model photo of Bush House. No known copyright holder but see Corbett, Harvey Wiley. "Architectural Models of Cardboard." *Pencil Points*, April–August 1922, 11–14; 28–32, 37; 14–17; 14–18.

FIGURE 4.10 Retouched model photo of the United Masonic Temple, *c.* 1929. Copyright © Doris Conrad Brown.

FIGURE 4.11 Checkman's guide to making model photo montages. Copyright © Wayne Checkman, Checkman, "How to Make the Most of Models," 84–6.

prominently for his design for the unbuilt George Washington National Masonic Monument.[34] His design for a ziggurat with a temple on top was presented with the help of a photo model. As in Corbett's other presentation models, the façade had been drawn onto the cardboard and included protruding elements and shadows. In order to illuminate the model from within, it was built higher than the building to include a light bulb in a lower part that was then obscured by painting its exterior black. The setbacks were built without ceilings so that the light would illuminate the façade from within and the model was photographed in front of a black background. For the montages, the box containing the light bulb was cut off and the remaining photo was inserted into a drawn background including figures and plants. The model's lighting was extended into the drawing with a shaft of light falling onto the people in front of the building. People and other elements were radically foreshortened according to the images' perspective.

A third technique, not mentioned in Corbett's article, was equally as widely used to insert a model into a broader panorama. By photographing a model in front of a real, drawn, or modeled background the image contained everything already in one negative, an improvement over the cumbersome montage work. In the 1920s, this was done by placing the model against the backdrop of a painted diorama as in Corbett's photo of the model of the George Washington National Masonic Monument (Figure 4.12). Perspectival backgrounds were done in water or poster colors. A cloudy sky as a backdrop was achieved by making a blue wash on a damp paper and then "cleaning" out the clouds with a wet sponge.[35] The diorama as a perspectival image created depth that was otherwise hard to achieve. Another option was to position a large model in front of a real urban backdrop (Figure 4.13). Placed on a tripod, the small-scale model had to be close to the wide-angled lens with the large-scale background in the far distance. Using forced perspective and the same incidence of light, the photo could give the impression of fusing fore- and background together.[36] One of the advantages of models over other architectural media, especially drawings, was that many pictures could be taken with one model—eliminating time-consuming rendering. Photo series, as in architectural photography, often presented various aspects of a building in separate images and consisted of several standard shots: a surveying bird's eye view, an image of the façade and details of important features. Similarly, model photos depicted imaginary walks through the model. In the 1920s, these photos offered the architect

FIGURE 4.12 Model of Corbett's George Washington National Masonic Monument photographed in front of a painted perspectival landscape. No known copyright holder but see Corbett, Harvey Wiley. "Architectural Models of Cardboard." *Pencil Points*, April–August 1922, 11–14; 28–32, 37; 14–17; 14–18.

FIGURE 4.13 Tower of the Metropolitan Life North Building, photographed in front of Manhattan, *c.* 1929. Private collection.

a new tool for visualizing a spatial experience that hitherto had been possible only through a laborious task of rendering different perspectival angles.

Faking versus Honesty

> Models help eliminate faking. [. . .] They tell the truth about a building, as old-fashioned renderings never did. The proportions are what they will be, not what an artistic eye has made them seem to be.[37]
>
> THEODORE CONRAD, 1956

The architectural model was clearly on the rise in the 1920s as both a tool in the drafting of architecture and its public dissemination. The discussion about modeling materials, techniques, and (albeit less so) model photography was linked to a much broader ideological debate about two forms of architectural media and their respective professions: the drawing and the model. Under the keywords "faking" and "honesty," a heated discussion was taking place between those favoring models and those favoring renderings as what was the correct depiction of an architectural design. In the 1920s, the mode of presenting a project to a client had started to shift away from large-scale Beaux-Arts presentation drawings that included colored perspectives, floor plans, and

FIGURE 4.14 Simon Breines' comparison between rendering and building. Copyright © Breines, Simon. "Paper Architecture." *The American Architect*, April 1931, 25.

sections arranged on one sheet in dramatic toward charcoal renderings following Hugh Ferriss' style. In his 1929 text on architectural rendering, Ferriss had explained the new interpretative tasks of a delineator as he saw them: "to convey advance realizations of proposed structures, to aid in crystallizing ideas in the architect's mind and to interpret the significance of existing structures."[38] An early critique of this practice of architectural rendering had been voiced by Alvin Covell in his 1914 article "Architecture in Miniature," in which he called perspectives deceptive and working drawings equally inaccurate in depicting what a building would look like to a pedestrian.[39] To Covell, models had a huge advantage: It was possible to make renderings and working drawings based on them and he recommended making the model before the drawings, not after, as it was customary. Moreover, Covell proposed, in order to avoid faulty renderings, the client could just be presented with the model. The word "faked" soon became synonymous for depictions that exaggerated parts of the building for the sake of a well-presented image (Figure 4.14).

Guilty of "faking" were delineators who used "freak skies, impossible lights and shadows, and unnatural surroundings."[40] Model maker Berthold Audsley added to the list of complaints colored renderings with added surroundings that did not exist, or "human interest" details such as people and cars.[41] In addition, Audsley argued, a perspective showed only one side of a building, usually the best, and should therefore be regarded as insufficient. According to the critics, the purpose of "faking" was to deceive the uninformed client.[42] But architects were just as much at fault as the delineators, according to the architect Simon Breines, who added that architects often asked the renderer to leave out aesthetically disadvantageous details like fire escapes.[43] Even Ferriss joined the discussion when he alluded to "faking" as a common technique of drawings: "if one arbitrarily makes alterations (as, for example, showing adjoining buildings less prominently than they are) he is guilty of 'faking.' Undeniably, many renderings are faked."[44] But he also maintained that highlighting a building's most important features by exaggerating them did not count as "faking." The growing distrust in renderings soon stretched to include all kinds of drawn representations: "Drawings of a building, after all, might be considered as guesses as to how to represent a thing in drawings which look well in a finished building, except in cases where a known and tested detail is used, and the best architect is the man who can best guess as to what will be the effect in the round of a drawing in the flat."[45] Following this trajectory, William Alciphron Boring, dean of the School of Architecture at Columbia University during the 1920s and another early critic, demanded that architectural education should be based on both, drawing and model making. His main argument was that since architecture is three-dimensional, drawings are of only limited help in giving a perception of buildings. Furthermore, he claimed that for the architect himself, a perspective was not a working tool, but a model truly was and could be used by both architect and client. He explained that the advantage of a model over a drawing was that projections and details could be shown to scale from different angles: "The wonderfully facile drawing of architecture taught by the French school to-day does not give a correct idea of the building when built, because it is not studied from the point of view of the constructed building, but from the point of view of a picture."[46] Three years later, in 1925, model maker Grumbine summed up what he considered the widely known weaknesses of drawings and perspectives for presentation purposes calling them vague, overly technical, or unintelligible.[47] This lack of definition, Grumbine concluded, made models appealing: "The conventional portrayal of architectural designs is artificial and often ambiguous, and sometimes even deceitful to the lay mind. Anyone can understand a model."[48]

Against the practice of "faked" renderings, architects increasingly voted for the use of models because it "is honest, in that it can be seen for what it is, and is not falsely enhanced by a fairyland of landscape and sky."[49] A model "in strict accordance with the architect's design, would make an honest statement of the facts which cannot mislead any one."[50] While models as physical objects were praised for their precision and truth to the built structure, their use in photographs soon raised concerns similar to those regarding perspectives. Conrad maintained that photos of models served as "perspectives" to study their mass from different angles and he regarded them as more accurate than a "touched up" perspective.[51] Grumbine instead was aware that models and photos were no less deceptive, hinting at the "extra finish" that the salesman demanded for presentations: "Models should be treated in the same manner as perspectives. They should of course be truthful, but photographic exactitude should not be attempted in one case any more than in the other."[52] As harsh and ambiguous as the criticism of renderings by the model advocates sounds, many of them, including Harvey Wiley Corbett and Raymond Hood, used models, model photos, and renderings simultaneously. Models and photos were even used to facilitate the composition of perspectives. Delineators like Ferriss had primarily used blueprints as the basis for their drawings.[53] But with the increasing availability of models, renderers began making perspectives after models and model photos as in the case of the New York County Courthouse by Guy Lowell or Corbett's Metropolitan Life North Building.[54] After the final plans for the latter were submitted in February 1931, a rendering showing the prospective building from a similar perspective as earlier model photos was published in the *New York Times*.[55] Model photos especially helped the renderer to imagine lighting and the mood of an image. In some cases, the model also served as a tool for conceiving difficult shapes. Here, even the working drawing had to be made after a model (Figures 4.15–4.16).[56]

FIGURE 4.15 Photo of Metropolitan Life North Building massing model inserted into a drawn background, repeating the shadows on the model. Private collection.

FIGURE 4.16 The model photo was then translated back into a drawing. Private collection.

Photo Models

> When I was young, you couldn't even print a photo in the newspaper, you had to use pen and ink. So we sat and penned and inked. Color was just out, so we all had to learn to watercolor. We got very good at it. That would sell the job before model making, and it gave us powers of imagination which are just totally lacking in architects today.[57]
>
> THEODORE CONRAD, 1978

The battle about "faking" that raged between rendering and model in the 1920s was never resolved fully and the two media continued to cohabitate in presentations and in architects' offices. In printed media, however, a slow change began. Until the 1930s, the dimensions of model photos were small, seldom larger than letter size and they were often mounted on canvas indicating their use in presentations rather than printed volumes. They were rarely published in architectural magazines or more widely disseminated newspapers. By and large, the primary way for presenting an unbuilt design in print remained the rendering. The three big American architectural publications at the time—*Pencil Points*, *Architectural Record,* and *Architectural Forum*—only used model photos now and again. The former stated its mission in the subtitle "A Journal for the Drafting Room," saying exactly what it was: a magazine addressing draftsmen and students of architecture as well as architects. The magazine's clear focus on Beaux-Arts renderings was instructive and included examples of good architectural practice following the traditional and widely accepted drawing conventions. Other professional magazines were more open to using architectural photography, as they focused on a survey of recently built architecture rather than design. Model photos did exist in the 1920s, such as those used by Corbett, but were rarely published. Their use oscillated between design needs or as perspective aids for renderings and semi-private presentations to clients. For magazines looking to present a design realistically, the often hybrid nature of chiaroscuro model photos, montages, and retouches of photos and drawings must have appeared too rough and ready when compared with elaborate renderings. The controversy around the 1931 publication of one of the Rockefeller Center models could be seen as indicative of a slow turning point toward an increased use of model photos by architects and, simultaneously, the wider public's unfamiliarity with them. Following the publication of a photo of a Plasticine massing model of Rockefeller Center in the *New York Times* and other papers in March 1931, a debate about the alleged ugliness of the proposed buildings "aroused the public as no other architectural undertaking has ever done and gave New Yorkers last month a subject for controversial conversation lasting far beyond the conventional nine days of newspaper publicity."[58] One reason for the audience's negative reaction was that, previously, models in exhibitions had been highly refined and tentative plans in print were presented in renderings such as Hugh Ferriss' work in such a way that missing details could be concealed. When published, model photos were often documentary and lacked the refinement and illusion of renderings by giving away their small scale (Figures 4.17–4.18); or, as was the case with the model for the *Chicago Tribune* competition, were refined white plaster models with a high degree of abstraction. The chiaroscuro model photos for Rockefeller Center combined both a lack of details and a dearth of accessories to smooth out its abstract masses. The public, unaccustomed to overly simplistic massing models and their photographic translation, dismissed the design in general. For them, the gap between what a model could represent and what was expected of an architectural photo or rendering diverged too much.

FIGURES 4.17 and 4.18 Documentary model photos published in architectural magazines before the 1930s. Copyright holder unknown but see *The Architectural Forum*, February 1919, 55 and *The Architectural Forum*, October 1919, 138.

Pioneering exceptions in the use of model photos in magazines that were closer to European avant-garde examples were such individual practices as Buckminster Fuller's photos of his Dymaxion House model, with which he demonstrated how his mass-produced house could be assembled. Similarly, Bel Geddes used model photos extensively as illustrations in his 1932 book *Horizons*, which advertised his design expertise.[59] In just a few years, model photos in architectural magazines had begun to play a much grander role and helped change model making and photos more fundamentally. By the mid-1930s, model photos had turned into the general public's preview of planned structures including such large-scale projects as the New York World's Fair, which released numerous model photos with press releases for its pavilions. The sharp increase in the use of photos could also be traced to many magazines' desperate need for illustrations in a time of crisis. During the Depression and war—when real-life constructions were scarce—architectural and lifestyle magazines, themselves struggling to survive, attempted to fill their pages by holding competitions or commissioning architects to present ideas for single-family homes. It was these publications that now took over and appropriated model photography from the architects' private practices and pushed for a development of greater realism to appeal to readers. Many modernist designs for unbuilt "houses of the future" featured open floor plans, large picture windows overlooking a garden, and amenities such as built-in garages, air-conditioning, and central heating in photos of models that were specially ordered by the magazines. Almost always planned without a site, these issues presented house layouts that could be bought cheaply, serving a variety of interests. For the magazines, the reason to run articles on modern housing, appliances, and interior decorating was to stimulate the slumping ad sales from builders and manufacturers of appliances. For architects like the young Edward Durell Stone, having photographs of modern houses published was a way to sell floor plans and attract attention, not easy during a time of unemployment and when the AIA's ban on advertising for architects restricted options for finding clients. For the building industry, the designs acted as a didactic tool, slowly altering the architectural tastes of the public. And for model makers and photographers, the commissions meant a longer-term employment in a time of economic uncertainty. Magazines such as the domestic periodicals *Ladies' Home Journal, McCall's, Woman's Home Companion, Good Housekeeping,* and *House & Garden,* but also more widely disseminated publications such as *Collier's, Life,* and *Fortune,* soon adopted the use of model photos. As the sponsors for new house designs, the editors of these magazines selected and commissioned architects and provided them with a model maker and photographer who would translate the designs. The aim in the translation of models into photos used for illustrations was, according to Conrad, utmost realism through lower vantage points, more elaborate props, and the simulation of sunlight that was rendered to perfection by Conrad's collaborator, the model photographer Louis Checkman.[60] Among the first to introduce model photos of modern houses were *Ladies' Home Journal* and *Collier's Weekly*.[61] With a readership of two and a half million, *Collier's*—one of the most successful magazines—focused largely on fiction and investigative journalism and predicted a new boom in construction.[62] Hoping for a share in this surge, the magazine commissioned three designs for small, affordable houses. The first was by Edward Durell Stone and based loosely on his earlier Mandel House. It was released in four articles between March and May 1936. The house was part of a campaign advocating modern architecture and working drawings were offered for $3. The exterior and garden were illustrated in model photos and floor plans, whereas interior and lighting were added as renderings. As in the 1920s, the camera could not get inside Conrad's small-scale wooden model. Therefore, the model photos by George van Anda and *Collier's* staff photographer Ifor Thomas ranged between bird's-eye views, almost-eye level images and close-ups from above. The edges of the model were often visible and the images were cropped out and set on a white page. The background, if it existed, was a non-descript black backdrop in front of which the house was spotlighted from a low light source creating long shadows. Set within lengthy descriptions of the new features of the house, the images were more supplemental than indulgent examples of realism. The architects Fordyce & Hamby developed a second, more traditional house that was published in *Collier's* a year later, in the spring of 1937—the first project that Conrad and Checkman are known to have worked on jointly for a magazine. Again, made largely from wood and cardboard with a painted exterior, the house was photographed in front of a dark grey background with life-like but long shadows. Checkman, too, took top-down shots but a number of eye-level images exist that successfully obscured the model's edges (Figure 4.19). However, the latter were not printed in *Collier's,* which preferred the top-down views. The interior, though visibly built in the model, was not shown in model photos but did appear in drawings and small floor plans. The new photo models' built-in realism depended largely on the development of model making from cardboard and wood to Plexiglas and metal, and reflected their changing material limitations. Unlike the model photos of the 1920s that served several purposes, for design and presentation, the magazine model's sole purpose was to be translated into a realistic photo. These early photos could not represent all aspects of a design as the models were small and did not include dismountable parts or roofs. Therefore, interiors could be represented only in renderings, as the opaque modeling materials did not allow for views into the models. Model photography had its limitations as well. Even though color was available by then, most model images were still taken in black and white. In combination with the rough texture and printing quality of the magazines, these images had the advantage of obscuring the model's inadequate materials. In a new strategy based on the model's availability for photo series, magazine spreads introduced the traditional idea of the series in architectural photography for the depiction of unbuilt designs, presenting several standard

FIGURE 4.19 Eye-level photo of Fordyce and Hamby's *Collier's* House, 1937. Copyright © Doris Conrad Brown, Wayne Checkman, Theodore Conrad papers, 1937–91, Avery Architectural and Fine Arts Library, Columbia University.

views—such as an establishing shot and subsequent approaches—until close-ups could display details. *Collier's*, though a pioneer, was not alone in the 1930s. Stone also worked on a house project for *Life* together with the *Architectural Forum*, where he was one of eight architects designing traditional and modern houses for which cut-out model replicas could be bought by readers for fifty cents.[63] The "grand old lady" of the women's magazines, *Ladies' Home Journal*, which had a history of architectural topics, publishing designs by Frank Lloyd Wright as early as 1901, printed another six houses every year in the 1930s similar to *Collier's* with plans costing $1.[64]

After the introduction and application of new modeling materials in the mid-1930s, more realistic images became available for modern designs, especially for depicting large and transparent windows. In 1939, Louis Checkman's photos of Conrad's model of the Pittsburgh House of Glass were the first to achieve an unparalleled realism. Arguably the most successful example of prewar model photos for magazines, the images show completely unprecedented exterior and interior eye level shots of a fully furnished and detailed model (Figures 4.20–4.21). Here, the model was not meant as a tool for selling floor plans but as a preview of the actual building. Eight years after the debacle of the Rockefeller model images, the magazine now had to print a disclaimer accompanying the photos to clarify for the reader that they were looking at a model, not the actual building: "The talk-provoking glass house at the World's Fair will be finished about the middle of May. We couldn't let you wait. So here's a Collier's model, real as life and just as beautiful."[65] In comparison with previous photos, the interior shots were exceptional in their realism down to the representation of the glare of the glass, sunbeams on the floor, and reflections of the windows in the interior (Figure 4.22). The idea of translucence, the main achievement of the "House of Glass," was thus recreated in the model photos. In only four years, the use of new modeling techniques and materials, the choice of lower camera standpoints and the use of interior shots changed model photography significantly. For the first time, a model could be taken apart to allow for interior shots. The backdrop was light and airy, contributing to the illusion of natural lighting and the strong chiaroscuro lighting of the 1920s massing models was abandoned in favor of more even light to draw out the model's materials, transparency, and detail. Shifting the focus of the lens

FIGURE 4.20 Original spread of *Collier's* May 6, 1939 issue. Copyright © Doris Conrad Brown, Wayne Checkman, Theodore Conrad papers, 1937–91, Avery Architectural and Fine Arts Library, Columbia University.

FIGURE 4.21 Exterior eye-level view of the House of Glass, 1939. Copyright © Doris Conrad Brown, Wayne Checkman, Theodore Conrad papers, 1937–91, Avery Architectural and Fine Arts Library, Columbia University.

FIGURE 4.22 Fully furnished interior shot of the House of Glass, 1939. Copyright © Doris Conrad Brown, Wayne Checkman, Theodore Conrad papers, 1937–91, Avery Architectural and Fine Arts Library, Columbia University.

helped to both obscure and elucidate individual parts of the model. The model's materiality played into the ability of the camera to focus on the parts that could guarantee utmost accuracy in their material representation, such as Plexiglas representing glass windows as well as blurring those parts that could be identified as miniatures in close-ups such as hedges. The tight frame cut off the edges of the model that were further obscured with artificial plants placed outside the model's base. The House of Glass model was arguably the first photo model that fully inhabited the gap between model and photo: Its built-in image creating capacities were based on new materials and model construction that catered to its sole function of becoming a photo. Built and published for a mainstream audience, it set the scene for a boom in model photos for magazines that, after the war, trickled into purely architectural contexts.

The Magazine Era

> But the biggest boost came in the immediate postwar years, during what Conrad and his competitors call their "magazine era."[66]
>
> JANE JACOBS, 1958

A new realism had entered model photography in the 1930s through the side-track of fictional photo models for lifestyle magazines—a process that continued throughout the 1940s and 1950s.

During the war, *Collier's* discontinued its model house series, never to be revived. But as the housing problem became acute in the immediate postwar years, women's magazines took over the practice of publishing photos of model houses, targeting those who were allegedly most affected by the housing shortage: wives and mothers. *Woman's Home Companion*, a sister publication of *Collier's* and the biggest women's interest magazine in the 1930s, featured a mix of literature and articles geared toward housewives.[67] Between 1947 and 1950, the magazine ran a monthly series offering designs for affordable houses. Under the tutelage of its interior design editor Harriet Burket and architect Wallace Heath, the magazine published layouts by modern architects such as O'Neil Ford and Jerry Rogers, Raymond & Rado, Perry Duncan, Edward Durell Stone, A. James Speyer, Joseph Esherick, and Gregory Ain. The models followed the precedent of the House of Glass but were built at the extremely large scale of 1/2"=1'-0".[68] Many of them could be disassembled for close-ups and their roofs could be taken off to show model "floor plans." Landscaping and accessories rose to an even higher importance as backdrops and focal points in the images. The opener of each article was an exterior view but interiors, unlike in the 1930s, became increasingly common in model photos. Color entered model photography through its application in full-color printed women's magazines (Figure 4.23). Built by Conrad for *Woman's Home Companion*, Checkman's model photos for A. James Speyer's eponymous house were published in September 1948.[69] Here, all the prewar developments came together. Even though no actual building site was considered, the model was extremely detailed and fully decorated. The colorful interior drew the view into the house. The modeling materials allowed for a completely realistic interior and exterior through large picture windows. The low vantage point and the built background left no gaps to reveal the edge of the model plates (Figure 4.24). Spotlights cast true-to-life shadows across the model and the frame of the image was close to the building. Printed in color as large illustrations, at about half-page size, the photos were highly realistic. Other magazines such as *Life*, *McCall's*, and *Ladies' Home Journal* followed the example of *Woman's Home Companion*. *McCall's* published house articles between 1945 and 1950 using even larger, 1"=1'-0" scale models to help readers "get the feeling of the house, and a good idea of what it would be like to live in."[70] Led by Mary Davis Gillies, decorating and architectural editor of *McCall's*, the magazine featured a column called *Home of the Month* that not only presented fictional designs but often built projects, too. The *Architectural Forum* had been cooperating with house exhibitions and lifestyle magazines since before the war. Now, the magazine became the first architectural content publication that picked up the topic and ran similar articles written by the editors of lifestyle magazines, featuring model photos from *Ladies' Home Journal*, *McCall's*, *Woman's Home Companion*, *Life*, *Better Homes & Gardens*, and others.[71] Disseminating not just modern designs but also the inventive use of models, the articles were brought before a different audience, showing architects the postwar possibilities in residential architecture and their representation. Due to their limited funds for printing, however, the same images were reprinted in black and white.

In the 1940s, photographic realism based on model making was not limited to architectural fiction, but applied to broader needs for illustrating overseas news items, stories of historical note, and other events that the average person would not otherwise see. In 1944, MoMA declared a "new form of picture journalism" had been invented in the photos of war models by Norman Bel Geddes.[72] Bel Geddes had shed his earlier chiaroscuro technique in the late 1930s, beginning with photos of his *Futurama* model that were less blurry and which drew out the model's details in life-

FIGURE 4.23 Color model photos in an article in *Woman's Home Companion*. Private collection.

FIGURE 4.24 Close-up of the Speyer house model, *c.* 1948. Copyright © Doris Conrad Brown, Wayne Checkman, Theodore Conrad papers, 1937–91, Avery Architectural and Fine Arts Library, Columbia University.

like images that were much more representative of surfaces and materials. At the pinnacle of his "new journalism" and moving beyond his earlier architectural, stage or landscape models, Bel Geddes began to build photo models of World War II battle fields for *Life* magazine that depicted campaigns, in some cases before they even happened. As Bel Geddes himself proclaimed, some of the photos appeared to be more authentic than actual photos of the battlegrounds because a greater amount of control was possible in staging the models.[73] Here, similar techniques as in architectural model photography were used: the lighting drew out and highlighted waves, steam, and the surface of the water as seen from an airplane. Again, the wider application of model photos embracing the new picture journalism resulted from a practical need for illustrations of imaginary or unbuilt projects. During the magazine era of the 1940s, photos finally superseded renderings in publications due to the superior techniques available since the mid-1930s. What all the photos had in common was that they were taken with highly detailed and large-scale photo models outfitted with interiors and accessories. With the introduction of materials other than cardboard—wood, Plexiglas, and aluminum—models could withstand a closer look than before and materials could be represented realistically in the photos through lighting and close-ups. Equally, the fore- and background reached a new importance. Often depicting unbuilt houses, the models and images presented an idyllic simulation of an already occupied house. The photo model, much in the same way as the model drawing, acted as a liminal tool whose task was to be used for the translation into realistic photos. Its material construction, therefore, decided the views possible in the images through openings, windows without Plexiglas panes, and demountable roofs. Their large scale was a concession to more detail but also to the large formats of the view cameras. As they were of no use to the magazines after photos were taken, they often remained with the model maker and were stored or their parts were disassembled for use on other models. Landscaping was of such utmost importance for realism that architects such as Wallace Harrison took great care in depicting the exact state of vegetation. As with architectural photography, most photos were taken during a (fictional) summertime long after a house had been finished and vegetation had grown in (Figure 4.25).

Model images had the great advantage that they could cater to the need for realistic images of inhabited houses before a project was built, as Conrad explained regarding the model of Gregory Ain's House for MoMA in 1956: "It takes about three months to print color pages in a magazine. If a house is finished in the winter it can't be photographed until spring. [. . .] In the case of this house it was built in the Museum of Modern Art Garden and finished in spring. The day it was opened to the public it appeared as a cover design for a leading magazine. The model had to be photographed in January to meet this publication date."[74] But, Conrad added: "The work of God, of course, is much more difficult to imitate than the work of man."[75] Therefore, to avoid flaws, about half of the modeling process was spent on landscaping.[76] Richard Pratt, architectural editor of *Ladies' Home Journal* and a landscape architect, model maker and photographer himself went as far as photographing the models for his magazine with real dwarfed trees and arctic shrubs that he grew as a backdrop of the large 1"=1'-0" scale models.[77] These increasingly elaborate backgrounds meant

FIGURE 4.25 Model of a house with a shed roof in a fall setting. Copyright holder unknown but see Gillies, *McCall's Book of Modern Houses*, 10.

a departure from earlier practices as the image was now created in one shot and without montaging a background into the images later on. These anti-montages no longer depended on composite techniques. As color photography became more important, the colors of the model and the accurate representation of surfaces, textures, and materials were highly influential and had to be accounted for during the model making process. The new materials and their abilities to represent almost any building material or surface could withstand the close look of the camera without "shrieking" model. As before, blurs in the photos' close range as well as the magazines' rather roughly graded color printing helped to obscure potential flaws that would otherwise have given away the model's scale. Built with or without window panes, the models allowed for certain views into or out of the model creating life-like reflections. As such, the model photos were often more perfect than photos of the actual building which made them more reliable and faster to obtain for magazines. The virtually indistinguishable verisimilitude of model photos from the finished building—the "jealousy of the model" as Christian Hubert called it—had its limits, however.[78] Human figures as an indicator of scale were generally omitted as they would have destroyed the illusion.

Model Photos in Architectural Practices

> If one picture is worth a thousand words, a good model (such as yours) is worth at least a hundred pictures.[79]
>
> DANIEL SHUSTER, 1954

The fact that realistic model photos were first introduced in lifestyle magazines and not as part of architectural office practices or periodicals is not surprising given their initial focus on lush and seductive imagery. For the model makers and photographers of the New York area, where most of the magazines were based, the new demand meant a considerable boost and a stabilization of their careers independent from architectural commissions that occupied them for most of the time immediately after the war and prepared them for the building boom of the 1950s. At the same time, architects became increasingly aware of the need not just for documentary or artistic but for realistically staged shots for publicity, whether with built architecture or through models, as they began using model photos for presentations to clients and in the design process on a much wider scale. After the immediate postwar dry spell in the construction industry, the new technological and representational techniques of model photography were quickly transferred to purely architectural contexts with only minor changes. Contrary to magazine models, the postwar models, albeit large in size, were often built at smaller scales as they were not just used for photos but also served as tools for designing and circulating architectural ideas. As such, their size was limited to facilitate easy transportation. Adopting realistic photo techniques from the very first design stages, models were now photographed as buildings with low vantage points located in an identifiable urban space with life-like lighting and framing. Even though, as Daniel Shuster remarked, a model was ideally "worth a hundred pictures," many models were photographed from only a few fixed standpoints that often anticipated a building's most important views. Most prominently, Ezra Stoller's photos of the models for SOM's Lever House simulated one particular view that examined the prominent tower from across Park Avenue—from the same vantage point later used in photographs by Stoller and many others of the real building (Figures 4.26–4.27).

FIGURES 4.26 and 4.27 Similar views of two different models of Lever House, *c.* 1949. Copyright © Ezra Stoller/Esto.

The anticipation of the building's views within the urban context through model photos made it possible to give the public a realistic preview as well as a tool via which the architects could examine their designs and adjust them as necessary. The perspectival normalcy of these model photos became a significant part of both design and presentation. Rather than creating a fictional environment to fit an imagined building, the models and photos now had to test how well a building would fit into an *existing* environment. For design photos, the often unnecessary abundance of props that had characterized the magazine photos was abandoned. Included now, however, were the human figures that had been missing hitherto. Other than the magazine photos, which set out to overwhelm by presenting fully inhabited spaces in order to make the buildings seem real, model images now relied on the human figure as a scale-giver for the building. Backgrounds remained crucial for a photo's success. Often, a simple white background was used as a backdrop. For the creation of more elaborate backdrops, however, older montage techniques were revived. Conrad and Checkman appropriated their technique for anti-montages from their magazine work for images that had their background built in: an airbrushed, transportable "sky" that was hung behind the model and spotlighted *together* with it thus creating a uniform appearance in the image (Figure 4.28). In opposition to the fictional house projects, lighting now had to be geographically accurate in simulating the position of the sunlight to draw out a building's appearance at different times of day. In connection with the interior lighting of the electrified models, night shots became an important feature for representing the alternating transparency in office buildings as in Conrad's Pepsi-Cola Building model (Figure 4.29). For the large assembled models that could not be taken apart, lighting could accentuate and translate contrasting features of the design into images: the façade, the open interior, or the internal structure of the building, as Ezra Stoller demonstrated on the model of SOM's Inland Steel Building. Since the representation of building

140 THE ARCHITECTURAL MODELS OF THEODORE CONRAD

FIGURE 4.28 Ezra Stoller's photo of a model of the General Life headquarters with extra props and an airbrushed sky for the background, c. 1957. Copyright © Ezra Stoller/Esto.

FIGURE 4.29 Night shot of Pepsi-Cola Building, c. 1956–7. Copyright © Ezra Stoller/Esto.

materials was one of the main aims of models and photos, the lack of definition that had previously been used to conceal unsatisfactory model making became less desirable. Instead, mirrors became a popular addition in models as a way of representing water so that it reflected and foregrounded the refined surfaces of the models. Since many models were no longer demountable but interiors became increasingly popular, interior shots were taken using the newly available sectional models in order to study the connection between what was inside a building and its surroundings. Image frames of the suburban house models had operated with tree branches, hedges, or other blurry props in the foreground. Now, the darkened shapes of adjacent buildings could be used as a similar indicator of the photographer's standpoint in the well-known urban fabrics of big cities like New York or Chicago. Additional model trees and landscaping of different scales could fill in holes in the backdrop, and out-of-scale props were used to enhance perspectival effects.

However well staged and detailed, the final prints of the postwar model photos were often altered significantly in post-production. Images were frequently cropped to tighten the frame and hide the edge of the model plate. Airbrushing became popular, especially for retouches and correcting mistakes on the final prints. One poignant example was a photo of Conrad's final presentation model of Huntington Hartford's Gallery of Modern Art in New York City (Figure 4.30). The model had been brought to Stone's office where it was photographed and presented to Huntington Hartford. The lower arcade was cut off accidentally in the photos but Checkman could not take them again because the model had already been given to the client. Instead, he had the arcades airbrushed in without anyone noticing, not even the architect himself.[80] The photos of Conrad's model for the American Pavilion at the World Expo in Brussels in 1958 could be seen as the culmination of realistic model photography (Figures 4.31–4.32). Including day and night shots,

FIGURE 4.30 Airbrushed arcades of Gallery of Modern Art model, *c*. 1958–9. Copyright © Wayne Checkman, *Architectural Record*, July 1959, 14.

FIGURES 4.31 and 4.32 Night and interior shot of the model of the American Pavilion at the Brussels Expo 1958, *c.* 1956–7. Copyright © Doris Conrad Brown, Wayne Checkman, Theodore Conrad papers, 1937–91, Avery Architectural and Fine Arts Library, Columbia University.

FIGURE 4.33 Cover of the *Architectural Forum*, May 1949, showing the Heinz Research Laboratory model. Copyright holder unknown but see *Architectural Forum*, May 1949, cover.

interiors, and a mirroring lake, the model photos presented an overwhelming preview of the building's appearance to detail. Checkman's photos were widely disseminated, not least on a three-cent stamp by the United States Post Office. The expansive use of model photos for publicity had finally come out of the niche of lifestyle magazines and entered architectural mass media, changing the size of the negatives and prints significantly. Whereas early photos were taken with 8x10 inch negatives, the later ones were much smaller and thus easier to handle at 4x5 inches.[81] The prints grew bigger, especially for public presentations. The shift toward a wider dissemination was also visible in the scene of architecture publishing. The former drafting magazine, *Pencil Points*, had been transformed into *Progressive Architecture* in 1945 to reflect its new focus.[82] The use of model photos to illustrate projects in architectural periodicals had been increasing slowly since the 1930s. Whereas in lifestyle magazines, color photos had arrived in the 1940s, in architectural magazines there were almost none at that time. In fact, it was not until the 1980s that color images became fully accepted and affordable.[83] With the growing focus on current building projects, magazines began to compete over the rights to publish a new building first. Model photos were now the prime medium of presenting these designs. One of the first model photos to make it onto the cover of an architectural magazine was a photo of Conrad's model of the Heinz Research Laboratories in Pittsburgh; taken by Stoller in 1949, it was printed on the cover of the May issue of *Architectural Forum* (Figure 4.33).[84] Following the established techniques of model photography, it used scaled figures to indicate its proportions and reflections of the metallic façade in the shiny surface of the street to showcase the new materials. A model photo as the teaser for a new building became the standard method of publication in magazines and newspapers alike. Roughly twenty years after the model photo of Rockefeller Center had caused a public outcry, the *New York Times* published a night shot of the proposed Manufacturers Trust building in 1953.[85] This time nobody cared—photos had become accepted by the readers. They were often accompanied by drawings, notably floor plans, but were also incorporated into drawings or labeled with legends. After a building was finished, they were replaced by a similar view of the finished building. However, model photos remained in the public realm long after a building's completion as architects and clients increasingly took advantage of their versatility for their own publicity, using them in their newsletters or sending them to prospective clients. Loaning model photos for advertising projects proved yet another way of attracting attention for an architect's services. Large corporations started handing out brochures advertising their new building projects not only to their employees but to the public through leaflets or in-house magazines such as General Life's company publication *Life in General*, which reported extensively on new building projects.

5

Model Displays

Selling an Idea

Occasions arise when the architect or surveyor finds a model indispensable—as, for example, when he wished to show a client exactly how his paper plans will materialize in bricks and mortar.[1]

PERCY COLLINS, 1915

Exhibitions, or presentations to clients, allowed the model to remain within a three-dimensional realm and to be combined with other media such as drawings or photographs without losing its most important quality: three-dimensionality. The visual connections between media in these displays created a spatial form of reviewing a building that allowed for observing a project from different angles before it was built. Even today, exhibitions remain the most tangible way in which the average viewer is confronted with the physical objects created by architects and model makers, aside from the buildings themselves. Models have entered the discussion centered around the history of exhibitions and display with regard to their presentation in specific time periods and geographical areas. Most notably, Wallis Miller researched the presentation of models in early twentieth-century Germany, especially in the Preußische Bauakademie and the Bauhaus, and Juliet Koss worked extensively on the design and display of models at the Russian architecture school Vkhutemas.[2] Aside from these more vanguard European movements, however, little is known about how the public display of small-scale architectural objects has changed over time, especially with regard to the United States. Exhibitions and presentation practices as part of the architect–client relationship raise pivotal questions regarding new techniques developed since the 1920s and their synergies with other media. As physical objects, their setup—for instance, the height at which a model was installed or the level of illusion brought to the object through the use of lighting and sound—significantly changed the way they were presented either as objects in their own right or as representations of architecture, not unlike the way in which photographic techniques governed the model's translation into an image. Even though drawings and renderings remained at the core of public presentations, in the United States models were used from at least 1900 for purposes of display (Figure 5.1).[3] They served in semi-public presentations to clients or as evidence in litigation to reconstruct crime scenes. Their intended use influenced their making, material, and price significantly. Whereas models for law enforcement needed to be exact, exhibition models required an "extra finish" and could be built more freely.[4] Model maker LeRoy Grumbine

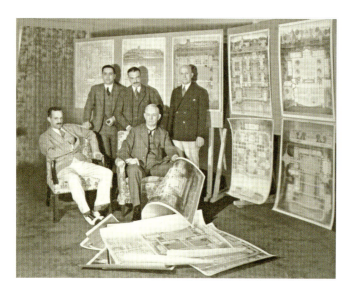

FIGURE 5.1 Judges of the A. W. Brown Scholarship competition in 1931 with entries. Copyright holder unknown, *Pencil Points*, June 1931, 466.

argued in 1929 that these models were the perfect tool for selling a design to a client.[5] His main argument for the model's supremacy over renderings as sales tools became a standard catchphrase among model advocates: "Most people cannot or will not take the trouble to visualize. Sales experts tell us that few people can be 'sold' on reason. Most people must be appealed to through their appetite or senses. A model does this. It diverts the attention from dollars to be expended and focuses it on something to be desired."[6] A model, so the argument ran, could help a client's decision by showing the overall scheme and its details in one object. The model's three-dimensional qualities, Grumbine argued, superseded the drawing's insufficient attempt at representing an object in space. In clear opposition to what he and other model advocates had voiced at precisely the same time to discredit architectural renderings as frauds—namely that the model was more "honest" than the "faked" drawing—Grumbine admitted to the equally deceptive nature of modeling that created a desire or longing to possess the object and which could be exploited by the architect. It was less spatial accuracy that appealed to the client than the physically tangible nature of the object.

In the 1920s, an ideal presentation model had a scale that resulted in an object between one and two feet long. Its price was that of two to three perspectives, so that an entire presentation cost about the same as before.[7] At times, several sketch models were substituted for one presentation model to offer the client a choice. Until the 1930s, models were rarely presented alone; they were accompanied by floor plans, sketches, and sections that complemented one another. The model served as the main perspectival representation but elevations or elaborate perspectives were often added. A supposedly complete set for a presentation survives for Harvey Wiley Corbett's entry to the Columbus Lighthouse competition in 1931. Between 1928 and 1931, a two-part competition was held by the Pan-American Union for a memorial and tomb for Christopher Columbus at the entrance to the harbor of Santo Domingo, Dominican Republic.[8] The first stage, a sketch competition, was launched on September 1, 1928. 455 entries from forty-eight countries were submitted by April 1 of the following year. No documents appear to have been preserved for this stage. Ten architects, among them Corbett, then went on to part two, for which plans and models had to be submitted by May 15, 1931.[9] The designs were to include specific solutions for a lighthouse, a "Pan-American" park, landing field and government building. Corbett submitted a set of Beaux-Arts renderings including a site plan, a section, a floor plan, and two perspectives as well as two photos of a white cardboard model. It is unclear whether the model itself was presented. Both renderings and model photos served separate purposes in accentuating a particular aspect of the design. Whereas the renderings gave an atmospheric interpretation of the structure in the landscape, the model photos gave a crisp sense of the building's mass.

Even though such large-scale public projects operated with refined presentation models and photos on a more widely accepted basis, the models were certainly seen as a novelty that was intended to overwhelm and take the client by surprise. As a theatrical tool, they could be disassembled to reveal hidden interiors or to show design alternatives. Corbett especially was a master of surprise known for his inventive use of models to dazzle his clients. One of these incidents was reported by Hugh Ferriss' daughter Jean Leich: "Corbett's light touch in selling tall buildings to his clients was observed by Ferriss on his first visit to the architect's office, then located on the top floor of the newly completed Bush Terminal Building on West 42nd Street. As the artist entered the spacious drafting room, he found Corbett—'a tall figure silhouetted against a bird's-eye view of Times Square'—intently contemplating what appeared to be a neatly constructed scale model of a twenty-story building. This object, however, turned out to be a box which, as Corbett pulled a hidden string, released a second building concealed inside the first. Inside the second, however, was a third, and the clients, impressed by the theatricality of the event, finally built considerably higher than the one originally intended."[10] Similarly, for the George Washington National Masonic Monument, Corbett had presented several schemes, the final of which included a model that could be taken apart in three pieces to show various heights.[11] In both instances, the architect took on the role of a magician who used the model's modification to get the intended reaction from the client. To engage his patrons physically, Corbett went even further with Conrad's models for the Metropolitan Life North Building. At the final meeting with the company on October 20, 1929, a book containing drawings and renderings for a 100-story glass tower and an unknown number of alternate designs of varying height were presented, including model photos. Much more successful, a model of the tower section of the favored design had been fixed to a handle which could be held against the urban background from the windows of the old MetLife tower to simulate the annex across the street (Figure 5.2). Here, the clients, holding the model, presented the design to themselves. Thus, models such as these could help to secure a design as they inscribed themselves into the planning process, making it harder for the client to imagine other solutions. Corbett's practice was unique in the 1920s and applied only to intimate meetings with clients; calls for proposals from large public commissions did not request models.[12] It was often not the models as physical objects that were important but rather the model photos that directly competed with renderings. In these cases, models were not intended as sales objects that would remain with the client, as became common in the 1950s. For the architect, keeping the model opened up the opportunity to advertise their services to a wider range of clients by placing a model in the office or a shop window, which did not conflict with the AIA's ban on advertising.[13] Initially introduced into the display of architecture as a sales tool, models and model photos quickly led to a departure from the paper-bound display of buildings presented on one highly polished sheet as practiced under the Beaux-Arts school. Now, several media coexisted alongside one another, each describing a different aspect of the project. Whereas model photos stood in direct competition with renderings, the model's advantage was its novelty and its direct engagement with the audience.

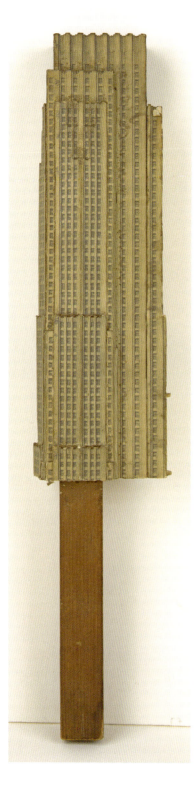

FIGURE 5.2 Model of the winning design for the Metropolitan Life North Building, c. 1929. Image reproduced courtesy of *Drawing Matter*.

The Modeling Craze

Whereas previously, architectural models had been clearly linked to the design of a building, in the 1930s the presentation of models was elevated to another level. Not only did the public display of design models skyrocket, but the manufacture of models and dioramas solely for display purposes increased rapidly too. This was not in the least due to several large-scale projects in the New York area that attracted wide attention outside immediate architectural circles. The controversy over the bleakness of the model photo of Rockefeller Center, mentioned in the previous chapter, was not based solely on publishing conventions of architectural projects in print but also on the wider traditions of architectural displays based on decorated renderings. Whereas the judges on the jury of the Columbus Lighthouse competition were architects who understood models and photos as an abstraction, the public misinterpreted the white models of Rockefeller Center as literal representations of the buildings: The audience expected a highly descriptive portrait of architecture. Here, the models had failed at translating—and thus *selling*—the architectural idea. This would change quickly with the introduction of highly realistic models and photos that catered to the lay audience's expectations. By the early 1930s, clients involved in the creation of architecture had been sufficiently sensitized to modeling and, as in the case of Rockefeller Center, models were heavily used in the search for prospective tenants (Figure 5.3). With the growing acceptance of models for public presentations, they adopted new functions as a medium of exhibition and education, by both documenting and staging architecture.

The *International Style* exhibition's importance for the canonization of modern architecture is ubiquitous in scholarly literature. For the postwar modeling boom, however, another event was much more fundamental. The New York World's Fair was a major event in the history of New York City as well as in the cultural memory of the United States. With a focus on "progress," the Fair aimed at giving a glimpse of a future facilitated by new technical inventions, cleaner and safer living, transportation, and a "consumer" lifestyle. The media coverage of the Fair was exceptional,

FIGURE 5.3 First press conference with plaster model of Rockefeller Center, March 1931. Copyright © Walter Kilham: Raymond Hood: Photostats & Paper negatives, folder 13, Raymond M. Hood architectural drawings and papers, 1890–1944, Avery Architectural and Fine Arts Library, Columbia University.

with frequent planning updates in newspapers and the publication of entire layouts of pavilions before the its opening. Renderings were still a major source of images and four official renderers were employed to depict the Fair: Hugh Ferriss, Theodore Kautzky, Chester Price, and John Wenrich. But it was the representation of the Fair *en miniature* in combination with the model exhibits inside the pavilions that attracted journalists' attention in particular. Both models that had been used for the planning of the Fair and models that had been made solely for presentation served a myriad of purposes for selling the Fair, as a display of ideas and as exhibits. The design models for the New York World's Fair were in constant use by those working for the World's Fair Corporation's Board of Design as all pavilions were presented and reviewed with the help of models and model photos (Figure 5.4). Beside their immediate use for planning purposes, they were part of a large-scale publicity campaign alongside drawings and photos in newspapers and professional journals. After construction commenced, many design models were displayed on-site in the Administration Building, at the Empire State Building, or were hung on the walls of the Board of Design room where delegations of visitors paraded past them (Figure 5.5).[14] Following

FIGURE 5.4 Signing the papers on top the model of the Continental Baking Company, December 2, 1937. Copyright © New York World's Fair 1939–1940 records, Manuscripts and Archives Division, The New York Public Library.

FIGURE 5.5 Brazilian delegation looking at a model at the Empire State Building on January 30, 1937. Copyright © New York World's Fair 1939–1940 records, Manuscripts and Archives Division, The New York Public Library.

Corbett's presentation practice, to enhance interest in the Fair, meetings with officials and foreign guests always included the presentation of a model. As for Rockefeller Center, models traveled all across the country; one even went as far as Paris, France.[15] Therefore, duplicates were frequently made in plaster to meet the demand for exhibitions. More than two years prior to the Fair's opening, in the spring of 1937, the design models were exhibited for the first time together with plans and drawings on the ground floor of the Empire State Building, on the corner of 5th Avenue and 34th Street.[16] Curated by Gretl Urban, fourteen display windows presented models and objects at different scales. A large copy of the original 1/200"=1'-0" scale progress model was shown in a darkened room. Covered with radioactive, fluorescent paint and used in combination with mercury vapor and lights, the model was a seductive nocturnal preview of the fairgrounds (Figure 5.6).[17] Around the same time, from April 21 to May 15, 1937, models of the Fair were exhibited at the Architectural League's New York office, including a model of the Theme Building, "Trylon and Perisphere."[18] Others toured the lobbies of American hotels and storefronts or were used as centerpieces at dinner parties (Figures 5.7–5.8). A year before the opening, the media coverage reached its peak when the World's Fair Organization staged a parade on April 30, 1938,

FIGURE 5.6 Model of the fairgrounds at night. Copyright © New York World's Fair 1939–40 records, Manuscripts and Archives Division, The New York Public Library.

FIGURE 5.7 Copy of a model of the central mall of the New York World's Fair used as a conversation piece at the dinner table. Copyright © New York World's Fair 1939–40 records, Manuscripts and Archives Division, The New York Public Library.

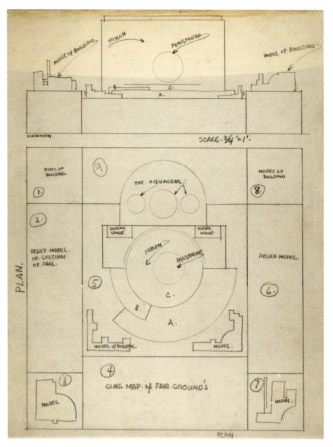

FIGURE 5.8 Plan and elevation for a model display of the New York World's Fair. Copyright © Museum of the City of New York. World's Fair Board of Design Collection. 41.44.120A.

with floats of the exhibitors from the Battery through Times Square to Broadway and all the way to 114th Street.[19] Two days later, forty-nine cars, one for each state, left New York with a stainless-steel cast of the Trylon and Perisphere to be presented at the state capitols.[20] Much like Corbett's practice, the exhibition of design models was an attempt at presenting the planning process of the Fair with unusual and spectacular measures. Often, the original design models were presented. But increasingly, numerous copies in different materials, mainly in plaster, were made to cater to the demand for public displays. To avoid the criticism that had threatened Rockefeller Center, the abstract models were highly staged for public presentations. Illumination, smoke, and animation turned them into scripted theatric events—a fitting preview for what was to be seen at the Fair itself. Watching "live" as the fairgrounds changed, the visitors got a similar sense of involvement that Corbett's clients must have felt when handling a model. The investors could literally insert their pavilions into progress models, inscribing their products or nations onto the landscape of Flushing, Queens. With the Fair's tremendous scale, the presentation of models came out of its niche to nationwide audience that learned to interpret models and model images.

When it opened, the New York World's Fair was an overwhelming spectacle of miniature representations, models, and around 300 dioramas, most notably Henry Dreyfuss' *Democracity*, Walter Dorwin Teague's *City of Light*, and Norman Bel Geddes' *Highways and Horizons*. Even though dioramas remain outside a strict definition of *architectural models*, they were of tremendous influence for their acceptance and popularity. Large-scale dioramas shared a highly theatrical nature with the display of earlier design models. But whereas the latter were clearly staged as isolated representations of buildings, dioramas created sealed-off environments in which the visitor was immersed in the physical model and the space surrounding it. The simulation of different times of day, weather, and sound effects was intended to create an atmosphere of realism that provided visitors with the experience of "being in the future." As a paradox, by projecting effects onto the dioramas, a heightened illusion of reality was created that simultaneously removed the physical objects further from modeled realism as it was practiced in architectural models. For the dioramas, it was more important to function in a theatrical ambience than as matter-of-fact objects that could be studied closely or photographed. Varying scales, perspectival distortions, and an increased distance from the audience created an illusion that was more important than physical accuracy. The degree of detail in most parts of the dioramas was comparatively low; windows or larger architectural features were well visible but most smaller elements were omitted. Each installation used its own strategies for creating an immersive environment. *Democracity*, depicting an ideal future metropolis for 1.5 million inhabitants, was located on the ground of the Fair's spherical Theme Building (Figure 5.9).[21] In a simulated flight, spectators looked down on it from moving balconies as the light changed in a day and night cycle. In opposition, the *City of Light* was installed along the curved wall of the Consolidated Edison Company Building (Figure 5.10). Perspectival distortion and foreshortening let the buildings recede radically into the background. Dedicated to the benefits of electricity, gas, and steam, it depicted illuminated parts of the New York metropolitan area and parts of Westchester County under changing daytime conditions—one day was compressed into twelve minutes.[22] Here, the audience did not move but a narrator

FIGURE 5.9 *Democracity* at the Theme Building representing an illuminated city at night, 1939. Copyright © New York World's Fair 1939–40 records, Manuscripts and Archives Division, The New York Public Library.

FIGURE 5.10 *City of Light*, 1939. Copyright © New York World's Fair 1939–40 records, Manuscripts and Archives Division, The New York Public Library.

commented upon the changes presented in the animated diorama including moving elevators, cars, underground trains, and ships. Each afternoon there was a thunderstorm and further special effects included a model theater play, an operating room, a mini Coney Island, and a mini World's Fair. There was even a miniature plane that landed at LaGuardia airport.[23] The third big display at the Fair, Norman Bel Geddes' *Highways and Horizons* took the medium's possibilities to a level neither any previous diorama or model exhibition, nor any other miniature at the Fair, could challenge. Its main purpose was to depict the achievements of automobile traffic as a story of growth and progress. Both visitors and diorama were animated. It was viewed from a long row of moving armchairs with speakers broadcasting the voice of a tour guide. The landscape was laid out over two stories covering 30,000 square feet including 500,000 buildings, one million trees, and 50,000 cars, 10,000 of which were moving.[24] Again mimicking a flight over the United States, the ride took sixteen minutes and was theatrically illuminated with color filters that changed to give the impression of different times of day; smoke also add to the impression of atmosphere. Unlike in architectural models, the *Futurama's* scale varied throughout, zooming in and out with the buildings' heights changing between one inch and nearly ten feet (Figure 5.11). Visitors did not stand or walk but were driven through a scripted scene. Individual contemplation or a closer look were precluded as the visitor was simultaneously immersed in an animated production including light and sound, and removed from it by a Plexiglas pane. The final part of the diorama presented a traffic intersection

MODEL DISPLAYS

FIGURE 5.11 Large-scale part of the *Futurama*, 1939. Copyright © New York World's Fair 1939–40 records, Manuscripts and Archives Division, The New York Public Library.

in the year 1960 at a bigger scale, after which the visitors stepped out and onto the exact same junction in full scale with actual cars by General Motors.[25] The *Futurama* introduced an unprecedented level of theatrics that physically involved the audience and negated the modeled object. Scale, size, and modeling materials lost their function to simulate architecture realistically as they were meant to be consumed through the prism of special effects. Animation contributed to the loss of detail and made a close examination of the object, as it was celebrated simultaneously in architectural models, impossible.

None of the Fair's dioramas or exhibition models survive.[26] However removed from architectural models, their wide popularity—the *Futurama* was considered the most successful exhibit at the Fair—helped to popularize models and modeling among a lay audience and confirmed the miniature's power as a communication tool between architectural professions and clients. The effect dioramas had on the public acceptance of model making was enduring. When the magazine *Pencil Points* prepared their July 1939 issue on model making, they requested model photos from architects across the country. To their surprise, almost everyone responded—by then, the model as a tool for presentation had clearly arrived in the architectural office.[27] Equally, the broader effect that publications and exhibitions such as the New York World's Fair had on the public cannot be overestimated. In the 1930s, models, miniatures, and dioramas were omnipresent. According to the statistics of the American Institute of Model Engineers, in 1935 there were more than 100,000 model makers of different kinds, from toys to railways to architecture and industrial prototyping.[28] As a large part of the movement, the growing number of hobbyist modeling organizations for "Boys from 8 to 80," such as the National Model Yacht Racing Association, the National Model Railroad Association, and the Junior Birdmen of America were prospering since the 1920s.[29] Their visibility was increased by public events such as the exhibitions of the New York Society of Model Engineers that included sections of model railways, maritime and aeronautical models, and engines.[30] In February 1940 the *New York Times* covered an exhibition held by the New Society of Model Engineers in the basement of the Knickerbocker Building on 152 West 42nd Street.[31] There, 500 exhibitors from all over the world presented their work to judges such as professional architectural model maker Berthold Audsley. Closer to architectural model making, model railroad enthusiasts rarely built trains themselves but rather focused on the surrounding environment. Miniature motorized planes and ships became as popular as railways with races and competitions. Fueled by the aviation adventures of pioneers Amelia Earhart and Charles Lindbergh, blueprints of planes and other models were for sale by about 2,000 manufacturers.[32] By the mid-1930s, there were about two million flying airplane models built each year.[33] NBC aired a radio show called the "Model Airplane Club of the Air" that gave advice on how to build model airplanes.[34] Soon, these models became part of the war preparations in the United States when companies such as the American Metalcraft Corporation made pre-stamped, small-scale military airplane and ship models that were carried around in cigar boxes, often by soldiers. Commercial enterprises such as the New York World's Fair Corporation reacted to this fertile ground by giving concessions to companies making merchandise and souvenirs in model form.

Architectural Exhibitions

> How, for instance, could the 'city of to-morrow' (at the New York World's Fair 1939/40) have been portrayed but by a model?[35]
>
> PETER RAYMOND WICKHAM, 1945

By the end of World War II, it was hard to imagine any kind of architectural exhibition without models. The modeling craze had not just been limited to personal hobbies or public spectacles such as the New York World's Fair but had reached art institutions and museums. The increased use of models as sales tools for entertainment and exhibitions was adopted for purely architectural displays and as educational tools in the permanent collections of museums. For the latter, new institutions tried to capitalize on the wide interest in models as in the case of the Museum of the City of New York, founded in 1932, which installed about thirty dioramas by model maker Ned Burns to illustrate the history of New York. Similarly, the Art Institute of Chicago mounted an exhibition of Mrs. James Ward Thorne's miniature period rooms in 1937 which is still there today. For architectural displays, MoMA acted as an important facilitator for the shift away from rendering toward models and linked them distinctly to modern architecture. In 1932, the *International Style* exhibition opened its doors to the first architectural exhibition at MoMA. Philip Johnson and Henry-Russell Hitchcock had invited nine contemporary architects to present their work. From the start, Johnson had planned for highly refined presentation models as the sole centerpiece, showcasing the architects' most prominent built projects. All models were previously unpublished, specially made for the museum and paid for by Philip Johnson.[36] All at the same scale, they were intended to become part of the collection.[37] As representations of finished buildings, they were of much greater detail than other publicly presented models in the early 1930s. Only later would photographs and drawings be incorporated with the floor plan as the most important drawing exhibited next to the models. Unlike the display practices of the 1920s, when small-scale models were part of the confidential meeting between architect and client or the spectacular displays at the New York World's Fair, here, realistic models were presented as the focus of attention, spotlighted on simple pedestals. Their close proximity to the visitors allowed for the inspection of details from varying standpoints and levels. The former theatrical element of unveiling a model to the client or the physical movement through a sequence of models yielded to a static presentation that did not fix the way the object was to be seen. Only the Villa Savoye and Villa Tugendhat models were regarded as more important in the exhibition and spotlights attached to their bases detailed the transparent windows (Figure 5.12). Following LeRoy Grumbine's advice to light a model with just one large lamp to represent the sun, this form of presentation was understood as a new and more realistic representation of a built structure in comparison with drawings or older modes of model displays.[38]

In the museum's other exhibitions in the 1930s, models became a frequent mode of presentation in shows such as *The Work of Young Architects in the Middle West* (April 1933), *The Recent Work of Le Corbusier* (October 1935), and *Alvar Aalto: Architecture and Furniture* (March–April 1938).[39] The museum's original collection policy mirrored the focus on models, yet regarded only the building as the original art work. Models and photos were not collected as artworks, but as didactic tools in an educational institution rather than a museum. This was a radical departure from older architectural collections, focused on architectural drawings. Based on the public's interest in miniatures in the 1930s, the use of models and photos was seen as a part of the museum's intended appeal to a broader audience; this was documented in a review in *Fortune* magazine, which claimed that the museum "perfected an informal and dramatic technique for exhibiting and explaining things in a way that makes people want to look at them."[40] In contrast with traditional

FIGURE 5.12 Model of the Villa Savoye in the International Style exhibition at MoMA, 1932. Copyright © 2020. Digital image, The Museum of Modern Art, New York/Scala, Florence.

displays of architecture in museum settings, the MoMA models must have seemed like a "dramatic technique for exhibiting." In comparison with displays such as the New York World's Fair, however, they paled in their sober abstinence from special effects that shifted the focus from immersion toward an appreciation of the crafted object and model making as (allegedly) the most truthful and realistic representation of architecture aside from the real building.

Architectural and lifestyle magazines joined MoMA at the forefront of new architectural exhibitions, frequently cooperating with museums and galleries in the 1930s and 1940s. At the center of this development were two institutions located at Rockefeller Center, the PEDAC Galleries and the Museum of Science and Industry. The PEDAC Galleries were founded by interior decorator Paul MacAllister and architect James Folger in 1933 and were located on the tenth floor of the RCA Building. The gallery displayed model homes, public housing, and home furnishings, of which models were a standard part.[41] Together with magazines that published model photos and sponsored by manufacturers of appliances, the gallery presented some of the original photo models alongside full-scale mock-ups of their interiors. One of them was Edward Durell Stone's design of a Garden House No. 1404, originally published in *Ladies' Home Journal*, and presented at PEDAC in March 1938. The detailed and landscaped model was shown on a revolving column inside an interior mockup of the house (Figure 5.13).[42] The model served a dual purpose: Published in the magazine, the photos acted as a teaser for the exhibition and sold copies of drawings. At PEDAC, the model was part of the exhibit within the house's interior referring the visitor's imagination to an exterior that did not exist but which they could build for themselves. The model made it possible for visitors to look at the exterior of the same building that they were walking through. As in the MoMA exhibitions, the model's great detail was meant to signify a real building—that was not yet built.

The second institution at Rockefeller Center, the Museum of Science and Industry, opened only three years after PEDAC, on February 12, 1936, in the basement of the RCA Building. It was heavily subsidized by companies such as General Electric, IBM, and United States Steel Co.[43] The announcement of its opening explicitly mentioned educational "working models" to illustrate

FIGURE 5.13 Model of Garden House No. 1404, *c.* 1937–8. Copyright © Doris Conrad Brown, Theodore Conrad papers, 1937–91, Avery Architectural and Fine Arts Library, Columbia University.

scientific principles as well as historic and current developments.[44] As illustrations, miniature houses were burnt to demonstrate fire hazards,[45] steam engines were exhibited and one of the first shows was a model exhibition featuring American architectural history, including "ultra-modern" houses by Harvey Wiley Corbett, Ralph Walker, William Van Alen, Lawrence White, Leonard Schultze, and Raymond Hood—the same models that had been presented at the 1933 Macy's *Forward House* exhibition co-organized with the *Architectural Forum*.[46] All models were built by Conrad and presented a unified look, even though the designs ranged from Georgian and classical villas to modern designs with flat roofs. At Macy's, the houses had served as a backdrop for advertising modern appliances. Yet, the houses had been for sale, too. Even though no installation shots are known, the model photos in the accompanying catalogue present soberly detailed models as they would have been displayed at MoMA (Figures 5.14–5.15). Less ideologically

FIGURE 5.14 Display of the Bissel House model in a storefront. Copyright © Doris Conrad Brown, Theodore Conrad papers, 1937–91, Avery Architectural and Fine Arts Library, Columbia University.

FIGURE 5.15 Conrad's Sun House model for Macy's Forward House exhibition, 1933. Copyright holder unknown but see Hollister, Paul. "Forward House Exhibition Catalogue." Published by Macy's and the Architectural Forum, 1933.

constrained, the Museum of Science's aim was to appeal to a broad audience with the help of models. As part of its educational program, it held its first summer modeling class for children in 1937, and in much larger groups, adults could learn how to make airplane, ship, and house models.[47] The museum's use of models peaked with a show organized by the American Institute of Architects in October 1948 called *Tomorrow's World* that was the New York chapter's largest public relations event to promote the work of architects. It featured a large number of models including a panoramic urban planning model of an ideal community of 20,000 inhabitants designed by J. Gordon Carr.[48] Curated by Eleanor Pepper, architect and editor of *House and Garden*, it included house models, mocked-up interiors, and photos.[49] Here, the MoMA's style of exhibition-making triumphed over more theatrical setups as they were practiced at PEDAC. Jokingly referred to as the "Theodore Conrad Show" because big parts were made in Conrad's Jersey City workshop, his large urban planning model could be viewed from above but no animation or light effects distracted from a close look at the model, highlighting the skills of both model maker and architect (Figures 5.16–5.17).

House model exhibitions proved so enormously popular in the 1930s and 1940s that eventually even MoMA, which had previously insisted on showing only built architecture, could not resist an exhibition of magazine models. In 1945, it opened the exhibition *Tomorrow's Small House* in collaboration with *Ladies' Home Journal*, that included mainly large 1"=1'-0" scale models of designs by George Fred Keck, Carl Koch, Philip Johnson, Mario Corbett, Hugh Stubbins Jr., Plan-Tech Associates, Vernon DeMars, and Frank Lloyd Wright, built by Devon Dennett and Raymond Barger Studios.[50] The popularity of model photos in magazines and model exhibits in galleries and museums pushed the limits of traditional modes of architectural display in the 1930s. Going even further, full-scale houses such as the Pittsburgh House of Glass at the New York World's Fair were directly linked and often the end point of the modeling craze in which models and photos served not only as a teaser for the show, but as an integral part of the imagery linked to the houses. Similar cases included a model of a vernacular redwood House of Ideas, designed by Edward Durell Stone and published in *Collier's* in 1940, that was built to advertise an exhibition house on the rooftop of the International Building at Rockefeller Center (Figure 5.18).[51] Another House of Tomorrow was designed by Harrison & Fouilhoux for which a full-scale indoor mock-up was sponsored by *Ladies' Home Journal* and the *New York Times* and built at the *North American Homes Exposition* in May 1937 at Madison Square Garden.[52] For all these projects, the model photos envisioned an imaginary scenery of a house in the suburbs. Yet in reality, all the houses were built in full scale somewhere in New York City. Together, model, photos and the full-scale house each added a layer of experience for the audience that the others could not provide. They were incomplete without one another. The model photos explained how the houses were to be looked at through their translation of the immaculately landscaped and furnished large-scale models. The full-scale house gave the visitor the experience of being able to step into the interior of the model with photos providing the visual background of the house's exterior. The houses, though not models themselves in a strict sense, were strongly influenced by the imitation of materials in the models and photos, translating the primarily visual experience from the photos into a bodily one in the full-scale houses.

In opposition to the *International Style* exhibition, most of the aforementioned shows illustrated non-existing architecture to help visitors visualize the future with the help of models. MoMA's models had been of rather small sizes presenting the latest high-art exemplary building types on

FIGURE 5.16 "Tomorrow's World" at the American Institute of Architects, 1948. Copyright © Doris Conrad Brown, Theodore Conrad papers, 1937–91, Avery Architectural and Fine Arts Library, Columbia University.

FIGURE 5.17 Speyer House and car models in "Tomorrow's World," 1948. Copyright © Doris Conrad Brown, Theodore Conrad papers, 1937–91, Avery Architectural and Fine Arts Library, Columbia University.

FIGURE 5.18 Large model photo as a teaser in *Collier's* for Stone's exhibition house at Rockefeller Center. Copyright © Doris Conrad Brown, Theodore Conrad papers, 1937–91, Avery Architectural and Fine Arts Library, Columbia University.

a pedestal like an artwork. Architecture exhibits at stores, commercial galleries, and in magazines featured larger, more colorful, and lavishly furnished medium-sized objects geared toward the average consumer. By transferring these commercial models back into the museum in the 1940s, they pushed exhibitions toward bigger, more life-like models and walk-in exhibits such as the House in the Museum Garden (1949) and the Exhibition House by Gregory Ain in collaboration with *Woman's Home Companion* (1950), both presented in the MoMA garden as models and full-scale mock-ups. By 1948, it was obvious to MoMA's curators that "the public is apathetic toward an exhibition of photographs of architecture. A scale model increases their interest, but it is obvious that proportion and enclosed space cannot be shown except at full size."[53] The model had superseded both renderings and photos as the most popular medium for display through its increased realism and its connection with full-scale buildings. With the growing interest in model making techniques among visitors, a new appreciation emerged that went beyond judging the design of the building represented. Institutions realized the tremendous success of detailed models in selling modern architecture because of the audience's admiration of the model maker's skills. Now, the physical object became the focus of attention.

Interactive Displays

In the same way that model photos became the main method for presenting an unbuilt structure in magazines, the model became the focal point in exhibitions and galleries in the 1930s. In the postwar years, architects embraced models as they became the most successful tool in the increasingly extended negotiations with large corporations and their boards of directors. Now, architects and model makers transferred the display techniques developed in the previous two decades back into the architectural discourse. The modeling craze had long-lasting effects on clients' expectations for presentations of an architect's ideas. As corporations and governmental agencies became some of the major sponsors for modern architecture, larger and more elaborate presentations to bigger groups became standard. These clients, educated by the wide dissemination of models, requested increasingly large models which sometimes could not even fit through the door of their meeting rooms.[54] After a decade of escalated realism in modeling, model photography, and model exhibitions, the average presentation model had to fulfill similar expectations of being a miniature building. From urban planning models to meticulous presentation and floor-plan models, the model as a tool for communication with the client had become indispensable. Model makers occupied an increasingly powerful position as architects depended on their work to represent the latest design changes in great detail—a fact that architect Philip Goodwin was made painfully aware of for his planned addition to the Yale University Art Gallery. By late 1943 Goodwin had sent Conrad blueprints for a presentation model.[55] The gallery model, Goodwin demanded, had to be finished by February 12, 1944. By mid-March, however, Conrad was only half done. Goodwin had invited his friend, the Horace Walpole scholar Wilmarth Lewis, who was associated with Yale University, to inspect the model.[56] The presentation, Goodwin argued, was of utmost importance as he needed to resolve his problems with the client to get authorization to prepare working drawings. Conrad was unable to finish the model due to wartime pressures on his studio. Eventually, it was finished at the end of October 1944 with the help of two other model makers, Louis C. Jaeger and Joseph Marino.[57] Though it cannot be confirmed conclusively that the late delivery was the only reason for the lost commission, it certainly delayed the university's decision. Eventually, the project was abandoned and between 1951–3 Louis Kahn built a different annex.

In the 1950s, models entered meetings with clients at earlier stages and often a succession of different model types was presented as ideas unfolded. Many architects developed individual practices of using models and photos that became a trademark of their work. Among the most personal is certainly Eero Saarinen's use of large-scale cardboard models that were presented in photos, as in the case of his TWA Terminal for which the client bought the design without ever seeing the model.[58] A more conventional method was SOM's combination of architectural media, reflected in their meeting with Inland Steel representatives for their new headquarters, held on May 21, 1954, that included the following documents: floor plans of all departments, a rental and economic analysis, isometrics and sketches of the structure, mechanical drawings, two perspectives of the building with surroundings, and a small Lucite model.[59] At a second meeting on February 16, 1955, a much more detailed 1/8"=1'-0" scale model that represented the building materials was used for the final approval of the design.[60] For SOM, the second model was of such importance that chief designer Bruce Graham himself delivered it to Chicago.[61] At first glance, similar drawings as in the 1920s remained at the heart of SOM's presentations. But now they were accompanied by a growing number of written documents to explain the design process. Models were meant to educate and communicate the architect's work in connection with all other media. As corporate clients began to take increasing interest in the technicalities of design they often became heavily involved in all aspects of development. Known for their inclusive practice, SOM invited participation from the onset as it facilitated their research into the client's needs and their translation into spatial arrangements, a process dubbed "programming." Possibly the most intense collaboration with a corporate client was the new headquarters for the Connecticut General Life Insurance Company in Hartford, Connecticut. Over a two-year process, the architects collaborated with a four-man committee to determine the building's program, design, and execution based on a written twenty-five-page program approved in June 1953.[62] After six months of preliminary design, three schemes were presented to the client.[63] Contrary to the usual course of interactions between architect and client, this process focused on floor plans and the façade was only revealed late in the development, as Gordon Bunshaft recalled: "Frazar Wilde and our office—he somehow liked me—worked. We got along beautifully. That doesn't mean he agreed with everything. He would raise intelligent questions and we would try to answer them or do studies to see what could be done. After a year of all this, we brought them a complete finished model of how the whole thing would look, site and all. This glass building and all that. In that they had gone through the planning, it just seemed natural to them. It was approved in about two minutes."[64] This process meant that new types of models became foregrounded. Initially, only a massing model had been presented that gave the overall layout of the building in the landscape (Figure 5.19). Then, floor-plan models with furniture were used by the interior designers to determine each department's layout (Figure 5.20). Here the interaction with the client reached a new level: the clients' internal planning department first developed a layout which was later translated into models and rearranged together with the client.[65] For SOM, models had become an interactive tool that was provided by the model maker and used by both architect and client.

As the nature of presentations and interactions with clients changed, so did the design process. Often, design decisions were made in meetings and needed to be presented in physical form to the client, which caused the number of models to rise. If, for Philip Goodwin, one detailed presentation model could have saved his commission it was now numerous, different models that were used to explain and decide every aspect of a building. Increasingly, the opinion of employees and the public mattered, as corporations sought not just to create floor space but also public manifestos of their company's products and place in society. Presentations to clients were still held in private offices but by adopting methods developed in museum exhibitions, architects increasingly sought the support of a larger public. Learning from earlier MoMA exhibitions, architects began to present their work as being more than architecture and thus attempted to elevate them to artworks that could be owned. In their negotiations with clients, this strategy added value to a design as it received the seemingly intangible quality of an artwork that could not as easily be questioned or

FIGURE 5.19 Gordon Bunshaft presenting an early massing model to a committee of General Life, *c.* fall 1953. Copyright © Gordon Bunshaft architectural drawings and papers, 1909–90, Avery Architectural and Fine Arts Library, Columbia University.

FIGURE 5.20 Large-scale floor-plan model in a meeting between architects and client inside a mock-up of the Connecticut General Life Building, *c.* 1954. Copyright © Gordon Bunshaft architectural drawings and papers, 1909–90, Avery Architectural and Fine Arts Library, Columbia University.

changed. Equally inspired by the success of model photos in lifestyle magazines, architects and model makers translated these two-dimensional images into the exhibition space to create a display in which the model could be looked at as both a highly elaborate physical object and as a "walk-in photo" that, in combination with photo murals, gave the illusion of standing in front of the building. Arguably the most elaborate use of models for such a presentation was SOM's show of models, renderings and photos at the Colorado Springs Fine Arts Center between May 13 and June 19, 1955.[66] The new US Air Force Academy was commissioned by the federal government in Washington, D.C., and the exhibition was the first presentation of the final designs to both the client and a wider audience. Prepared in under two months, it had the remarkably high budget of $100,000 and at least two model makers were employed for building five models: Rush Studios of Chicago and Conrad.[67] George Cooper Rudolph, one of SOM's preferred delineators, created renderings and the photographers Ezra Stoller, Ansel Adams, and William Garnett were employed to take background photos as well as exhibition shots and model photos. Stoller's model photos taken with the backgrounds in the exhibition were intended for marketing purposes. At the entrance of the exhibition, a small model of the site gave an overview over the plateau on which the academy was planned. The first room showed two models, one of the airfield and one of the community center both with black-and-white aerial panoramas in the background. The following room contained a rendering of cadets and buildings by Rudolph, a photo by Adams and the centerpiece of the show, a 1/32"=1'-0" scale model of the cadet area mounted at waist height against a blue wall and flanked by curtains.[68] All of the models were used in connection with photo murals that gave them depth and translated the realistic model photos of magazines back into a spatial setting where the visitors could themselves "create" the illusion of looking at a real building by taking an eye-level position in front of the model—a kind of walk-in model photo-setting (Figures 5.21–5.22). Visitors could move around in the gallery examining the model from different vantage points in its setting. They were not presented with one fixed view, as in a photo, but with the option for multiple viewpoints. For the model of the cadet area, the visitors were presented with two options of looking at it: in unison with the photo mural or from an elevated walkway giving the illusion of a flight over the site. Part of an elaborate program, the exhibition was accompanied by a dinner, a presentation to the client, a visit to the show, and an inspection of the site. The response from architectural magazines was very positive. Members of Congress, however, were more critical and the cadet area and chapel became the focus of an extended public debate concerned with political considerations surrounding building materials and monumentality as the politicians expected a more conservative architectural style. In hearings before the House of Representatives, John Merrill used model photos to show revised designs using considerably less glass.[69] Initially, another show had been planned at MoMA from October 18 to November 27, 1955, which was postponed to February 1957 due to fears of further criticism.

In comparison with SOM's earlier exhibition at MoMA, the increased blur between model presentations for sales purposes and to achieve institutional elevation of their designs as art, is striking as both architects and museums adopted similar display techniques. The exhibition *Architectural Work by Skidmore, Owings and Merrill* had opened on September 26, 1950, as the first solo show of a young up-and-coming office after the war. The models on show had not been made specially for the exhibition but instead came from the architects' practice. They were staged on pedestals in the middle of the room in front of large blow-ups of photos and drawings. Four models were presented of recently developed projects: Lever House, the Heinz Research Center in Pittsburgh, the Ford headquarters in Dearborn, and the New York Bellevue Hospital.[70] The model of Lever House, one of the first models of a high-rise ever to be constructed almost entirely from Plexiglas, did not disappoint as the eye-catcher mounted at the entrance to the exhibition as

FIGURE 5.21 Model in front of a photo mural, 1955. Copyright holder unknown but see Nauman, *On the Wings of Modernism*, 53, 54, 55.

FIGURE 5.22 Model of the cadet area in front of a photo mural in the exhibition, 1955. Copyright holder unknown but see *SOM News*, June 15, 1955.

Natalie de Blois of SOM remembered (Figure 5.23): "I think the model of Lever House was first presented to the public at the MoMA exhibit in September 1950. [. . .] The Lever House model, shown in the exhibition, was really spectacular. I was very impressed."[71] As for the Air Force models, the juxtaposition of models with blow-up photos opened up a simulated space comparable to model photos. Oscillating between presenting the models as art objects and walk-in photo settings, the exhibition left room to look at them as crafted objects and to highlight their novelty materials. MoMA had experimented with large blow-up images at least since Ludwig Mies van der Rohe's exhibition three years earlier. There, Mies' models had been set in the middle of the gallery space interacting with furniture and large-scale murals of his buildings (Figure 5.24). Mies' display acted much the same way as Edward Durell Stone's model of a Garden House No. 1404 at the PEDAC galleries where the visitor was immersed in an interior space while simultaneously looking at the structure's exterior through the model.

Aside from viewing models as meticulously crafted objects, the two approaches toward staging models—walk-in photo settings using blown-up photos of exterior spaces, and the construction of interiors in the exhibition space using models as a reference to an imagined outside—were applied widely during the 1950s. In the former, visitors were not a part of the display but could "enter" it by adapting their viewpoint to the model's scale. In the latter, they were immersed in an interior space that they could "leave" by looking at the model's exterior. Both display strategies depended heavily on the new techniques for making realistic models. A combination of both strategies was

FIGURE 5.23 Lever House model in the exhibition "Architectural Work by Skidmore, Owings and Merrill" at MoMA, fall 1950. Copyright © 2020. Digital image, The Museum of Modern Art, New York/Scala, Florence.

FIGURE 5.24 Ludwig Mies van der Rohe and Philip Johnson in front of a photo mural of Tugendhat house at MoMA. Copyright © 2020. Digital image, The Museum of Modern Art, New York/Scala, Florence.

FIGURE 5.25 Model of the American Embassy in New Delhi inside a mock-up of the building's terracotta screens in the exhibition "Buildings for Business and Government" at MoMA, 1957. Copyright © 2020. Digital image, The Museum of Modern Art, New York/Scala, Florence.

used for what Mary Anne Staniszewski called "the most ambitious of MoMA's photo and model exhibitions": the 1957 exhibition *Buildings for Business and Government*.[72] Curated by Arthur Drexler, all six projects combined large models, photo murals and mock-ups of the buildings' most prominent features such as the American Embassy's pierced terracotta tiles (Figure 5.25). The use of full-scale mock-ups in the gallery space included exteriors such as a twenty-foot façade mock-up of Mies' Seagram Building as well as interiors. Depending on the visitor's position in the gallery, the models either functioned as walk-in model photos, referred to an exterior of a building that the visitor was immersed in or created a fictional urban landscape through the juxtaposition of geographically unrelated projects that were displayed alongside one another (Figures 5.26–5.27). Common to all these exhibitions, models emerged from their immediate dependence on other architectural media such as photography or special effects projected onto them. Based on their heightened realism they no longer needed to be obscured or transformed. Rather, the objects and their materials became the focus of attention. Their connection with photo murals combined two independent media that equally influenced and challenged one another through their juxtaposition but left the ultimate simulation to the visitors. Taking this practice outside the gallery space, models became an effigy for the building in a dialogue with the public as they were set up at the building site. Cases such as Rockefeller Center, the New York World's Fair, or the Seagram Building were somewhat unusual but employed the same techniques as architectural exhibitions, positioning a small-scale model in front of the scenery of the construction site where it could be imagined as the real building (Figure 5.28).

Many of the models presented in the MoMA exhibitions during the 1950s traveled extensively. After the war, model exhibitions abroad acted in the context of the Cold War to win over an international audience. As such, models became part of American cultural promotion. Like the full-scale practices of architects such as Edward Durell Stone or SOM, model exhibitions received an increasingly wide and international audience. And much like the small house models that had

FIGURES 5.26 and 5.27 Air Force Academy model as seen from two different directions. Copyright © 2020. Digital image, The Museum of Modern Art, New York/Scala, Florence.

FIGURE 5.28 Model of the Seagram Building in front of the construction site on Park Avenue. Copyright holder unknown but see Town & Country 1957. Photography: Gleb Derujinsky.

encouraged American audiences to invest in modern appliances during the 1940s, the models and photos of office towers of the 1950s suggested to predominantly European audiences that they could be a part of American Modernism. MoMA played an important role in exporting American culture, not least by supporting the Pan-American "good neighbor" efforts of the 1940s, and models became its most successful architectural export item, best exemplified by the model of the MoMA building traveling to the *Exhibition of American Art* at the Musée du Jeu de Paume in Paris in 1938.[73] Similar shows were such towering events as the *Amerika Baut* exhibition in 1957 in Berlin, the Brussels World's Fair in 1958, and the *American National Exhibition* in Moscow in 1959.[74] A key player in organizing these promotional events were Jack Masey and his office of exhibits at the US Information Agency that was responsible for the exhibits in Berlin and Moscow.[75] Both, the Brussels World's Fair display and the *American National Exhibition* were not significant for their display models. Because it was staged in the context of the building fair *Interbau 57*, the Berlin exhibition remains the most impressive of these foreign shows. *Amerika Baut* opened in September 1957 at the George C. Marshall House in West Berlin to present a positive image of Western modernist building practices.[76] Curated by Peter Blake, editor of the *Architectural Forum*, and Julian Neski, it followed the display strategies of American exhibitions, utilizing six full-size façade mock-ups of high-rises—including Lever House, the Union Carbide Building, the Seagram Building, and the Alcoa Building in Pittsburgh—that were visually extended with mirrors.[77] The exhibition also included as least two models: the Mile High Center by I. M. Pei and Lever House. The latter was displayed inside a window in the mock-up of Lever House, continuing the play with scales in different representations of a building (Figure 5.29). While the visitor could walk through an imagined exterior of an American city, the model displayed in the window referred both to the

FIGURE 5.29 Installation shot of "America Builds" with façade mock-ups and model in mock-up of Lever House, 1957. Copyright © 2020. Digital image, The Museum of Modern Art, New York/Scala, Florence.

imagination of what the entire building looked like and alluded to a shop window, suggesting that the building was a precious object that could be owned. Instead of the model just referring to a building that was absent in the gallery space, here the building was condensed into a model that could be desired. Architectural models in these international exhibitions were, arguably, the biggest success for the postwar modeling boom as it exported not just American architecture but model making alike.[78] Part of what had made models attractive for exhibitions was their increased detail. At the same time, the fragile nature of the assembled models often could not withstand the frequent travels. Yet, the object's renewed material aura required it to be in the exhibition space to be fully appreciated and attested to a revived interest in the crafted object, not just images produced with its help. The translation of model photos back into a three-dimensional space retained the simulation of reality but at the same time opened them up to the physical engagement of the visitor that largely contributed to the success of the model as an architectural medium. The drawing never fully disappeared from model presentations but with the creation of environments in the gallery space it was relegated to an explanatory tool. Models, now the established effigy of the building, were arranged as the focal point of the shows.

Notes

Introduction

1. Jane Jacobs, "The Miniature Boom," *The Architectural Forum*, May 1958, 106–11, 196.
2. Elizabeth McFadden, "Lilliputian Buildings Are His Forte. Made to Assist Architects," *Newark Sunday News*, August 30, 1964. Alex Ladd, "The Dean of Models: Was New York City Built in a Heights Shop?," *The Jersey City Reporter*, July 21, 1991. Anna Quindlen, "For a Maker of a Model City it is Indeed a Small World," *The New York Times*, January 15, 1981. Karen Moon, *Modeling Messages: The Architect and the Model* (New York: Monacelli Press, 2005). Oliver Elser, "On the History of the Architectural Model in the Twentieth Century," in *The Architectural Model: Tool, Fetish, Small Utopia*, ed. Oliver Elser and Peter Cachola Schmal (Zurich: Scheidegger und Spiess, 2012), 17. Davide Deriu, "Transforming Ideas into Pictures: Model Photography and Modern Architecture," in *Camera Constructs: Architecture and the Modern City*, ed. Andrew Higgott and Timothy Wray (Farnham: Ashgate, 2012), 171.
3. John Havas, "Hudson Man Big Builder in Small Way Among Top Modelmakers," 1956, newspaper clipping, Theodore Conrad Archive.
4. Jeremy Lebensohn, "Mighty Miniatures," *American Craft*, June/July 1988, 35. Carter Horsley, "Modelmaker's Work Gaining New Recognition," *The New York Times*, July 28, 1974. Ladd, "The Dean of Models."
5. Quindlen, "For a Maker of a Model City."
6. Newsletter of the American Institute of Architects, March 23, 1962, 2, Archives of the American Institute of Architects.
7. The following collections own models made in Conrad's workshop: The Museum of Modern Art, The New York Historical Society, The Heinz Architectural Center-Carnegie Museum of Art in Pittsburgh, The Special Collections. University of Arkansas Libraries in Fayetteville, The Art Institute of Chicago, and The Centre Georges Pompidou in Paris, as well as a private collection in the UK.
8. LeRoy Grumbine, "Cardboard Models," *The Architectural Review*, August 2, 1922. LeRoy Grumbine, "A Florida House and Garden in Model," *House and Garden*, February 1924. LeRoy Grumbine, "The Use of Scale Models as an Aid to the Architect," *Western Architect: Architecture and Allied Arts*, June 1925, 59–62. LeRoy Grumbine, "Using Scale Models Advantageously," *The Architectural Forum*, January 1929, 105–09.
9. Harvey Wiley Corbett, "Architectural Models of Cardboard," *Pencil Points*, April–August 1922, 11–14; 28–32, 37; 14–17; 14–18. Kenneth Reid, "Architectural Models," *Pencil Points*, July 1939, 407–12. Robert Dennis Murray, "Models and Scotch," *Pencil Points*, July 1939, 427–37. James Rose "Landscape Models," *Pencil Points*, July 1939, 438–44. Robert Hoyt, "World's Fair Models," *Pencil Points*, July 1939, 413–26.
10. Edward Hobbs, *Pictorial House Modelling* (London: Crosby Lockwood and Son, 1926). Rolf Janke, *Architectural Models* (New York: Frederick A. Praeger, 1968).

11 Horst Bredekamp, *St. Peter in Rom und das Prinzip der produktiven Zerstörung. Bau und Abbau von Bramante bis Bernini* (Berlin: Wagenbach, 2000). Leon Battista Alberti, *Ten Books on Architecture* (London: Tiranti, 1955), 22.

12 Walter Grasskamp, "Sentimentale Modelle," *Kunstforum International*, no. 2 (1980): 54–79. Oliver Elser, "On the History of the Architectural Model," in *The Architectural Model: Tool, Fetish, Small Utopia*, ed. Oliver Elser and Peter Cachola Schmal (Zurich: Scheidegger und Spiess, 2012), 11–22. Martino Stierli, "Preservation Parade: The Mediatization of the Lieb House into a Monument," *Future Anterior*, no.1 (summer 2010): 46.

13 Moon, *Modeling Messages*, 113–14, 132. Kenneth Frampton, *Idea as Model* (New York: Rizzoli, 1981).

14 Moon, *Modeling Messages*, 38.

1 Architectural Model Making as a Profession

1 Andrew Reinhard, "Organization for Cooperation," *The Architectural Forum*, January 1932, 1.

2 Spiro Kostof, *The Architect: Chapters in the History of the Profession* (New York: Oxford University Press, 1977), 59–94.

3 Mary Woods, *From Craft to Profession: The Practice of Architecture in Nineteenth-Century America* (Berkeley: University of California Press, 1999). Peggy Deamer, *The Architect as Worker: Immaterial Labor, the Creative Class, and the Politics of Design* (London: Bloomsbury, 2015).

4 Woods, *From Craft to Profession*, 7.

5 Ibid., 127.

6 Joan Ockman, *Architecture School: Three Centuries of Educating Architects in North America* (Cambridge, MA: MIT Press, 2012), 86.

7 Harvey Wiley Corbett, "Choosing a Profession," *Herald Tribune*, June 1, 1926.

8 Woods, *From Craft to Profession*, 1–2.

9 Carol Willis, "Drawing towards Metropolis," in *Hugh Ferriss: The Metropolis of Tomorrow* (New York: Princeton Architectural Press, 1986), 150.

10 Alina Payne, "Materiality, Crafting, and Scale in Renaissance Architecture," *Oxford Art Journal*, no. 3 (2009): 372.

11 Leon Battista Alberti, *On the Art of Building in Ten Books* (Cambridge, 1988), 34.

12 Alberto Pérez-Gómez, "The Revelation of Order: Perspective and Architectural Representation," in *This is Not Architecture: Media Constructions*, ed. Kester Rattenbury (London: Routledge, 2002), 3–25.

13 See the oral history interviews by Pauline Saliga, Betty Blum, and Sharon Zane for the Art Institute of Chicago.

14 Dana Cuff, *Architecture: The Story of Practice* (Cambridge, MA: MIT Press, 1991), 27.

15 Mary Davis Gillies, *McCall's Book of Modern Houses* (New York: Simon and Schuster, 1951), foreword.

16 Jacobs, "Miniature Boom," 107.

17 Reinhard Wendler, *Das Modell zwischen Wissenschaft und Kunst* (Munich: Wilhelm Fink, 2013), 73.

18 Paul Stoller, "The Architecture of Harvey Wiley Corbett" (thesis, University of Wisconsin, 1995), 2.

NOTES

19 Harvey Wiley Corbett, "Architectural Models of Cardboard," *Pencil Points*, April–August 1922, 11–14; 28–32, 37; 14–17; 14–18.
20 Ibid., 11.
21 *A New Description of Sir John Soane's Museum* (Marlborough: Sir John Soane's Museum, 2007), 87.
22 Moon, *Modeling Messages*, 143.
23 Ibid., 147. Robert Dennis Murray, "Models and Scotch," *Pencil Points*, July 1939, 429.
24 Stan Buck, *E.W. Twining: Model Maker, Artist and Engineer* (Cedarburg: Landmark Publishing, 2004).
25 LeRoy Grumbine, *Scale Models*, booklet, Oberlin College Archives.
26 Hobbs, *Pictoral House Modelling*, 2.
27 LeRoy Grumbine, *Scale Models*, booklet, Oberlin College Archives.
28 LeRoy Grumbine, "The Use of Scale Models."
29 Moon, *Modeling Messages*, 145.
30 Joseph Esherick, "Architectural Education in the Thirties and Seventies: A Personal View," in *The Architect: Chapters in the History of the Profession*, ed. Spiro Kostof (New York: Oxford University Press, 1977), 239. Ockman, *Architecture School*, 79–80.
31 Ockman, *Architecture School*, 93.
32 Circular of Information, Day Courses, New York 1928–1929/1929–1930, Pratt Institute, School of Fine and Applied Arts.
33 Office of the Registrar, Pratt Institute, email to author, January 23, 2014.
34 Theodore Conrad, "His Models Made the Difference," *Historic Preservation*, November/December 1981, 14.
35 Janet Henrichs to Theodore Conrad, June 19, 1937, letter, Villa Savoye Folder, Study Center Architecture and Design, MoMA.
36 Transcript of interview, April 4, 1956, Theodore Conrad Archive.
37 Theodore Conrad to Delta Manufacturing Co., June 30, 1934, letter, Theodore Conrad Archive.
38 Kenneth Reid, "Architectural Models," *Pencil Points*, July 1939, 412. "Edward Howes, 87, Artist, Architect," *The New York Times*, May 11, 1964.
39 Box 34, Folder 3: Model Makers, New York World's Fair 1939 and 1940 Incorporated Records (1935–1945), Manuscripts and Archives Division, New York Public Library.
40 Hal Borland, "Worlds in Miniature for the Fair," *The New York Times*, March 12, 1939.
41 Hoyt, "World's Fair Models," 420.
42 David Gelernter, *1939: The Lost World of the Fair* (New York: The Free Press, 1995), 340–1.
43 "'Bubble Floating on Fountains' to be Central Building at Fair," *New York American*, March 16, 1937, newspaper clipping, Theodore Conrad Archive.
44 Theodore Conrad to Janet Henrichs, March 9, 1938, invoice, Villa Savoye Folder, Study Center Architecture and Design, MoMA. "'Bubble Floating on Fountains' to be Central Building at Fair."
45 Gelernter, *1939*, 341. "Bid for Signal Job on Fair Tube Spur," *Brooklyn Daily Eagle*, July 30, 1938.
46 Joseph Cusker, "The World of Tomorrow," in *Dawn of a New Day: The New York World's Fair, 1939/40*, ed. Helen Harrison (New York: New York University Press, 1980), 3.
47 "World's Fair Rents Design Workshop," *The New York Times*, May 26, 1936.
48 Richard Wurts and Stanley Appelbaum, *The New York World's Fair 1939/1940 in 155 Photographs* (New York: Dover Publications, 1977), xiii.

49 Box 34, Folder 3: Model Makers, New York World's Fair 1939 and 1940 Incorporated Records (1935–1945), Manuscripts and Archives Division, New York Public Library.

50 "Fair of 1939 Will Depict the 'World of Tomorrow,'" *The New York Times*, October 9, 1936.

51 "Model Makers Build NY World's Fair in Miniature," *New York Herald Tribune,* March 6, 1938.

52 John Markland, "Expert Model-Making. Construction of World's Fair Structures in Miniature Aids Building Hobbyists," *The New York Times*, March 21, 1937. "Model Makers Build NY World's Fair in Miniature," *New York Herald Tribune,* March 6, 1938. Box 1703, Folder 1, New York World's Fair 1939 and 1940 Incorporated Records (1935–45), Manuscripts and Archives Division, New York Public Library.

53 Hoyt, "World's Fair Models," 413.

54 New York World's Fair Bulletin, January 1937, 3, Patricia Klingenstein Library, New-York Historical Society.

55 Box 211, Folder 11: Corbett & MacMurray, New York World's Fair 1939 and 1940 Incorporated Records (1935–45), Manuscripts and Archives Division, New York Public Library.

56 The following models can be verified: several versions of the Theme Building; a model of a fountain by Fernand Léger; models for the Focal Food Building; the National Dairy Products Pavilion; the Heinz Dome; the General Cigar Company Pavilion, the Johns Manville Building; and the Pittsburgh House of Glass. "'Bubble Floating on Fountains' to be Central Building at Fair." Louis Checkman to Theodore Conrad 1938, invoice, Theodore Conrad Archive.

57 "How Realism is Achieved in Diorama Making," *Torrance Herald*, August 15, 1935.

58 Donald Albrecht, *Norman Bel Geddes Designs America* (New York: Abrams, 2012).

59 Jennifer Davis Roberts, *Norman Bel Geddes: An Exhibition of Theatrical and Industrial Designs* (Austin: The University of Texas at Austin, 1979), 27. Christopher Innes, *Designing Modern America. Broadway to Main Street* (New Haven, CT: Yale University Press, 2005), 194.

60 Nicolas Paolo Maffei, "Designing the Image of the Practical Visionary: Norman Bel Geddes, 1893–1958," (dissertation, Royal College of Art, February 2000), 226.

61 Jeffrey Meikle, "'A Few Years Ahead:' Defining a Modernism with Popular Appeal," in *Norman Bel Geddes Designs America*, ed. Donald Albrecht (New York: Abrams, 2012), 115.

62 Maffei, "Designing the Image of the Practical Visionary," 242. Donald Albrecht, "Introduction," in *Norman Bel Geddes Designs America*, ed. Donald Albrecht (New York: Abrams, 2012), 23.

63 Harrison, *Dawn of a New Day*, 52.

64 Estimate for General Motors, N.Y. World's Fair Exhibit, Norman Bel Geddes Papers, Harry Ransom Center, The University of Texas at Austin.

65 "Fair's Super-Speed Highway Exhibit to be Huge Panorama," *The New York Sun*, January 21, 1939. Press Release, April 29, 1939, Image ID 1674408, backside, Digital Collections, New York Public Library. Roberts, *Norman Bel Geddes*, 44.

66 Moon, *Modeling Messages*, 147.

67 Stephen Waring, "Improved Techniques in Architectural Modelling," *Journal. Royal Architectural Institute of Canada*, February 1948, 58–60.

68 Drawing on experiences with extremely small-scale topographic models, his suggestions for postwar models were rather conservative, including improved wood-cutting techniques, landscaping, and more electrification. In addition, Waring was not referring to the US but most likely to the modeling shop at Medmenham, U.K. Waring, "Improved Techniques in Architectural Modelling," 59.

69 Martin Briggs, "Architectural Models," *The Burlington Magazine*, April 1929, 180.

NOTES

70 Alastair Pearson, "Allied Military Model Making during World War II," *Cartography and Geographic,* March 2002, 227.

71 Buck, *E.W. Twining*, 82.

72 John Kreis, *Piercing the Fog: Intelligence and Army Air Forces Operations in World War II* (Washington, D.C.: U.S. Government Printing Office, 1996), 86.

73 Constance Babington Smith, *Evidence in Camera: The Story of Photographic Intelligence in World War II* (London: David & Charles, 1974), 234.

74 Pearson, "Allied Military Model Making," 228, 238. Waring, "Improved Techniques in Architectural Modelling," 58–9. Richard Rush, "Made Shedd's Reef and Museum's Heart," *The Chicago Tribune*, December 5, 2001. Andy Wallace, "L.n. Abrams, 72, Master Modelmaker," *The Philadelphia Inquirer*, August 29, 1992.

75 Guy Hartcup, *Camouflage: A History of Concealment and Deception in War* (London: David & Charles, 1979), 51.

76 Smith, *Evidence in Camera*, 145. Kreis, *Piercing the Fog*, 81.

77 Sally Deering, "Model Maker Disguised a City," *The Jersey Journal*, November 18, 1991. *Fortune*, December 1940. Commander Lammers and E.J. M., "Fortune Naval Base. Structures and Facilities to be Provided," October 9 and October 14, 1940, manuscript, Theodore Conrad Archive.

78 Theodore Conrad to Louis Checkman, November 9, 1943, letter, Theodore Conrad Archive. Theodore Conrad to Local Board No. 28, undated, letter, Theodore Conrad Archive.

79 Theodore Conrad to Louis Checkman, November 9, 1943, letter, Theodore Conrad Archive.

80 Deering, "Model Maker Disguised a City." Robert Barnard O'Connor to Theodore Conrad, July 14, 1942, letter, Theodore Conrad Archive.

81 Theodore Conrad to Louis Checkman, December 10, 1943. Theodore Conrad to Louis Checkman, March 5, 1943. Theodore Conrad to Louis Checkman, June 14, 1943, letters, Theodore Conrad Archive.

82 "Women Engaged in the Art of Camouflage," *The New York Times*, April 20, 1942.

83 Christina Cogdell, "Theater of War," in *Norman Bel Geddes Designs America*, ed. Donald Albrecht (New York: Abrams, 2012), 316–39.

84 Theodore Conrad to Louis Checkman, December 10, 1943, letter, Theodore Conrad Archive.

85 Louis Checkman to Theodore Conrad, April 20, 1945, letter. "Photo Lab Soldier Designs Scale Model of Page Field," August 27, 1945, newspaper clipping, Louis Checkman Archive.

86 Thomas William Hendrick, *Model Making as a Career* (London: Percival Marshall & Co. Ltd, 1952), 23–8.

87 Robert Larkins, "Diamonds, Bologna Star in Heights' History," *The Jersey Journal*, July 30, 1979. Gene Flinn, "Pulse of the City. An Architectural Model Home Maker," April 26, 1951, newspaper clipping, Theodore Conrad Archive.

88 Theodore Conrad, "Delta Competition Entry 1944," Theodore Conrad Archive.

89 Jacobs, "The Miniature Boom," 196.

90 Theodore Conrad to Argentine Consulate General, September 7, 1965, letter, Theodore Conrad Archive. "Certificate of Registration," Federal Committee on Apprenticeship, September 23, 1953, registry number 76782.

91 "Model Maker. Artificial Trees Specialty of Jersey City Woman," newspaper clipping, Theodore Conrad Archive.

92 Devon Dennett to Theodore Conrad, invoice for 700 small trees à 5ct. and 75 coupés and taxis à 10ct., November 15, 1954, invoice, Theodore Conrad Archive.

93 Theodore Conrad, "Work Processes for Model Maker Apprentices," 1953, Theodore Conrad Archive.

94 Raymond Lester, "Built Model of New York City," *The New York Times*, October 1, 1983. Arthur Herman, "Models of Plastic and Aluminium," *Progressive Architecture*, December 1959, 9–11. "Model of City Shows Every House, Park, Bridge, Pier, Stadium and Police Station," *The New York Times*, April 26, 1964.

95 "Art Work at Fair Stirs Union Fight," *The New York Times*, October 10, 1963. Jeremy Lebensohn, "Mighty Miniatures," *American Craft*, June/July 1988, 34–9. Louise Weinberg et al., "Panorama of the City of New York," leaflet Queens Museum, c. 2014.

96 "Mrs. Dennett, 75, Suffrage Leader," *The New York Times*, July 26, 1947. Devon Dennett, "Architects' Aide," *The New York Times*, April 25, 1960.

97 Jacobs, "The Miniature Boom," 106.

98 Obituary, "Thomas W. Salmon II. Of NY and IN," accessed February 17, 2015, http://boards.ancestry.com/surnames.salmon/553/mb.ashx?pnt=1.

99 Moon, *Modeling Messages*, 147. Lebensohn, "Mighty Miniatures," 37.

100 Turpin Bannister, *The Architect at Mid-Century: Evolution and Achievement and Converstations Across the Nation* (New York: Reinhold, 1954), 36.

101 Moon, *Modeling Messages*, 37. Franz Schulze and Edward Windhorst, *Mies van der Rohe: A Critical Biography* (Chicago: University of Chicago Press, 2012), 377. John Comazzi, *Balthazar Korab: Architect of Photography* (New York: Princeton Architectural Press, 2012), 7. Lebensohn, "Mighty Miniatures."

102 "Architectural Photography," assembled by Norbert Adler Associates, Binghamton, New York, exhibition flyer, Louis Checkman Archive.

103 "Photo Lab Soldier Designs Scale Model of Page Field," August 27, 1945, newspaper clipping, Louis Checkman Archive. Theodore Conrad, "Letter of Recommendation for Louis Checkman," November 3, 1943, Theodore Conrad Archive.

104 Letters between Louis Checkman and Theodore Conrad 1942–5, Theodore Conrad Archive.

105 Nina Rappaport and Erica Stoller, *Ezra Stoller. Photographer* (New Haven, CT: Yale University Press, 2012), 8.

106 Robert Sobieszek, *The Architectural Photography of Hedrich-Blessing* (New York: Holt, Reinhart and Winston, 1984), 4.

107 Ibid., 12.

108 Flinn, "Pulse of the City."

109 John Havas, "Hudson Man Big Builder in Small Way Among Top Modelmakers," newspaper clipping, Theodore Conrad Archive.

110 Manfredo Tafuri, "The Disenchanted Mountain: The Skyscraper and the City," in *The American City. From the Civil War to the New Deal*, ed. Giorgio Ciucci (Cambridge, MA: MIT Press, 1979), 389–505.

111 E. Raymond Bossange, "Changes in Architectural Education," *Pencil Points Reader: A Journal for the Drafting Room 1920–1943*, ed. George Hartman and Jan Cigliano (New York: Princeton Architectural Press, 2004), 327–8.

112 William Alciphron Boring, "The Use of Models in the Study of Architecture," *Architecture*, June 1922, 200.

113 Moon, *Modeling Messages*, 79.

114 Ockman, *Architecture School*, 97–8.

115 Joseph Esherick, "Architectural Education in the Thirties and Seventies: A Personal View," in *The Architect: Chapters in the History of the Profession*, ed. Spiro Kostof (New York: Oxford University Press, 1977), 248–64.

116 Reid, "Architectural Models," 405–12.

NOTES

117 Albert Halse to Theodore Conrad, September 8, 1948, letter, Theodore Conrad Archive.
118 Betty Blum, "Oral History of Myron Goldsmith," The Art Institute of Chicago, 133.
119 Peter Raymond Wickham, *Commercial Model Making: Professional Model Making for Architects, Building Trades, Industrial Purposes, Exhibitions, General Advertising Display* (London: Vawser and Wiles, 1945), 6.
120 Hendrick, *Model Making as a Career*. Thomas William Hendrick, *The Modern Architectural Model* (London: The Architectural Press London, 1957).
121 Janke, *Architectural Models*, 3.
122 Carol Krinsky, *Gordon Bunshaft of Skidmore, Owings & Merrill* (New York: MIT Press, 1988), 6.
123 Hicks Stone, in discussion with the author, February 2014.
124 Mary Ann Hunting, *Edward Durrell Stone: Modernism's Populist Architect* (New York and London: W.W. Norton & Company, 2013), 20.
125 Edward Durell Stone, *The Evolution of an Architect* (New York: Horizon Press, 1962), 30.
126 Hunting, *Edward Durrell Stone*, 14.
127 Ernest Jacks, "The Elegant Bohemian," unpublished manuscript, 353.
128 Ibid., 145.
129 Ibid., 141.
130 Hunting, *Edward Durrell Stone*, 41. Ernest Jacks in discussion with the author, August 20, 2014.
131 Jacks, "The Elegant Bohemian," 292.
132 Betty Blum, "Oral History of Gordon Bunshaft," The Art Institute of Chicago, 109.
133 Ibid., 110.
134 Krinsky, *Gordon Bunshaft*, xiii.
135 Betty Blum, "Oral History of Natalie de Blois," The Art Institute of Chicago, 10.
136 Nicholas Adams, *Skidmore, Owings & Merrill: SOM since 1936* (Milan: Electaarchitecture, 2006), 24.
137 Sharon Zane, "Oral History of Roger Radford," The Art Institute of Chicago, 41.
138 Robert Morgan to Elliot Binzen, April 7, 1953, letter, Pei Cobb Freed Archive.
139 L.W. King to Norman Bel Geddes, June 15, 1955, letter, Norman Bel Geddes Papers, Harry Ransom Center, The University of Texas at Austin.
140 *The Denver Post*, July 8, 1953, letter, Theodore Conrad Archive.
141 Moon, *Modeling Messages*, 139.
142 Theodore Conrad to Carter Horsley, July 29, 1974, letter, Theodore Conrad Archive.
143 Ernest Jacks in discussion with the author, February 6, 2014.
144 Flinn, "Pulse of the City."
145 Theodore Conrad to John Rea, October 6, 1965, letter, Theodore Conrad Archive.
146 Ruth Conrad in discussion with the author, June 3, 2013.
147 Lebensohn, "Mighty Miniatures," 34–9.

2 Modeling Materials

1 Richard Armiger, email to author, September 14, 2020.
2 Wendler, *Das Modell*, 14, 39.

3   Robert Harbison, *Thirteen Ways: Theoretical Investigations in Architecture* (Cambridge, MA: MIT Press, 1997), 84.

4   Susan Stewart, *On Longing: Narratives of the Miniature, the Gigantic, the Souvenir, the Collection* (Baltimore: John Hopkins University Press, 1984), 68.

5   Geoffrey Batchen, "Does Size Matter?" *Konsthistorisk Tidskrift*, no. 4 (2003): 251. Moon, *Modeling Messages*, 54.

6   Jacobs, "The Miniature Boom," 107.

7   Tom Holert, "Mikro-Ökonomie der Geschichte. Das Unausstellbare en miniature," *Texte zur Kunst*, March 2001, 57–68.

8   Silke Voßkötter, *Maßstäbe der Architektur* (Dresden: Tectum, 2009).

9   Nadine Rottau, *Materialgerechtigkeit. Ästhetik im 19. Jahrhundert* (Hamburg: DFG Graduiertenkolleg Kunst und Technik, 2012).

10 Monika Wagner et al., *Materialästhetik. Quellentexte zu Kunst, Design und Architektur* (Berlin: Dietrich Reimer, 2005), 135.

11 *3. Darmstädter Gespräch, Mensch und Technik*, ed. Hans Schwippert (Darmstadt: Neue Darmstädter Verlagsanstalt, 1952).

12 Monika Wagner, *Das Material in der Kunst. Eine andere Geschichte der Moderne* (Munich: C.H. Beck, 2011), 185.

13 Jeffrey Meikle, *American Plastic Age* (New Brunswick: Rutgers University Press, 1995).

14 Roland Barthes, "Plastik," in *Materialästhetik. Quellentexte zu Kunst, Design und Architektur*, ed. Monika Wagner et al. (Berlin: Dietrich Reimer, 2005), 87–9.

15 Jean Baudrillard, "Stimmungswert Material," in *Materialästhetik. Quellentexte zu Kunst, Design und Architektur*, ed. Monika Wagner et al. (Berlin: Dietrich Reimer, 2005), 30.

16 Albert Smith, *Architectural Model as Machine: A New View on Models from Antiquity to the Present Day* (Amsterdam: Elsevier, 2004), xxi.

17 Elser, *The Architectural Model*, 13–14, 229–33.

18 Moon, *Modeling Messages*, 168.

19 Thomas Raff, *Die Sprache der Materialien. Anleitung zu einer Ikonologie der Werkstoffe* (Münster: Waxmann, 2008), 49.

20 Mario Carpo, *Architecture in the Age of Printing: Orality, Writing, Typography, and Printed Images in the History of Architectural Theory* (Cambridge, MA: MIT Press, 2001), 6.

21 Hobbs, *Pictoral House Modelling*, 28. "How Realism is Achieved in Diorama Making," *Torrance Herald*, August 15, 1935.

22 Hobbs, *Pictoral House Modelling*, 28.

23 Lebensohn, "Mighty Miniatures," 34–9.

24 Wendler, *Das Modell*, 34. Ansgar Oswald, *Meister der Miniaturen. Architektur Modellbau* (Berlin: DOM publishers, 2008), 37.

25 Wendler, *Das Modell*, 11.

26 Barnabas Calder, "Medium or Message? Uses of Design and Presentation Models by Denys Lasdun and Partners," in *2nd International Conference of the European Architectural History Network*, Brussels, 2012.

27 Wendler, *Das Modell*, 30. Translation by the author.

28 Ibid., 30, 32.

29 Albena Yaneva, "Scaling Up and Down: Extraction Trials in Architectural Design," *Social Studies of Science*, no. 6 (December 2005): 871.

NOTES

30 Hoyt, "World's Fair Models," 420.
31 Borland, "Worlds in Miniature for the Fair."
32 Hobbs, *Pictoral House Modelling*, 15.
33 Harvey Wiley Corbett, "Zoning and the Envelope of the Building," *Pencil Points*, April 1923.
34 Hugh Ferriss, "Architecture of this Age," in *Machine Age Exposition*, ed. Jane Heap (New York, 1927), 5–6.
35 Stoller, "The Architecture of Harvey Wiley Corbett," 33.
36 Berthold Audsley, "Miniatures and their Value in Architectural Practice," *Brickbuilder*, September 1914, 214.
37 Grumbine, "The Use of Scale Models as an Aid to the Architect."
38 Corbett, "Architectural Models of Cardboard," 11.
39 Ibid.
40 Harvey Wiley Corbett, "Metropolitan Life Insurance Company: New Home Office Building in New York," *Architectural Record*, September 1933, 182.
41 Roger Shepherd, *Skyscraper: The Search for an American Style 1891–1941. Annotated Extracts from the First 50 Years of Architectural Record* (New York: McGraw-Hill, 2003), 277.
42 Theodore Conrad to Timothy Rub, June 18, 1984, letter, Theodore Conrad Archive. Corbett, "Metropolitan Life Insurance Company," 182. "Skyscraper Plans Hazy," *The New York Times*, October 5, 1929.
43 Hugh Ferriss, *The Metropolis of Tomorrow*, ed. Carol Willis (New York: Princeton Architectural Press, 1998), 84–5.
44 "Skyscraper Plans Hazy," *The New York Times*, October 5, 1929. "To Build on 4th Av. Block," *The New York Times*, October 23, 1929.
45 Lebensohn, "Mighty Miniatures," 35.
46 Hobbs, *Pictoral House Modelling*, 15, 118–23. Percy Collins, "Architectural Modeling," *American Homes and Gardens*, August 1915.
47 Grumbine, "The Use of Scale Models," no pages.
48 Ibid.
49 Walter Kilham, *Raymond Hood, Architect: Form through Function in the American Skyscraper* (New York: Architectural Book Publishing Co., 1973), 23.
50 Victoria Newhouse, *Wallace Kirkman Harrison, Architect, USA, 1895–1981* (New York: Rizzoli, 1989), 44.
51 Bob Perrone, email to author, January 23, 2015.
52 Newhouse, *Wallace Kirkman Harrison*, 39.
53 Stone, *Edward Durell Stone*, 38–9.
54 Reinhard, "Organization for Cooperation," 3.
55 Wallace Harrison, "Drafting Room Practice," *The Architectural Forum*, January 1932, 5–6. Alan Balfour, *Rockefeller Center: Architecture as Theater* (New York: McGraw-Hill, 1978), 29–30. Rem Koolhaas, *Delirious New York* (Aachen: Arch+ Verlag, 1999), 202–03.
56 Balfour, *Rockefeller Center: Architecture as Theater*, 44.
57 Ibid., 37.
58 John Bero and Katie Eggers Comeau, *Historic Resources Report. Means Restriction Project* (Ithaca: Cornell University, May 26, 2011), 23.

59 Wolfgang Kemp, *Architektur analysieren. Eine Einfürung in acht Kapiteln* (Munich: Schirmer/Mosel, 2009), 60.

60 Ferriss, *The Metropolis of Tomorrow*, 100–01.

61 Ibid., 148, footnote 2. Robert Stern, *The Philip Johnson Tapes* (New York: Monacelli Press, 2008), 537. Theodore Conrad to Timothy Rub, June 18,1984, letter, Theodore Conrad Archive.

62 Hobbs, *Pictoral House Modelling*, 71.

63 Ibid., 74–7. Theodore Conrad to Louis Checkman, letter, Theodore Conrad Archive.

64 Collins, "Architectural Modeling."

65 Hobbs, *Pictoral House Modeling*, 113.

66 Ibid., xi.

67 Jeffrey Meikle, *American Plastic Age* (New Brunswick: Rutgers University Press, 1995), 91.

68 Ibid., 84–5.

69 J.P. Tilley, "Versatility of Acrylics, 1934–1980," in *The Development of Plastics*, EDS. S.T.I. Mossmann and P.J.T. Morris (Cambridge, MA: MIT Press, 1994), 95.

70 "1936 Lucite," 2.dupont.com, accessed March 31, 2015, http://wwww2.dupont.com/Phoenix_Heritage/en_US/1936_detail.html.

71 Meikle, *American Plastic Age*, 97–8.

72 Ibid., 99.

73 Kai Buchholz, *Plexiglas. Werkstoff in Architektur und Design* (Darmstadt: Wienand Verlag, 2007), 51.

74 Eva Brachert, *Hausrat aus Plastic. Alltagsgegenstände in Deutschland in der Zeit von 1950–1959* (Weimar: VDG Weimar, 2002), 109.

75 Meikle, *American Plastic Age*, 110.

76 "What the Chemist Will Show You at the Fair," Ely Jacques Kahn Files, newspaper clipping, Avery Architectural Archives.

77 Brachert, *Hausrat aus Plastic*, 66–7.

78 Gerhard Kaldewei, *Linoleum: History, Design, Architecture 1882–2000* (Ostfildern: Hatje Cantz, 2000), 15. Pamela Simpson, "Comfortable, Durable, and Decorative: Linoleum's Rise and Fall from Grace," *APT Bulletin*, no. 2/3 (1999), 20–1.

79 Simpson, "Comfortable, Durable, and Decorative," 21.

80 John Peter and Edward Hamilton, *Aluminum in Modern Architecture* (New York: Reinhold Publishing, 1956), 13. Luitgard Marschall, *aluminium. Metall der Moderne* (Munich: oekom verlag, 2008), 17.

81 Marschall, *aluminium*, 68.

82 Ibid., 38, 161–3.

83 Peter and Hamilton, *Aluminum in Modern Architecture*, 14.

84 Marschall, *aluminium*, 38, 109.

85 Ibid., 90.

86 "Materials for 194X. Wartime Developments Have Provided an Idea Storehouse for Postwar Designs," *The Architectural Forum*, March 1944, 14.

87 "Many Big Buildings Got Start on Small Parcel in Jersey City," *Jersey Journal*, 1957.

88 Hitchcock and Johnson, *The International Style*, 29.

89 "Test-Tube Marvels of Wartime Promise a New Era in Plastics. Postwar Horizons," *Newsweek*, May 17, 1943, 43. Buchholz, *Plexiglas*, 17–18.

NOTES

90 Jacks, "The Elegant Bohemian," 294.
91 Eva Baronowski, "Conrad Biography," November 1984, Theodore Conrad Archive.
92 "A Model of the Structure Which Will House the Exhibits of the Corning Glass Works, Owens-Illinois Glass Company and Pittsburgh Plate Glass Company," *The New York Times*, June 27, 1938.
93 "Models and Model Making," *Pencil Points*, July 1939, 423. *Collier's*, May 6, 1939.
94 Ruth Carson, "House of Glass," *Collier's*, May 6, 1939, 16–17, 38.
95 "Models and Model Making," 423.
96 Betty Blum, "Oral History of Monroe Bowman," The Art Institute of Chicago, 6, 10, 12.
97 "Glass and Steel Flats for Evanston," *Chicago Sunday Tribune*, May 29, 1932. "All-Metal Apartment," *The New York Times*, July 6, 1930.
98 Robert Stern et al., *New York 1930* (New York: Rizzoli, 1987), 144.
99 Dominic Ricciotti, "The 1939 Building of the Museum of Modern Art," *The American Art Journal 17*, summer 1985, 67.
100 Philip Goodwin to Theodore Conrad, June 18, 1943, letter, Theodore Conrad Archive.
101 Ibid. Philip Goodwin to Theodore Conrad, August 12, 1943, letter, Theodore Conrad Archive.
102 Dave Croke, "On the Road to the Future," in *Norman Bel Geddes Designs America*, ed. Donald Albrecht (New York: Abrams, 2012), 103.
103 Carolyn Lanchner, *Fernand Léger* (New York: Abrams, 1998), 277. Carter Horsley, "Modelmakers' Work Gaining New Recognition," *The New York Times*, July 28, 1974. "Public Gets a Rare Peek at Fine Art Lent to Show by Prominent Jerseyans," *The New York Times*, July 30, 1972.
104 Terence Riley, *The International Style: Exhibition 15 and the Museum of Modern Art* (New York: Rizzoli, 1992), 81.
105 Ibid.
106 Theodore Conrad to Ione Ulrich, March 8, 1939, letter, Villa Savoye Folder, Study Center Architecture and Design, MoMA. Theodore Conrad to Thomas Dabney Mabry Jr., April 27, 1938, letter, Villa Savoye Folder, Study Center Architecture and Design, MoMA.
107 Theodore Conrad to Janet Henrichs, February 21, 1938, letter, Villa Savoye Folder, Study Center Architecture and Design, MoMA.
108 *Frühe Kunststoffe. Die Sammlung Eva Stille*, ed. Historisches Museum Frankfurt (Frankfurt am Main: Historisches Museum Frankfurt, 2012, 16). "Molded Airplanes for Defense," *Modern Plastics*, July 1940, 25–31.
109 Tilley, "Versatility of Acrylics," 107.
110 Phyllis Lambert, *Building Seagram* (New Haven, CT: Yale University Press, 2013), 46–7.
111 "Murray Hill Site Will Get Skyscraper," *The New York Times*, December 17, 1948.
112 Betsy Bradley, "New Heights in American Architecture: The Urban Design and Aesthetic Theories of Harvey Wiley Corbett," Thesis, Columbia University, 1990, 157. Christopher Innes, "Modular and Mobile," in *Norman Bel Geddes Designs America*, ed. Donald Albrecht (New York: Abrams, 2012), 200–13.
113 Jacobs, "The Miniature Boom," 106.
114 Peter and Hamilton, *Aluminum in Modern Architecture*, 20.
115 Jacobs, "The Miniature Boom," 109. Lebensohn, "Mighty Miniatures."
116 William Hartmann to Walter Netsch, August 3, 1954, memo, SOM Archive Chicago.
117 Blum, "Oral History of Gordon Bunshaft," 48.

118 *SOM News*, no. 17, April 15, 1956, 3.
119 Krinsky, *Gordon Bunshaft*, 72.
120 *Newark Sunday News* 1964, newspaper clipping, Theodore Conrad Archive.
121 McFadden, "Lilliputian Buildings Are His Forte. Made to Assist Architects," 1964.
122 Elser, *The Architectural* Model, 219. Lambert, *Building Seagram*, 38, 41.
123 Hendrick, *The Modern Architectural Model*, 66–7.
124 Havas, "Hudson Man Big Builder," "The Talk of the Town," *The New Yorker*, July 6, 1956.
125 Jacobs, "The Miniature Boom," 108.
126 Krinsky, *Gordon Bunshaft*, 56.
127 *Life in General*, February/March 1953.
128 Blum, "Oral History of Gordon Bunshaft," 217.
129 Moon, *Modeling Messages*, 162.
130 Ibid., 183.
131 Frampton, *Idea as Model*.
132 Moon, *Modeling Messages*, 103.

3 Model Drawings

1 Alberto Pérez-Gómez, "The Revelation of Order: Perspective and Architectural Representation," in *This is Not Architecture: Media Constructions*, ed. Kester Rattenbury (London: Routledge, 2002), 3.
2 Albena Yaneva, "Scaling Up and Down," 887.
3 Wendler, *Das Modell*, 95.
4 "Planungsmethoden, Ausführungsprozesse und Formvorstellungen bilden in der Architektur ein komplexes System wechselseitig kausaler Abhängigkeiten. Die Idee eines geplanten Baus prägt seine Entwurfsmethoden wie umgekehrt die möglichen Planungsmittel sowohl die Formvorstellung wie die tatsächliche Ausführung beeinflussen." Translation by the author. Andres Lepik, *Das Architekturmodell in Italien 1335–1550* (Worms: Wernersche Verlagsgesellschaft, 1994), 9.
5 Beatriz Colomina, *Privacy and Publicity. Modern Architecture as Mass Media* (Cambridge, MA: MIT Press, 1996), 13.
6 Ibid., 204.
7 Ibid., 14, 73. Martino Stierli, "Preservation Parade: The Mediatization of the Lieb House Into a Monument," *Future Anterior*, no. 1 (summer 2010): 44–58.
8 Colomina, *Privacy and Publicity*, 13.
9 Kester Rattenbury, *This is Not Architecture: Media Constructions* (London: Routledge, 2002), xi.
10 Robin Evans, "Translations from Drawing to Building," in *Translations from Drawing to Building and Other Essays* (London: AA Publications, 1997), 156.
11 Wallis Miller, "Fitting in: Architecture in the Art Gallery," in *Architecture from the Outside In: Selected Essays by Robert Gutman*, ed. Robert Gutman, Dana Cuff and John Wriedt (New York: Princeton Architectural Press, 2010), 87–8.
12 Hélène Lipstadt, "Architectural Publications, Competitions, and Exhibitions," in *Architecture and Its Image: Four Centuries of Architectural Representation. Works from the Collection of the Canadian Centre for Architecture*, ed. Eve Blau and Edward Kaufman (Cambridge, MA: MIT Press, 1989), 128.

NOTES

13 Rattenbury, *This is Not Architecture*, xxiii.
14 Ibid., 1.
15 Alberto Pérez-Gómez and Louise Pelletier, *Architectural Representation and the Perspective Hinge* (Cambridge, MA: MIT Press, 2000), 7.
16 Tom Porter, *The Architect's Eye: Visualization and Depiction of Space in Architecture* (London: E&FN Spon, 1997), 21–2.
17 Davide Deriu, "Transforming Ideas into Pictures: Model Photography and Modern Architecture," in *Camera Constructs: Architecture and the Modern City*, edited by Andrew Higgott and Timothy Wray (Farnham: Ashgate, 2012), 169.
18 Mario Carpo, *Architecture in the Age of Printing: Orality, Writing, Typography, and Printed Images in the History of Architectural Theory* (Cambridge, MA: MIT Press, 2001), 12–13.
19 Arthur Drexler, "Engineer's Architecture: Truth and Its Consequences," in *The Architecture of the École des Beaux-Arts*, edited by Arthur Drexler (New York: MIT Press, 1975), 15, 24.
20 Moon, *Modeling Messages*, 86.
21 Harbison, *Thirteen Ways*, 98.
22 Colomina, *Privacy and Publicity*, 65.
23 Ibid., 207.
24 Evans, "Translations from Drawing to Building." Robin Evans, *The Projective Cast* (Cambridge, MA: MIT Press, 1995). Colomina, *Privacy and Publicity*, 64–5. Yaneva, "Scaling Up and Down," 888. Pérez-Gómez and Pelletier, *Architectural Representation*, 3–8.
25 Evans, "Translations from Drawing to Building," 154.
26 Ibid., 160.
27 Colomina, *Privacy and Publicity*, 43.
28 Evans, "Translations from Drawing to Building," 182.
29 Stan Allen, *Practice: Architecture, Technique + Representation* (London: Routledge, 2000), 7.
30 Wendler, *Das Modell*, 12.
31 John Havas, "The Talk of the Town," *The New Yorker*, July 6, 1956, 13–14.
32 Evans, "Translations from Drawing to Building," 154, 159.
33 Colomina, *Privacy and Publicity*, 65.
34 Matilda McQuaid, *Envisioning Architecture: Drawings from the Museum of Modern Art* (New York: MoMA, 2002), 11. Mario Carpo, "Vom Handwerker zum Zeichner. Das Alberti'sche Paradigma und die Erfindung des Bauplans in der Moderne," in *Der Bauplan. Werkzeug des Architekten*, ed. Annette Spiro and David Ganzoni (Zurich: Park Books, 2013), 279.
35 Winfried Nerdinger, *Die Architekturzeichnung. Vom barocken Idealplan zur Axonometrie. Zeichnungen aus der Architektursammlung der Technischen Universität München* (Munich: Prestel, 1985), 494. Pérez-Gómez, "The Revelation of Order," 19. Paul Emmons, "Drawn to Scale: The Imaginative Inhabitation of Architectural Drawings," in *From Models to Drawings: Imagination and Representation in Architecture*, ed. Marco Frascari (London: Routledge, 2007), 64–78. Uta Hassler and Daniel Stockhammer, "Aus der Entwicklungsgeschichte des Bauplans. Wissenstransfer, Demonstration einer Bauidee oder Anleitung zum Bauen?" in *Der Bauplan. Werkzeug des Architekten*, ed. Annette Spiro and David Ganzoni (Zurich: Park Books, 2013), 287.
36 Ockman, "Architecture School," 76. Susan Piedmont-Palladino, *Tools of the Imagination: Drawing Tools and Technologies from the Eighteenth Century to the Present* (New York: Princeton Architectural Press, 2007), 81.
37 Robert Forman, *Architectural Models* (New York: The Studio Publications, 1946), 10.

38 Kenneth McCutchon, "Architectural Models," *Architect's Journal*, October 1, 1936, 459.
39 Murray, "Models and Scotch," 429.
40 Guidelines, Norman Bel Geddes Papers, Harry Ransom Center, The University of Texas at Austin. Hoyt, "World's Fair Models," 415.
41 Hassler and Stockhammer, "Aus der Entwicklungsgeschichte des Bauplans," 285.
42 Theodore Conrad to Ione Ulrich, March 8, 1939, letter, Villa Savoye Folder, Study Center Architecture and Design, MoMA. Theodore Conrad to Thomas Dabney Mabry Jr., April 27, 1938, letter, Villa Savoye Folder, Study Center Architecture and Design, MoMA. Theodore Conrad to Philip Goodwin, January 17, 1944, letter, Theodore Conrad Archive.
43 Hobbs, *Pictorial House Modelling*, 29.
44 Hoyt, "World's Fair Models," 413–26.

4 Model Photography

1 "Der Kamera als Vermittler ist es gegeben, das Modell in seiner günstigsten Ansicht zu zeigen." Giebelhausen, *Architekturfotografie*, 136. Translation by the author.
2 "Das Modell und seine Ausführung bestimmt in jedem Falle die Aufnahmetechnik." Ibid., 143. Translation by the author.
3 Deriu, "Transforming Ideas into Pictures," 159–78. Rolf Sachsse, "A Short History of Architectural Model Photography," in *The Architectural Model: Tool, Fetish, Small Utopia*, ed. Oliver Elser and Peter Cachola Schmal (Zurich: Scheidegger und Spiess, 2012), 23–8.
4 LeRoy Grumbine, "The Use of Scale Models."
5 Forman, *Architectural Models*, 52.
6 Joachim Giebelhausen, *Architekturfotografie* (Munich: Verlag Grossbild-Technik GmbH, 1964). Janke, *Architectural Models*. Julius Shulman, *The Photography of Architecture and Design: Photographing Buildings, Interiors, and the Visual Arts* (New York: The Whitney Library of Design, 1977), 190–9.
7 Deriu, "Transforming Ideas into Pictures," 161, 175.
8 Mark Morris, "Worlds Collide: Reality to Model to Reality," in *Camera Constructs: Architecture and the Modern City*, ed. Andrew Higgott and Timothy Wray (Farnham: Ashgate, 2012), 182.
9 Jacobs, "The Miniature Boom," 107.
10 Louis Checkman, "Scale Models in Architectural Photography," *The Professional Photographer*, July 1966, no pages.
11 Murray, "Models and Scotch," 427.
12 Deriu, "Transforming Ideas into Pictures," 159–60.
13 Elser, *The Architectural Model*, 14.
14 Deriu, "Transforming Ideas into Pictures," 176.
15 Colomina, *Privacy and Publicity*, 56.
16 Moon, *Modeling Messages*, 67.
17 Deriu, "Transforming Ideas into Pictures," 160.
18 Giebelhausen, *Architekturfotografie*, 136–59.
19 Ibid., 140, 152.
20 Ibid., 142.

NOTES

21 Ernst Born, *Geschichte des Bilderdrucks* (Basel: ambripress, 2006), 82. David Sumner, *The Magazine Century: American Magazines since 1900* (New York: Peter Lang, 2010), 80. Andrew Higgott and Timothy Wray, "Introduction: Architectural and Photographic Constructs," in *Camera Constructs*, ed. Andrew Higgott and Timothy Wray (Farnham: Ashgate, 2012), 7. Giebelhausen, *Architekturfotografie*, 143.

22 Corbett, "Architectural Models of Cardboard," 15.

23 Ibid.

24 Higgott and Wray, *Camera Constructs*, 5.

25 Willis, *The Metropolis of Tomorrow*, 149.

26 Ibid., 185.

27 Andrea Gustavson, "The Bel Geddes Process," in *Norman Bel Geddes Designs America*, ed. Donald Albrecht (New York: Abrams, 2012), 340–53. Roberts, *Norman Bel Geddes*, 46. Norman Bel Geddes, *Magic Motorways* (New York: Random House, 1940).

28 Cogdell, "Theater of War," 325.

29 Gustavson, "The Bel Geddes Process," 340.

30 Maffei, "Designing the Image of the Practical Visionary," 232.

31 Massimo Scolari, *Oblique Drawing: A History of Anti-Perspective* (Cambridge, MA: MIT Press, 2012), xii.

32 Corbett, "Architectural Models of Cardboard," 11.

33 Louis Checkman, "How to Make the Most of Models," *AIA Journal*, April 1967, 84–6.

34 tim1965.livejournal.com, accessed February 15, 2015, http://tim1965.livejournal.com/1644249.html?thread=2308569.

35 Hobbs, *Pictorial House Modelling*, 140.

36 Giebelhausen, *Architekturfotografie*, 147.

37 "In Scale," *The New Yorker*, July 7, 1956, 13–14.

38 "Rendering, Architectural," in *Encyclopedia Britannica* (Chicago: Encyclopedia Britannica) 147.

39 Alvin Covell, "Architecture in Miniature: The Plastic Model Studies of an English Artist," *The Architectural Record*, March 1914, 264.

40 Grumbine, Using Scale Models.

41 Minutes of Meeting, page 2, Norman Bel Geddes Papers, Harry Ransom Center, The University of Texas at Austin.

42 Audsley, "Miniatures and Their Value," 214.

43 Simon Breines, "Paper Architecture," *The American Architect*, April 1931, 25.

44 "Rendering, Architectural," 148.

45 Boring, "The Use of Models," 200.

46 Ibid., 200.

47 Grumbine, "The Use of Scale Models," no pages.

48 Grumbine, "Using Scale Models," 108.

49 Edwin Parker, "The Model for Architectural Representation," *The Architectural Forum*, April 1919, 119.

50 Audsley, "Miniatures and Their Value," 214.

51 "Architectural Models," Delta Competition Entry 1944, Theodore Conrad Archive.

52 Grumbine, "Using Scale Models," 106.

53 Willis, *The Metropolis of Tomorrow*, 148–99.

54 Parker, "The Model for Architectural Representation," 119. Deriu, "Transforming Ideas into Pictures," 161. Drexler, "Engineer's Architecture," 18.

55 "Metropolitan Life Will Erect $9.000.000 Building on 4th Av.," *The New York Times*, February 7, 1931. "New Metropolitan Life Building," *The New York Times*, April 19, 1931.

56 Wickham, *Commercial Model Making*, 7.

57 Elena Testa, "Theodore Conrad," *Forum. Jersey City Chamber of Commerce*, January/February 1978, 21–5.

58 "Plan and Two Views of Model of Design for Radio City, Fifth Avenue, New York," *Pencil Points*, May 1931, 387.

59 Buckminster Fuller, "Dymaxion House," *The Architectural Forum*, March 1932, 285–8. Norman Bel Geddes, *Horizons* (Boston: Little, Brown, and Company), 1932.

60 Letter of Recommendation by Theodore Conrad for Louis Checkman, November 3, 1943, Theodore Conrad Archive.

61 "Collier's House:" John Flynn, "A Good Place to Live," *Collier's*, March 28, 1936, 10–11, 52–3, 56. Ruth Carson, "What's a Garden For?" *Collier's*, April 11, 1936, 20–1, 76, 78. Marie Beynon Ray, "Night Life at Home," *Collier's*, April 25, 1936, 18–19. Helen Thompson, "Home is Like This," *Collier's*, May 16, 1936, 20–1, 46. For Fordyce & Hamby's "Collier's House:" John Flynn, "Collier's $7500 House," *Colliers*, April 3, 1937, 15–18, 54–5. Catherine Bauer and Ruth Carson, "Land for Your House," *Colliers*, May 15, 1937, 19, 26, 29. For Stone's "Collier's Weekend House:" Ruth Carson, "Collier's Week-End House," *Collier's*, April 23, 1938, 13–16, 30. *Ladies' Home Journal* published at least two houses by Edward Durell Stone and Harrison & Fouilhoux. For Stone's "Garden House:" John Fistere, "Space for Living," *Ladies' Home Journal*, April 1938. Henrietta Murdock, "Living in Space," *Ladies' Home Journal*, April 1938. For Harrison & Fouilhoux's "House of Tomorrow:" "House of Tomorrow," *Ladies' Home Journal*, April 1937.

62 Hunting, *Edward Durrell Stone*, 41. "The Active Market is Laying the Foundation for America's Building Boom!" *Collier's*, March 21, 1936, 70–1.

63 Hunting, *Edward Durrell Stone*, 43.

64 Kathleen Endres and Therese Lueck, *Women's Periodicals in the United States: Consumer Magazines* (Westport, CT: Greenwood Press, 1995), 173.

65 Ruth Carson, "House of Glass," *Collier's*, May 6, 1939, 17.

66 Jacobs, "The Miniature Boom," 109.

67 Endres and Lueck, *Women's Periodicals in the United States*, 447.

68 Conversation with Ruth Conrad, June 7, 2013.

69 Wallace Heath, "Big as All Outdoors. . .," *Woman's Home Companion*, September 1948, 62–5.

70 Mary Davis Gillies, *McCall's Book of Modern Houses* (New York: Simon & Schuster), 1951, foreword.

71 John Normile, "Home is Where You Hang Your Mortgage," *The Architectural Forum*, April 1945, 91–100. Mary Davis Gillies, "Mr. and Mrs. McCall Know What They Want," *The Architectural Forum*, April 1945, 101–08. Richard Pratt, "Let's Look Ahead," *The Architectural Forum*, April 1945, 109–18. Harriet Burket and Elizabeth Beveridge, "Some Like It Hot, Some Like it Cold," *The Architectural Forum*, April 1945, 130–40.

72 Albrecht, *Norman Bel Geddes Designs America*, 24.

73 Gustavson, "The Bel Geddes Process," 348.

74 Transcript of interview, April 4, 1956, Theodore Conrad Archive.

75 Flinn, "Pulse of the City."

76 Theodore Conrad to Louis Checkman, April 29, 1945, letter, Theodore Conrad Archive.
77 Theodore Conrad to Louis Checkman, November 28, 1944, letter, Theodore Conrad Archive. Theodore Conrad to Louis Checkman, April 29, 1945, letter, Theodore Conrad Archive. Pratt, "Let's Look Ahead," 109.
78 Christian Hubert in *Idea As Model*, cited after: Morris, "Worlds Collide," 179.
79 Daniel Shuster to Theodore Conrad, June 24, 1954, letter, Theodore Conrad Archive.
80 Jacks, "The Elegant Bohemian," 145.
81 Conversation with Wayne Checkman, June 30, 2015.
82 John Morris Dixon, "Introduction," in *Pencil Points Reader: A Journal for the Drafting Room 1920–1943*, ed. George Hartman and Jan Cigliano (New York: Princeton Architectural Press, 2004), xiii.
83 Nina Rappaport and Erica Stoller, *Ezra Stoller: Photographer* (New Haven, CT: Yale University Press, 2012), 25.
84 *The Architectural Forum,* May 1949, cover.
85 Lee Cooper, "New Design Used for Bank Edifice. Pedestrians to View Work in Manufacturers Trust Unit Through Glass Walls," *The New York Times*, August 16, 1953.

5 Model Displays

1 Collins, "Architectural Modeling," 261.
2 Wallis Miller, "Cultures of Display: Exhibiting Architecture in Berlin, 1880–1931," in *Architecture and Authorship*, edited by Tim Anstey, et.al (London: Black Dog Press, 2007), 98–107. Juliet Koss, "VKhUTEMAS Snapshots," in *Modelling Time: The Permanent Collection, 1925–2013*, edited by Mari Lending and Mari Hvattum (Oslo: Torpedo Press, 2014), 267–70.
3 Moon, *Modeling Messages*, 111. Miller, "Cultures of Display," 98–107.
4 Collins, "Architectural Modeling," 261.
5 Grumbine, "Using Scale Models," 105.
6 Ibid.
7 Ibid., 107.
8 Luis Carranza and Fernando Luiz Lara, *Modern Architecture in Latin America: Art, Technology, and Utopia* (Austin: University of Texas Press, 2014), 42–6.
9 Robert Alexander González, *Designing Pan-America* (Austin: University of Texas Press, 2011), 107, 113. "Huge Air Beacon at Santo Domingo in Honor of Columbus is Sponsored by 21 American Nations," *The Niagara Falls Gazette*, August 9, 1930.
10 Jean Ferriss Leich and Paul Goldberger, *Architectural Visions. The Drawings of Hugh Ferriss* (New York: Whitney Library of Design, 1980), 21–2. Stoller, "The Architecture of Harvey Wiley Corbett," 61.
11 Corbett, "Architectural Models of Cardboard," 37.
12 James Kornwolf, *Modernism in America 1937–1941. A Catalog and Exhibition of Four Architectural Competitions* (Williamsburg: Joseph and Margaret Muscarelle Museum of Art, College of William and Mary, 1985), 3.
13 Grumbine, "Using Scale Models," 109.
14 Folder 5, Model Display, Box 898, New York World's Fair 1939 and 1940 Incorporated Records (1935–1945), Manuscripts and Archives Division, New York Public Library. L.H. Robbins, "It Begins to Look Like a Great Fair!" *The New York Times*, May 1, 1938.

15 Folder 10, Box 898, New York World's Fair 1939 and 1940 Incorporated Records (1935–1945), Manuscripts and Archives Division, New York Public Library.

16 "Miniature of Fair Shown in Exhibit," *The New York Times*, March 25, 1937. "In Miniature Form," *The New York Times*, March 30, 1937.

17 "Miniature of Fair Shown in Exhibit." VI: General, Collection on the 1939–1940 New York World's Fair, 1934–93, Museum of the City of New York.

18 "United States Pavilion," *The New York Times*, April 15, 1937. Folder 2, Museum of Science and Industry, Box 208, New York World's Fair 1939 and 1940 Incorporated Records (1935–1945), Manuscripts and Archives Division, New York Public Library.

19 "Fair Motorcade to Cover 16 Miles," *The New York Times*, April 4, 1938.

20 Folder 13, Box 898, New York World's Fair 1939 and 1940 Incorporated Records (1935–1945), Manuscripts and Archives Division, New York Public Library.

21 Roberts, *Norman Bel Geddes*, 45. Cusker, "The World of Tomorrow," 14.

22 The City of Light Brochure 1939, Series IV Box 17: Consolidated Edison, Collection on the 1939–1940 New York World's Fair, 1934–1993, Museum of the City of New York.

23 "Exhibits: A World of Wonders," *The New York Times*, May 5, 1940.

24 "Fair's Super-Speed Highway Exhibit to Be Huge Panorama," *The New York Sun*, January 21, 1939. "Exhibits: A World of Wonders."

25 Roberts, *Norman Bel Geddes*, 43.

26 "Futurama is Kept as Museum Piece," *The New York Times*, December 16, 1940. Lawrence Speck, "Futurama," in *Norman Bel Geddes Designs America*, ed. Donald Albrecht (New York: Abrams, 2012), 314. Maffei, "Designing the Image of the Practical Visionary," 237. Innes, *Designing Modern America*, 146.

27 Reid, "Architectural Models," 407.

28 Ruth Lampland, "The 'Hobby Army' Grows," *The New York Times*, May 5, 1935.

29 Horace Boucher, "On Model Making, Boucher Hobby Book," distributed by the Boucher Playthings Mfg. Corp., 1933. Brochure, "Miniature Marine Reproductions," distributed by the H.E. Boucher Mfg. Co., 2, both Theodore Conrad Archive. William Young and Nancy Young, *The 1930s* (Westport, CT: Greenwood Press, 2012), 32.

30 *The Modelmaker*, January 1929, no. 1, 14, magazine, Theodore Conrad Archive.

31 "Model Fans Open 12th Annual Show," *The New York Times*, February 10, 1940.

32 Barron Watson, "Plane Time Here Again," *The New York Times*, April 5, 1936. Steven Gelber, *Hobbies: Leisure and the Culture of Work in America* (New York: Columbia University Press, 1999), 232.

33 Gelber, *Hobbies*, 232.

34 Young and Young, *The 1930s*, 32.

35 Wickham, *Commercial Model Making*, 5.

36 Robert Stern, *The Philip Johnson Tapes* (New York: Monacelli Press, 2008), 41. "Decorator's Group Takes Rockefeller Center Floor," *The New York Times*, June 20, 1933. Riley, *The International Style*, 19, 43, 79.

37 Riley, *The International Style*, 25.

38 Grumbine, "The Use of Scale Models," no pages.

39 McQuaid, *Envisioning Architecture*, 21–2.

40 *Fortune* 18, no. 6 (December 1938), 75. Cited after: McQuaid, *Envisioning Architecture*, 22.

41 Stone, *Edward Durell Stone*, 85.

NOTES

42 "Miniature Home Shown," *The New York Times*, March 13, 1938.

43 "Dr. Jewett Heads Science Museum," *The New York Times*, October 19, 1935.

44 "New York City Guide," ed. The Guilds' Committee for Federal Writer's Publications Inc., 1939, 342–4.

45 "Home Fire Causes Shown at Museum," *The New York Times*, October 16, 1936.

46 "Housing Display Opens," *The New York Times*, September 20, 1936.

47 "Young and Old Join in Model-Building," *The New York Times*, July 7, 1937.

48 Invitation to Dinner Meeting, Three Extremely Important Subjects, The American Institute of Architects, New York Chapter.

49 Mary Roche, "Exhibit Portrays Living in Future," *The New York Times*, October 2, 1948.

50 Elizabeth Mock, "Tomorrow's Small House," *The Bulletin of the Museum of Modern Art*, Summer 1945, 3.

51 Stern, *New York 1930*, 476. Hunting, *Edward Durrell Stone*, 53.

52 "'Garden of Tomorrow' to Greet Show Visitors," *The New York Times*, May 9, 1937. "Model Dwellings Rise in 'Garden,'" *The New York Times*, May 9, 1937, 1, 10.

53 Mary Anne Staniszewski, *The Power of Display: A History of Exhibition Installations at the Museum of Modern Art* (Chicago: MIT Press, 1998), 199.

54 Havas, "Hudson Man Big Builder."

55 Philip Goodwin to Theodore Conrad, December, 28 1943, letter, Theodore Conrad Archive.

56 Philip Goodwin to Wilmarth Lewis, March 20, 1944, letter, Theodore Conrad Archive.

57 Cost Estimate, October 19, 1944, Theodore Conrad Archive.

58 Comazzi, *Balthazar Korab*, 43.

59 Inland Steel Company, Presentation Drawings, memo, SOM Archive Chicago.

60 Jack Train, Meetings of January 3, 1955, November 14, 1954, memo, SOM Archive Chicago

61 Mary Jane Mahoney to Bruce Graham, February 9, 1955, letter, SOM Archive Chicago.

62 Adams, *Skidmore, Owings & Merrill*, 90.

63 Krinsky, *Gordon Bunshaft of Skidmore, Owings & Merrill*, 56.

64 Blum, "Oral History of Gordon Bunshaft," 101.

65 *Life in General*, October 1955.

66 Robert Allen Nauman, *On the Wings of Modernism: The United States Air Force Academy* (Champaign: University of Illinois Press, 2004), 36.

67 Ibid., 47.

68 Ibid., 52.

69 Ibid., 72.

70 Press release, no date, MoMA Study Center.

71 Blum, "Oral History of Natalie de Blois," 44.

72 Staniszewski, *The Power of Display*, 199. Felicity Scott, "An Army of Soldiers or a Meadow: The Seagram Building and the 'Art of Modern Architecture,'" *JSAH*, no. 3 (September 2011): 333–4.

73 Information for Mr. Conrad for Corrections on Model of Museum of Modern Art, November 16, 1938, Philip Goodwin to Theodore Conrad, February 6, 1939, letter, Theodore Conrad Archive.

74 Peter Blake, *No Place Like Utopia: Modern Architecture and the Company We Kept* (New York: Knopf, 1993), 228, 233. Jack Masey and Conway Lloyd Morgan, *Cold War Confrontations: US Exhibitions and Their Role in the Cultural Cold War* (Zurich: Lars Müller Publishers, 2008), 214.

75 Eva Franch i Gilabert et.al, *Office US Agenda* (Zurich: Lars Müller, 2014), 241.

76 "Ausstellungen. Interbau Berlin 1957," *Bauen und Wohnen*, November 1957, 190. Masey, *Cold War Confrontations*, 88–107.

77 "U.S. Architecture in West Berlin," *Arts & Architecture*, January 1958, no pages. Klaus Franck, *Ausstellungen–Exhibitions* (Stuttgart: Hatje, 1961). Eason Leonard to Edward Stansbury, October 7, 1957, letter, Pei Cobb Freed Archive, New York. Blake, *No Place Like Utopia*, 118–26. Masey, *Cold War Confrontations*, 98.

78 Teresa Fankhänel, "Dreischeibenhaus," in *The Architectural Model: Tool, Fetish, Small Utopia*, ed. Oliver Elser and Peter Cachola Schmal (Zurich: Scheidegger und Spiess, 2012), 112–16.

References

"149 Critical Skills Get First Priority." *The New York Times*, August 15, 1943.
"1936 Lucite." www2.dupont.com/Phoenix_Heritage/en_US/1936_detail.html. Accessed March 31, 2015.
Adams, Nicholas. *Skidmore, Owings & Merrill. SOM since 1936*. Milan: Electaarchitecture, 2006.
Alberti, Leon Battista, *Ten Books on Architecture*. London: Tiranti, 1955.
Albrecht, Donald. *Norman Bel Geddes Designs America*. New York: Abrams, 2012.
Allen, Stan. *Practice: Architecture, Technique + Representation*. London: Routledge, 2000.
"All-Metal Apartment." *The New York Times*, July 6, 1930.
"A Model of the Structure Which Will House the Exhibits of the Corning Glass Works, Owens-Illinois Glass Company and Pittsburgh Plate Glass Company." *The New York Times*, June 27, 1938.
A New Description of Sir John Soane's Museum. Marlborough: Sir John Soane's Museum, 2007.
Anstey, Tim et al. *Architecture and Authorship*. London: Black Dog Publishing, 2007.
"Art Work at Fair Stirs Union Fight." *The New York Times*, October 10, 1963.
Audsley, Berthold. "Miniatures and Their Value in Architectural Practice." *The Brickbuilder*, September 1914, 214.
"Ausstellungen. Interbau Berlin 1957." *Bauen und Wohnen*, November 1957, 190.
Babington Smith, Constance. *Evidence in Camera. The Story of Photographic Intelligence in World War II*. London: David & Charles, 1974.
Balfour, Alan. *Rockefeller Center: Architecture as Theater*. New York: McGraw-Hill, 1978.
Bannister, Turpin. *The Architect at Mid-Century: Evolution and Achievement and Conversations Across the Nation*. New York: Reinhold, 1954.
Barthes, Roland. "Plastik." In Monika Wagner et al. (eds) *Materialästhetik. Quellentexte zu Kunst, Design und Architektur*, 87–9. Berlin: Dietrich Reimer, 2005.
Batchen, Geoffrey. "Does Size Matter?" *Konsthistorisk Tidskrift*, no. 4 (2003): 251.
Baudrillard, Jean. "Stimmungswert Material." In Monika Wagner et al (eds), *Materialästhetik. Quellentexte zu Kunst, Design und Architektur*, 29–31. Berlin: Dietrich Reimer, 2005.
Bauer, Catherine, and Ruth Carson. "Land for Your House." *Colliers*, May 15, 1937, 19, 26, 29.
Bayley, Thomas. *Model Making in Cardboard*. Leicester: Dryad Press, 1958.
Bel Geddes, Norman. *Horizons*. Boston: Little, Brown, and Company, 1932.
Bel Geddes, Norman. *Magic Motorways*. New York: Random House, 1940.
Bero, John, and Katie Eggers Comeau. *Historic Resources Report: Means Restriction Project*. Ithaca: Cornell University, May 26, 2011.
"Bid for Signal Job on Fair Tube Spur." *Brooklyn Daily Eagle*, July 30, 1938.
Blake, Peter. *No Place like Utopia: Modern Architecture and the Company We Kept*. New York: Knopf, 1993.
Boring, William Alciphron. "The Use of Models in the Study of Architecture." *Architecture*, June 1922, 200.
Borland, Hal. "Worlds in Miniature for the Fair." *The New York Times*, March 12, 1939.
Born, Ernst. *Geschichte des Bilderdrucks*. Basel: ambripress, 2006.
Bossange, E. Raymond. "Changes in Architectural Education." In George Hartman and Jan Cigliano (eds), *Pencil Points Reader. A Journal for the Drafting Room 1920–1943*, 327–8. New York: Princeton Architectural Press, 2004.

REFERENCES

Brachert, Eva. *Hausrat aus Plastic. Alltagsgegenstände in Deutschland in der Zeit von 1950–1959*. Weimar: VDG Weimar, 2002.

Bradley, Betsy. "New Heights in American Architecture: The Urban Design and Aesthetic Theories of Harvey Wiley Corbett." Thesis, Columbia University, 1990.

Bredekamp, Horst. *St. Peter in Rom und das Prinzip der produktiven Zerstörung. Bau und Abbau von Bramante bis Bernini*. Berlin: Wagenbach, 2000.

Breines, Simon. "Paper Architecture." *The American Architect*, April 1931, 25.

Briggs, Martin. "Architectural Models." *The Burlington Magazine*, 1929, 174–83, 245–52.

"'Bubble Floating on Fountains' To Be Central Building at Fair." *New York American*, March 16, 1937.

Buchholz, Kai. *Plexiglas. Werkstoff in Architektur und Design*. Darmstadt: Wienand Verlag, 2007.

Buck, Stan. *E.W. Twining: Model Maker, Artist and Engineer*. Cedarburg: Landmark Publishing, 2004.

Burket, Harriet, and Elizabeth Beveridge. "Some Like It Hot, Some Like It Cold." *The Architectural Forum*, April 1945, 130–40.

Calder, Barnabas. "Medium or Message? Uses of Design and Presentation Models by Denys Lasdun and Partners." In *2nd International Conference of the European Architectural History Network*, Brussels, 2012.

Carpo, Mario. *Architecture in the Age of Printing: Orality, Writing, Typography, and Printed Images in the History of Architectural Theory*. Cambridge, MA: MIT Press, 2001.

Carpo, Mario. "Vom Handwerker zum Zeichner. Das Alberti'sche Paradigma und die Erfindung des Bauplans in der Moderne." In Annette Spiro and David Ganzoni (eds), *Der Bauplan. Werkzeug des Architekten*, 278–80. Zurich: Park Books, 2013.

Carranza, Luis, and Fernando Luiz Lara. *Modern Architecture in Latin America. Art, Technology, and Utopia*. Austin: University of Texas Press, 2014.

Carson, Ruth. "House of Glass." *Collier's*, May 6, 1939, 16–17, 38.

Checkman, Louis. "Scale Models in Architectural Photography." *The Professional Photographer*, July 1966, no pages.

Checkman, Louis. "How to Make the Most of Models." *AIA Journal*, April 1967, 84–6.

Cogdell, Christina. "Theater of War." In Donald Albrecht (ed.), *Norman Bel Geddes Designs America*, 316–39. New York: Abrams, 2012.

Collier's, May 6, 1939.

Colomina, Beatriz. *Privacy and Publicity. Modern Architecture as Mass Media*. Cambridge, MA: MIT Press, 1996.

Collins, Percy. "Architectural Modeling." *American Homes and Gardens*, August 1915, 261.

Comazzi, John. *Balthazar Korab: Architect of Photography*. New York: Princeton Architectural Press, 2012.

Cooper, Lee. "New Design Used for Bank Edifice. Pedestrians to View Work in Manufacturers Trust Unit Through Glass Walls." *The New York Times*, August 16, 1953.

Corbett, Harvey Wiley. "Architectural Models of Cardboard." *Pencil Points*, April–August 1922, 11–14; 28–32, 37; 14–17; 14–18.

Corbett, Harvey Wiley. "Zoning and the Envelope of the Building." *Pencil Points*, April 1923, 68–9.

Corbett, Harvey Wiley. "Choosing a Profession." *The Herald Tribune*, June 1, 1926.

Corbett, Harvey Wiley. "An Architecture Finer Than the World Has Ever Seen." *The Architectural Forum*, April 1931, no pages.

Corbett, Harvey Wiley. "Metropolitan Life Insurance Company. New Home Office Building in New York." *Architectural Record*, September 1933, 182.

Covell, Alvin. "Architecture in Miniature: The Plastic Model Studies of an English Artist." *The Architectural Record*, March 1914, 263–6.

Croke, Dave. "On the Road to the Future." In Donald Albrecht (ed.), *Norman Bel Geddes Designs America*, New York: Abrams, 2012.

Cuff, Dana. *Architecture: The Story of Practice*. Cambridge, MA: MIT Press, 1991.

Cusker, Joseph. "The World of Tomorrow." In Helen Harrison (ed.), *Dawn of a New Day. The New York World's Fair, 1939/40*. New York: New York University Press, 1980.

REFERENCES

Deamer, Peggy. *The Architect as Worker: Immaterial Labor, the Creative Class, and the Politics of Design*. London: Bloomsbury, 2015.
"Decorator's Group Takes Rockefeller Center Floor." *The New York Times*, June 20, 1933.
Deering, Sally. "Model Maker Disguised a City." *The Jersey Journal*, November 18, 1991.
Deriu, Davide. "Transforming Ideas into Pictures: Model Photography and Modern Architecture." In Andrew Higgott and Timothy Wray (eds), *Camera Constructs: Architecture and the Modern City*, 159–78. Farnham: Ashgate, 2012.
"Diorama Making." *Torrance Herald*, August 15, 1935.
Dixon, John Morris. "Introduction." In George Hartman and Jan Cigliano (eds), *Pencil Points Reader. A Journal for the Drafting Room 1920–1943*, XVI–XXIII. New York: Princeton Architectural Press, 2004.
Drexler, Arthur. "Engineer's Architecture: Truth and Its Consequences." In Arthur Drexler (ed.), *The Architecture of the École des Beaux-Arts*, 12–59. New York: MIT Press, 1975.
"Dr. Jewett Heads Science Museum." *The New York Times*, October 19, 1935.
"Edward Howes, 87, Artist, Architect." *The New York Times*, May 11, 1964.
Elser, Oliver, and Peter Cachola Schmal. *The Architectural Model: Tool, Fetish, Small Utopia*. Zurich: Scheidegger und Spiess, 2012.
Emmons, Paul. "Drawn to Scale. The Imaginative Inhabitation of Architectural Drawings." In Marco Frascari (ed.), *From Models to Drawings. Imagination and Representation in Architecture*, 64–78. London: Routledge, 2007.
Endres, Kathleen, and Therese Lueck. *Women's Periodicals in the United States: Consumer Magazines*. Westport, CT: Greenwood Press, 1995.
Esherick, Joseph. "Architectural Education in the Thirties and Seventies: A Personal View." In Spiro Kostof (ed.), *The Architect: Chapters in the History of the Profession*, 238–79. New York: Oxford University Press, 1977.
Evans, Robin. *The Projective Cast*. Cambridge, MA: MIT Press, 1995.
Evans, Robin. "Translations from Drawing to Building." In *Translations from Drawing to Building and Other Essays*. London: AA Publications, 1997.
"Exhibits: A World of Wonders." *The New York Times*, May 5, 1940.
"Fair Motorcade to Cover 16 Miles." *The New York Times*, April 4, 1938.
"Fair of 1939 Will Depict the 'World of Tomorrow.'" *The New York Times*, October 9, 1936.
"Fair's Super-Speed Highway Exhibit to Be Huge Panorama." *The New York Sun*, January 21, 1939.
Fankhänel, Teresa. "Dreischeibenhaus." In Oliver Elser and Peter Cachola Schmal (eds), *The Architectural Model: Tool, Fetish, Small Utopia*, 112–16. Zurich: Scheidegger und Spiess, 2012.
Ferriss, Hugh. "Architecture of this Age." In Jane Heap (ed.), *Machine Age Exposition*, 5–6. New York, 1927.
Ferriss, Hugh. *The Metropolis of Tomorrow*, ed. Carol Willis. New York: Princeton Architectural Press, 1998.
Fistere, John. "Space for Living." *Ladies' Home Journal*, April 1938.
Flinn, Gene. "Pulse of the City. An Architectural Model Home Maker." April 26, 1951.
Flynn, John. "A Good Place to Live." *Collier's*, March 28, 1936, 10–11, 52–3, 56.
Flynn, John. "Collier's $7500 House." *Collier's*, April 3, 1937, 15–18, 54–5.
Forman, Robert. *Architectural Models*. New York: The Studio Publications, 1946.
Frampton, Kenneth. *Idea as Model*. New York: Rizzoli, 1981.
Franch i Gilabert, Eva et al. *Office US Agenda*. Zurich: Lars Müller, 2014.
Franck, Klaus. *Ausstellungen–Exhibitions*. Stuttgart: Hatje, 1961.
Frascari, Marco. *From Models to Drawings: Imagination and Representation in Architecture*. London: Routledge, 2007.
Frühe Kunststoffe. Die Sammlung Eva Stille, edited by the Historisches Museum Frankfurt, Frankfurt am Main, 2012.
Fuller, Buckminster. "Dymaxion House." *The Architectural Forum*, March 1932, 285–8.
"Futurama is Kept as Museum Piece." *The New York Times*, December 16, 1940.
"'Garden of Tomorrow' to Greet Show Visitors." *The New York Times*, May 9, 1937.

Gelber, Steven. *Hobbies: Leisure and the Culture of Work in America*. New York: Columbia University Press, 1999.
Gelernter, David. *1939: The Lost World of the Fair*. New York: The Free Press, 1995.
Giebelhausen, Joachim. *Architekturfotografie*. Munich: Verlag Grossbild-Technik GmbH, 1964.
Gillies, Mary Davis. "Mr. and Mrs. McCall Know What They Want." *The Architectural Forum*, April 1945, 101–08.
Gillies, Mary Davis. *McCall's Book of Modern Houses*. New York: Simon & Schuster, 1951.
"Glass and Steel Flats for Evanston." *Chicago Sunday Tribune*, May 29, 1932.
González, Robert Alexander. *Designing Pan-America*. Austin: University of Texas Press, 2011.
Grasskamp, Walter. "Sentimentale Modelle." *Kunstforum International*, no. 2 (1980): 54–9.
Grumbine, LeRoy. "Cardboard Models." *The Architectural Review*, August 2, 1922.
Grumbine, LeRoy. "A Florida House and Garden in Model." *House and Garden*, February 1924.
Grumbine, LeRoy. "The Use of Scale Models as an Aid to the Architect." *Western Architect. Architecture and Allied Arts*, June 1925, 59–62.
Grumbine, LeRoy. "Using Scale Models Advantageously." *The Architectural Forum*, January 1929, 105–09.
Gustavson, Andrea. "The Bel Geddes Process." In Donald Albrecht (ed.), *Norman Bel Geddes Designs America*, 340–53. New York: Abrams, 2012.
Harbison, Robert. *Thirteen Ways: Theoretical Investigations in Architecture*. Cambridge, MA: MIT Press, 1997.
Harrison, Helen. *Dawn of a New Day: The New York World's Fair, 1939/40*. New York: New York University Press, 1980.
Harrison, Wallace. "Drafting Room Practice." *The Architectural Forum*, January 1932, 5–6.
Hartcup, Guy. *Camouflage. A History of Concealment and Deception in War*. London: David & Charles, 1979.
Harvey, William. *Models of Buildings: How to Make and Use Them*. London: The Architectural Press, 1927.
Hassler, Uta, and Daniel Stockhammer. "Aus der Entwicklungsgeschichte des Bauplans. Wissenstransfer, Demonstration einer Bauidee oder Anleitung zum Bauen?" In Annette Spiro and David Ganzoni (eds), *Der Bauplan. Werkzeug des Architekten*, 284–93. Zurich: Park Books, 2013.
Havas, John. "Hudson Man Big Builder in Small Way Among Top Modelmakers." 1956.
Havas, John. "The Talk of the Town." *The New Yorker*, July 6, 1956, 13–14.
Heath, Wallace. "Big as All Outdoors. . ." *Woman's Home Companion*, September 1948, 62–5.
Hendrick, Thomas William. *The Modern Architectural Model*. London: Architectural Press, 1957.
Herman, Arthur. "Models of Plastic and Aluminium." *Progressive Architecture*, December 1959, 9–11.
Hitchcock, Henry-Russell, and Philip Johnson. *The International Style*. New York: W.W. Norton & Company, 1966.
Hobbs, Edward. *Pictorial House Modelling*. London: Crosby Lockwood and Son, 1926.
Holert, Tom. "Mikro-Ökonomie der Geschichte. Das Unausstellbare en miniature." *Texte zur Kunst*, March 2001, 57–68.
"Home Fire Causes Shown at Museum." *The New York Times*, October 16, 1936.
Horsley, Carter. "Modelmaker's Work Gaining New Recognition." *The New York Times*, July 28, 1974.
"House of Tomorrow." *Ladies' Home Journal*, April 1937.
"Housing Display Opens." *The New York Times*, September 20, 1936.
"How Realism Is Achieved in Diorama Making." *Torrance Herald*, August 15, 1935.
Hoyt, Robert. "World's Fair Models." *Pencil Points*, July 1939, 413–26.
"Huge Air Beacon at Santo Domingo in Honor of Columbus is Sponsored by 21 American Nations." *The Niagara Falls Gazette*, August 9, 1930.
Hunting, Mary Ann. *Edward Durell Stone: Modernism's Populist Architect*. New York and London: W.W. Norton & Company, 2013.
"In Miniature Form." *The New York Times*, March 30, 1937.
Innes, Christopher. *Designing Modern America: Broadway to Main Street*. New Haven, CT: Yale University Press, 2005.

REFERENCES

Innes, Christopher. "Modular and Mobile." In Donald Albrecht (ed.), *Norman Bel Geddes Designs America*, 200–13. New York: Abrams, 2012.

Jacks, Ernest. "The Elegant Bohemian." unpublished manuscript.

Jacobs, Jane. "The Miniature Boom: A Growing Demand for Precision Models Has Propelled the Architectural Modelmaker into the Machine Age." *The Architectural Forum*, May 1958, 106–11, 196.

Janke, Rolf. *Das moderne Architektur-Modell*. Stuttgart: Hatje, 1962.

Janke, Rolf. *Architectural Models*. New York: Frederick A. Praeger, 1968.

Kaldewei, Gerhard. *Linoleum: History, Design, Architecture 1882–2000*. Ostfildern: Hatje Cantz, 2000.

Kemp, Wolfgang. *Architektur analysieren. Eine Einführung in acht Kapiteln*. Munich: Schirmer/Mosel, 2009.

Kilham, Walter. *Raymond Hood, Architect: Form Through Function in the American Skyscraper*. New York: Architectural Book Publishing Co., 1973.

Koolhaas, Rem. *Delirious New York*. Aachen: Arch+ Verlag, 1999.

Kornwolf, James. *Modernism in America 1937–1941: A Catalog and Exhibition of Four Architectural Competitions*. Williamsburg: Joseph and Margaret Muscarelle Museum of Art, College of William and Mary, 1985.

Koss, Juliet. "VKhUTEMAS Snapshots." In Mari Lending and Mari Hvattum (eds), *Modelling Time: The Permanent Collection, 1925–13*, 267–70. Oslo: Torpedo Press, 2014.

Kostof, Spiro. *The Architect: Chapters in the History of the Profession*. New York: Oxford University Press, 1977.

Kreis, John. *Piercing the Fog: Intelligence and Army Air Forces Operations in World War II*. Washington, D.C.: U.S. Government Printing Office, 1996.

Krinsky, Carol. *Gordon Bunshaft of Skidmore, Owings & Merrill*. New York: MIT Press, 1988.

Ladd, Alex. "The Dean of Models: Was New York City Built in a Heights Shop?" *The Jersey City Reporter*, July 21, 1991.

Lambert, Phyllis. *Building Seagram*. New Haven, CT: Yale University Press, 2013.

Lampland, Ruth. "The 'Hobby Army' Grows." *The New York Times*, May 5, 1935.

Lanchner, Carolyn. *Fernand Léger*. New York: Abrams, 1998.

Larkins, Robert. "Diamonds, Bologna Star in Heights' History." *The Jersey Journal*, July 30, 1979.

Lebensohn, Jeremy. "Mighty Miniatures." *American Craft*, June/July 1988, 34–9.

Leich, Jean Ferriss, and Paul Goldberger. *Architectural Visions: The Drawings of Hugh Ferriss*. New York: Whitney Library of Design, 1980.

Lepik, Andres. *Das Architekturmodell in Italien 1335–1550*. Worms: Wernersche Verlagsgesellschaft, 1994.

Lester, Raymond. "Built Model of New York City." *The New York Times*, October 1, 1983.

Lipstadt, Hélène. "Architectural Publications, Competitions, and Exhibitions." In Eve Blau and Edward Kaufman (eds), *Architecture and Its Image: Four Centuries of Architectural Representation. Works from the Collection of the Canadian Centre for Architecture*, 109–37. Cambridge, MA: MIT Press, 1989.

Maffei, Nicolas Paolo. "Designing the Image of the Practical Visionary: Norman Bel Geddes, 1893–1958." Dissertation, Royal College of Art, February 2000.

"Many Big Buildings Got Start on Small Parcel in Jersey City," *Jersey Journal*, 1957.

Masey, Jack, and Conway Lloyd Morgan. *Cold War Confrontations: US Exhibitions and Their Role in the Cultural Cold War*. Zurich: Lars Müller Publishers, 2008.

Markland, John. "Expert Model-Making: Construction of World's Fair Structures in Miniature Aids Building Hobbyists." *The New York Times*, March 21, 1937.

Marschall, Luitgard. *aluminium. Metall der Moderne*. Munich: oekom verlag, 2008.

"Materials for 194X. Wartime Developments Have Provided an Idea Storehouse for Postwar Designs." *The Architectural Forum*, March 1944, 14.

McCutchon, Kenneth. "Architectural Models." *Architect's Journal*, October 1, 1936, 459.

McFadden, Elizabeth. "Lilliputian Buildings Are His Forte, Made to Assist Architects." *Newark Sunday News*, August 29, 1964.

McQuaid, Matilda. *Envisioning Architecture: Drawings from the Museum of Modern Art*. New York: MoMA, 2002.
Meikle, Jeffrey. *American Plastic Age*. New Brunswick, NJ: Rutgers University Press, 1995.
Meikle, Jeffrey. "'A Few Years Ahead': Defining a Modernism with Popular Appeal." In Donald Albrecht (ed.), *Norman Bel Geddes Designs America*, 114–35. New York: Abrams, 2012.
"Metropolitan Life Will Erect $9.000.000 Building on 4th Av." *The New York Times*, February 7, 1931.
Miller, Wallis. "Cultures of Display: Exhibiting Architecture in Berlin, 1880–1931." In Tim Anstey, Katja Grillner, and Rolf Hughes (eds), *Architecture and Authorship*, 98–107. London: Black Dog Press, 2007.
Miller, Wallis. "Fitting In: Architecture in the Art Gallery." In Robert Gutman, Dana Cuff, and John Wriedt (eds), *Architecture from the Outside In: Selected Essays by Robert Gutman*, 87–8. New York: Princeton Architectural Press, 2010.
"Miniature Home Shown." *The New York Times*, March 13, 1938.
"Miniature of Fair Shown in Exhibit." *The New York Times*, March 25, 1937.
Mock, Elizabeth. "Tomorrow's Small House." *The Bulletin of the Museum of Modern Art*, Summer 1945.
"Model Dwellings Rise in 'Garden.'" *The New York Times*, May 9, 1937.
"Model Fans Open 12th Annual Show." *The New York Times*, February 10, 1940.
"Model Makers Build NY World's Fair in Miniature." *The New York Herald Tribune*, March 6, 1938.
"Model of City Shows Every House, Park, Bridge, Pier, Stadium and Police Station." *The New York Times*, April 26, 1964.
"Molded Airplanes for Defense." *Modern Plastics*, July 1940, 25–31.
Moon, Karen. *Modeling Messages: The Architect and the Model*. New York: Monacelli Press, 2005.
Morris, Mark. "Worlds Collide: Reality to Model to Reality." In Andrew Higgott and Timothy Wray (eds), *Camera Constructs: Architecture and the Modern City*, 179–92. Farnham: Ashgate, 2012.
"Mrs. Dennett, 75, Suffrage Leader." *The New York Times*, July 26, 1947.
Murdock, Henrietta. "Living in Space." *Ladies' Home Journal*, April 1938.
"Murray Hill Site Will Get Skyscraper." *The New York Times*, December 17, 1948.
Murray, Robert Dennis. "Models and Scotch." *Pencil Points*, July 1939, 427–37.
Nauman, Robert Allen. *On the Wings of Modernism: The United States Air Force Academy*. Champaign: University of Illinois Press, 2004.
Nerdinger, Winfried. *Die Architekturzeichnung. Vom barocken Idealplan zur Axonometrie. Zeichnungen aus der Architektursammlung der Technischen Universität München*. Munich: Prestel, 1985.
Newhouse, Victoria. *Wallace Kirkman Harrison, Architect, USA, 1895–1981*. New York: Rizzoli, 1989.
"New Metropolitan Life Building." *The New York Times*, April 19, 1931.
New York City Guide. edited by The Guilds' Committee for Federal Writer's Publications Inc., 1939.
Normile, John. "Home is Where You Hang Your Mortgage." *The Architectural Forum*, April 1945, 91–100.
Ockman, Joan. *Architecture School: Three Centuries of Educating Architects in North America*. Cambridge, MA: MIT Press, 2012.
Oswald, Ansgar. *Meister der Miniaturen. Architektur Modellbau*. Berlin: DOM publishers, 2008.
Parker, Edwin. "The Model for Architectural Representation." *The Architectural Forum*, April 1919, 119–21.
Payne, Alina. "Materiality, Crafting, and Scale in Renaissance Architecture." *Oxford Art Journal*, no. 3 (2009): 365–86.
Pearson, Alastair. "Allied Military Model Making during World War II." *Cartography and Geographic Information Science*, March 2002, 238.
Pérez-Gómez, Alberto, and Pelletier, Louise. *Architectural Representation and the Perspective Hinge*. Cambridge, MA: MIT Press, 2000.
Pérez-Gómez, Alberto. "The Revelation of Order. Perspective and Architectural Representation." In Kester Rattenbury (ed.), *This is Not Architecture: Media Constructions*, 3–25. London: Routledge, 2002.

REFERENCES

Peter, John, and Edward Hamilton. *Aluminum in Modern Architecture*. New York: Reinhold Publishing, 1956.
Piedmont-Palladino, Susan. *Tools of the Imagination: Drawing Tools and Technologies from the Eighteenth Century to the Present*. New York: Princeton Architectural Press, 2007.
"Plan and Two Views of Model of Design for Radio City, Fifth Avenue, New York." *Pencil Points*, May 1931, 387.
Porter, Tom. *The Architect's Eye: Visualization and Depiction of Space in Architecture*. London: E & FN Spon, 1997.
Pratt, Richard. "Let's Look Ahead." *The Architectural Forum*, April 1945, 109–18.
"Preservation of Architectural Models." *American Architect*, August 28, 1918, 252.
Quindlen, Anna. "For a Maker of a Model City it is Indeed a Small World." *The New York Times*, January 15, 1981.
"Public Gets a Rare Peek at Fine Art Lent to Show by Prominent Jerseyans." *The New York Times*, July 30, 1972.
"Radio City Design Now Being Altered." *The New York Times*, April 2, 1931, 29.
Raff, Thomas. *Die Sprache der Materialien. Anleitung zur Ikonologie der Werkstoffe*. Münster: Waxmann, 2008.
Rappaport, Nina, and Erica Stoller. *Ezra Stoller: Photographer*. New Haven, CT: Yale University Press, 2012.
Rattenbury, Kester. *This is Not Architecture: Media Constructions*. London: Routledge, 2002.
Ray, Marie Beynon. "Night Life at Home." *Collier's*, April 25, 1936, 18–19.
Reid, Kenneth. "Architectural Models." *Pencil Points*, July 1939, 407–12.
Reinhard, Andrew. "Organization for Cooperation." *The Architectural Forum*, January 1932, 78–81.
"Rendering, Architectural." In *Encyclopedia Britannica*, 147. Chicago: Encyclopedia Britannica.
Ricciotti, Dominic. "The 1939 Building of the Museum of Modern Art." *The American Art Journal* 17, no. 3, (summer 1985): 48–73.
Riley, Terence. *The International Style: Exhibition 15 and the Museum of Modern Art*. New York: Rizzoli, 1992.
Robbins, L. H. "It Begins to Look Like a Great Fair!" *The New York Times*, May 1, 1938.
Roberts, Jennifer Davis. *Norman Bel Geddes: An Exhibition of Theatrical and Industrial Designs*. Austin: The University of Texas at Austin, 1979.
Roche, Mary. "Exhibit Portrays Living in Future." *The New York Times*, October 2, 1948.
Rose, James. "Landscape Models." *Pencil Points*, July 1939, 438–44.
Rottau, Nadine. *Materialgerechtigkeit. Ästhetik im 19. Jahrhundert*. Hamburg: DFG Graduiertenkolleg Kunst und Technik, 2012.
Rush, Richard. "Made Shedd's Reef and Museum's Heart." *The Chicago Tribune*, December 5, 2001.
Sachsse, Rolf. "A Short History of Architectural Model Photography." In Oliver Elser and Peter Cachola Schmal (eds), *The Architectural Model: Tool, Fetish, Small Utopi*a, 23–8. Zurich: Scheidegger und Spiess, 2012.
Schulze, Franz, and Edward Windhorst. *Mies van der Rohe: A Critical Biography*. Chicago: University of Chicago Press, 2012.
Schwippert, Hans ed. *3. Darmstädter Gespräch, Mensch und Technik*. Darmstadt: Neue Darmstädter Verlagsanstalt, 1952.
Scolari, Massimo. *Oblique Drawing: A History of Anti-Perspective*. Cambridge, MA: MIT Press, 2012.
Scott, Felicity. "An Army of Soldiers or a Meadow: The Seagram Building and the 'Art of Modern Architecture.'" *JSAH*, no. 3 (September 2011): 330–53.
Shepherd, Roger. *Skyscraper: The Search for an American Style 1891–1941. Annotated Extracts from the First 50 Years of Architectural Record*. New York: McGraw-Hill, 2003.
Shulman, Julius. *The Photography of Architecture and Design: Photographing Buildings, Interiors, and the Visual Arts*. New York: The Whitney Library of Design, 1977.
Simpson, Pamela. "Comfortable, Durable, and Decorative: Linoleum's Rise and Fall from Grace." *APT Bulletin*, no. 2/3 (1999): 17–24.

"Skyscraper Plans Hazy." *The New York Times*, October 5, 1929.

Smith, Albert. *Architectural Model as Machine: A New View on Models from Antiquity to the Present Day*. Amsterdam: Elsevier, 2004.

Sobieszek, Robert. *The Architectural Photography of Hedrich-Blessing*. New York: Holt, Reinhart and Winston, 1984.

Speck, Lawrence. "Futurama." In Donald Albrecht (ed.), *Norman Bel Geddes Designs America*, 288–315. New York: Abrams, 2012.

Spiro, Annette, and David Ganzoni. *Der Bauplan. Werkzeug des Architekten*. Zurich: Park Books, 2013.

Staniszewski, Mary Anne. *The Power of Display: A History of Exhibition Installations at the Museum of Modern Art*. Chicago: MIT Press, 1998.

Stern, Robert et al. *New York 1930*. New York: Rizzoli, 1987.

Stern, Robert. *The Philip Johnson Tapes*. New York: Monacelli Press, 2008.

Stewart, Susan. *On Longing: Narratives of the Miniature, the Gigantic, the Souvenir, the Collection*. Baltimore: John Hopkins University Press, 1984.

Stierli, Martino. "Preservation Parade: The Mediatization of the Lieb House into a Monument." *Future Anterior*, no. 1 (summer 2010): 44–58.

Stoller, Paul. "The Architecture of Harvey Wiley Corbett." Thesis, University of Wisconsin, 1995.

Stone, Edward Durell. *The Evolution of an Architect*. New York: Horizon Press, 1962.

Sumner, David. *The Magazine Century: American Magazines since 1900*. New York: Peter Lang, 2010.

Tafuri, Manfredo. "The Disenchanted Mountain: The Skyscraper and the City." In Giorgio Ciucci (ed.), *The American City: From the Civil War to the New Deal*, 389–503. Cambridge, MA: MIT Press, 1979.

Testa, Elena. "Theodore Conrad." *Forum. Jersey City Chamber of Commerce*, January/February 1978, 21–5.

"Test-Tube Marvels of Wartime Promise a New Era in Plastics. Postwar Horizons." *Newsweek*, May 17, 1943.

"The Active Market is Laying the Foundation for America's Building Boom!" *Collier's*, March 21, 1936, 70–1.

"Thomas W. Salmon II. Of NY and IN." www.boards.ancestry.com/surnames.salmon/553/mb.ashx?pnt=1. Accessed February 17, 2015.

Thompson, Helen. "Home is Like This." *Collier's*, May 16, 1936, 20–1, 46.

Tilley, J. P. "Versatility of Acrylics, 1934–1980." In S. T. I. Mossmann and P. J. T. Morris (eds), *The Development of Plastics*, 95–104. Cambridge: Royal Society of Chemistry, 1994.

www.tim1965.livejournal.com/1644249.html?thread=2308569. Accessed February 15, 2015.

"To Build on 4th Av. Block." *The New York Times*, October 23, 1929.

"United States Pavilion." *The New York Times*, April 15, 1937.

"U.S. Architecture in West Berlin." *Arts & Architecture*, January 1958, no pages.

Voßkötter, Silke. *Maßstäbe der Architektur*. Dresden: Tectum, 2009.

Wagner, Monika. *Materialästhetik. Quellentexte zu Kunst, Design und Architektur*. Berlin: Reimer, 2005.

Wagner, Monika. *Das Material in der Kunst. Eine andere Geschichte der Moderne*. Munich: C.H. Beck, 2011.

Wallace, Andy. "L.n. Abrams, 72, Master Modelmaker." *The Philadelphia Inquirer*, August 29, 1992.

Waring, Stephen. "Improved Techniques in Architectural Modelling." *Journal of the Royal Architectural Institute of Canada*, February 1948, 58–60.

Watson, Barron. "Plane Time Here Again." *The New York Times*, April 5, 1936.

Weinberg, Louise et al. "Panorama of the City of New York." Leaflet Queens Museum, *c.* 2014.

Wendler, Reinhard. *Das Modell zwischen Wissenschaft und Kunst*, Munich: Wilhelm Fink, 2013.

Wickham, Peter Raymond. *Commercial Model Making: Professional Model Making for Architects, Building Trades, Industrial Purposes, Exhibitions, General Advertising Display*. London: Vawser and Wiles, 1945.

REFERENCES

Willis, Carol. "Drawing Towards Metropolis." In Carol Willis (ed.), *Hugh Ferriss: The Metropolis of Tomorrow*, New York: Princeton Architectural Press, 1986.
"Women Engaged in the Art of Camouflage." *The New York Times*, April 20, 1942.
Woods, Mary. *From Craft to Profession: The Practice of Architecture in Nineteenth-Century America*. Berkeley: University of California Press, 1999.
"World's Fair Rents Design Workshop." *The New York Times*, May 26, 1936.
Wray, Timothy, and Andrew Higgott. *Camera Constructs: Architecture and the Modern City*. Farnham: Ashgate, 2012.
Wurts, Richard, and Stanley Appelbaum. *The New York World's Fair 1939/1940 in 155 Photographs*. New York: Dover Publications, 1977.
Yaneva, Albena. "Scaling Up and Down: Extraction Trials in Architectural Design." *Social Studies of Science*, no. 6 (December 2005): 867–94.
"Young and Old Join in Model-Building." *The New York Times*, July 7, 1937.
Young, William, and Nancy Young. *The 1930s*. Westport, CT: Greenwood Press, 2012.

Archives

Alexander Architectural Archive, Austin, Texas
Architectural Archives, University of Pennsylvania, Philadelphia, Pennsylvania
Art Institute of Chicago, Chicago, Illinois
Avery Architectural and Fine Arts Library, Columbia University, New York City (papers of Gordon Bunshaft, Louis Checkman, Theodore Conrad, Harvey Wiley Corbett, Wallace Harrison, Raymond Hood, and Skidmore, Owings & Merrill)
Beinecke Library at the Yale University Archives, New Haven, Connecticut
Cigna Corporate Archive, Hartford, Connecticut
Harry Ransom Center. The University of Texas at Austin (Norman Bel Geddes Papers)
Heinz Architectural Center, Carnegie Museum of Art, Pittsburgh, Pennsylvania
Jahn Architects, Chicago, Illinois
Manuscripts and Archives Division, The New York Public Library, New York City
Manuscripts & Archives, Yale University Library, New Haven, Connecticut
Metropolitan Life Insurance Company Archive, New York City
Museum of the City of New York, New York City (New York World's Fair collection)
Museum of Modern Art, New York City
New York Public Library (paper files of the former World's Fair Corporation)
Pei Cobb Freed & Partners Architects LLP, New York City
Pratt Institute Library, New York City
Queens Museum (New York World's Fair ephemera)
Rockefeller Center Archive, New York City
Skidmore, Owings & Merrill LLP, Chicago, Illinois
Special Collections. University of Arkansas Libraries, Fayetteville, Arkansas (Edward Durell Stone Papers)
The Art Institute of Chicago. Department of Architecture and Design, Chicago, Illinois
The New York Historical Society, New York City (New York World's Fair collection)

Index

Ackerman, Jay 70
Adams, Ansel 165
Ain, Gregory 43, 134, 137, 162
Air Force Academy 33, 47, 92, 165, 167, 170
Alberti, Leon Battista 7, 15, 99
aluminum
    Lever House 1, 83
    manufacture 14, 53–5, 72–3, 76–7, 79
    post-war use 80–1, 83, 86, 88, 92–3, 108, 136
    war 81
Architectural Forum
    exhibition 159, 171
    Miniature Boom 3, 35–6, 45
    model making 42, 78
    model photos 6, 38–9, 128–9, 131, 134, 143
Armiger, Richard 51
Audsley, Bertold 58, 68, 125, 156

Barr, Alfred 73
Barthes, Roland 53
Bassett, Kendall 77
Bassett-Lowke 17, 27
Baudrillard, Jean 53
Bayley, Thomas 43
Beaux-Arts system 8, 13, 15–16, 18, 40–3, 124, 128, 147
Bel Geddes, Norman
    biography, 119
    Conrad 5, 47
    Futurama 25–6, 34, 153–4
    model making 23, 25, 77, 83, 86, 102
    model photography 119–20, 129, 134
    plastics 70
    World War II 29, 136
Benjamin, Walter 11, 112
Blake, Peter 171
blueprint 13, 28, 99, 101–2, 108, 126, 156, 163
Boring, William Alciphron 42, 126
Bossange, E. Raymond 40
Bowman Brothers 77
Breines, Simon 125
Breuer, Marcel 43

Briskman, Norman 35, 38
Brussels World Fair 2, 38–9, 141–2, 171
Bunshaft, Gordon 5, 38, 43–7, 49, 85, 87, 164–5
Burdick, Edward Heckler 25, 55
Burket, Harriet 134
Burns, Ned 25, 156

Calder, Alexander 70
camouflage 27, 29
cardboard
    Corbett 6, 16–17, 19, 52, 58, 60, 73
    manufacture 41, 43, 53, 56–9, 64–8, 76, 86
    model drawing 103, 105
    model photography 114, 116–19, 121, 123, 136
    models 9, 18, 26, 46, 62–3, 77, 87–8, 92–3, 130, 147, 163
Carr, J. Gordon 160
celluloid 53, 68–9, 73, 81, 83, 108
Century of Progress Exhibition 24, 39, 69, 77
C.F. Murphy Associates 43
Chaffee, Bill 47, 85
Chambellan, Rene Paul 16, 24, 45, 62
Chase Manhattan Bank 33, 86–7
Checkman, Louis
    biography 5–6, 32, 37–9
    Edward Durell Stone Art 45–6, 109
    photography 47, 112, 120, 122, 130–4, 139, 141–3
    Pittsburgh House of Glass 76
    World War II 29–30
Chiaroscuro 118–20, 128, 131, 134
Chicago Tribune competition 16, 40, 62, 128
City of Light 25, 153–4
Collier's 6, 29, 45, 75, 104, 130–2, 134, 160, 162
Collins, Percy 145
Connecticut General Life 5, 90, 163, 165
Conrad, Theodore
    Air Force Academy 165
    assembled models 83
    Beinecke Library 92
    biography 3–5, 8, 10, 49–50, 93

Chase Manhattan Bank 86
clients 42, 43–9
Connecticut General Life 90–1, 163
education 18–19, 128
exhibitions 147, 159–61
Fernand Léger 78
Lever House model 1–2, 7, 81–3
Liebman House 99–101, 106, 108
linoleum 77
Manufacturers Trust 88
Metropolitan Life North Building 59–60, 64, 66, 68, 147
model drawings 98–108
model photography 37–41, 116, 124, 126, 128, 130–1, 133–4, 137, 139, 141, 143
MoMA 79–80
New York World's Fair 23–4, 75
Pepsi-Cola 88–9, 139
Plexiglas 7, 72–6, 81, 83–6, 93
Reynolds Metals Building 90
workshop 19–22, 30–6, 42, 63–4, 86, 98, 124
World War II 26–30
Yale University Art Gallery 163
Corbett, Harvey Wiley
  Conrad 4–6, 19, 42–4, 59
  exhibitions 146–7, 151–2, 159
  Metropolitan Life North Building 67, 118–19, 126
  model making 16–17, 52, 56–60, 62–3, 73, 83, 123
  model photography 36, 117–20, 123, 126, 128
  New York World's Fair 24, 70
Corbett, Mario 160
Covell, Alvin 125

de Blois, Natalie 167
Delta Power Tools Competition 4, 19, 21, 30
DeMars, Vernon 160
Democracity 25, 153
Dennett, Devon 35, 83, 160
Deskey, Donald 70
Diorama Corporation 25, 55
division of labor 13, 15, 25–6, 30–3, 83, 99
Drexler, Arthur 97, 169
Dreyfuss, Henry 153
Duckett, Edward 36, 87
Duncan, Perry 134
DuPont 69, 72

École des Beaux-Arts 16, 18
Esherick, Joseph 134

Ferriss, Hugh 14, 56, 59, 66–9, 119, 125–6, 128, 147, 150
Folger, James 158
Fordyce & Hamby 26, 130
Forman, Robert 43, 100
Fortune 27, 28, 38, 70–1, 130, 157
Fouquet, Jean-Pierre 17
Frey, Albert 72
Fromm, Louis 24
Fuller, Buckminster 129

Gabriel, Georg 35–6
Gallery of Modern Art 45, 141
Garet, Emile 17
Garnett, William 165
Giedion, Sigfried 113
Gillies, Mary Davis 15, 134
Gilstein, Harold 36
glass
  buildings 1, 7, 10, 49, 54, 66–8, 80–1, 85–8, 147, 164, 166
  models 7, 41, 54–5, 73–7
  photography 115, 131–4
Goldsmith, Myron 42
Goodman, Percival 29
Goodwin, Philip 4, 26, 43, 45, 77, 108, 163–4
Graham, Bruce 163
Gropius, Walter 1, 49
Grumbine, LeRoy 6, 17, 58, 62, 111, 126, 145–6, 157
Guild, Lurelle 70

Harr, Bob 40
Harrison, Wallace
  New York World's Fair 24, 35
  practice 1, 4–5, 19, 42–4, 49, 83, 101, 137, 160
  Rockefeller Apartments 64
  Rockefeller Center 62
Harvey, William 42
Heath, Wallace 134
Hedrich Blessing 37, 39, 40, 47
Hedrich, Ken 39
Hellmuth, Obata + Kassabaum 43
Hendrick, Thomas William 30, 32, 43, 88
Hitchcock, Henry-Russell 156
Hobbs, Edward W. 6, 17, 42, 54, 68, 105
Hood, Raymond
  exhibitions 159
  model making 16, 62, 73, 81, 119, 126
  practice 99
Hopper, Richard 36

INDEX

Howes, Edward 23
Hoyt, Robert 55
Hudnut, Joseph F. 41–2

Idea as Model 10, 88, 93
Ifor, Thomas 130
Inland Steel Building 47, 85, 139, 163
International Style
    architecture 3–4, 10, 47, 49, 54–5
    exhibition 72–3, 77, 79, 81, 99, 149, 156–7, 160

Jacks, Ernest 46
Jacobs, Harry Allen 99
Jacobs, Jane 3, 6, 10, 16, 34, 112, 133
Jaeger, Louis C. 163
Janke, Rolf 6, 43, 111
John F. Kennedy Memorial 33, 49
Johnson, Philip 35, 43, 77, 156–7, 160, 168

Kahn, Ely Jacques 26, 70
Kahn & Jacobs 43, 47, 81–2
Kahn, Louis 43, 163
Kautzky, Theodore 150
Keck, George Fred 160
Kilham, Walter 26, 62
Koch, Carl 160
Kocher, A. Lawrence 72
Kogan, Belle 70
Korab, Balthazar 36

Ladies' Home Journal 6, 35, 72, 130–1, 134, 137, 158, 160
Landefeld & Hatch 26, 75
Le Corbusier 49, 99, 157
Lefebvre, Gerard 32
Léger, Fernand 26, 78
Lester, Raymond 34–5
Leuschner, Walter 25
Lever House 1–2, 7, 81–3, 92, 138–9, 166–8, 171–2
Liebman, Aline Meyer 99, 106
Liebman, Charles J. 99
Life 6, 130–1, 134, 136
linoleum 69, 72–3, 76–7
Loewy, Raymond 70
Loos, Adolf 53, 97, 99

MacAllister, Paul 158
Marchand, Henri 25
Marino, Joseph 163
Masey, Jack 171

McCall's 6, 15, 72, 130, 134
McCallum, William 17
Messineo, Joseph 24, 34
Metropolitan Life North Building 59–60, 64, 66–8, 81, 118–19, 124, 126–7, 147–8
Mies van der Rohe, Ludwig
    exhibitions 167, 168–9
    model making 36, 39, 42–3, 54, 81, 87
    practice 6, 15, 49–50, 72
Minissale, Katherine 33
model drawings 5, 9, 47–8, 95–109
model photos
    archival 5–6, 19, 98
    exhibitions 147, 150, 159–60, 165–7, 169, 172
    magazines 6, 15, 45, 149, 155, 158–60, 162, 165
    photographers 5, 37–40
    photographic techniques 9, 2, 45, 47, 54, 76, 85, 95, 109, 111–44
modeling clay 16, 26, 41, 45–6, 55–6, 62, 65, 73, 93
Moses, Robert 35
Museum of Modern Art
    Conrad 22, 79, 137
    building 45, 77–8, 103–5, 108
    exhibitions 35, 72–3, 77, 81, 156–8, 160–2, 164, 166–9, 171
    general 1–2, 4, 70, 99, 134

Netsch, Walter 85, 92
New York World's Fair
    Conrad 4–6, 23–4, 43
    dioramas 25
    exhibition 149–53, 155–8, 160, 169
    history 9, 26
    model photos 129
    plastics 69, 74, 78
    workshop 22–3, 46, 70, 102
Noguchi, Isamu 48–9

O'Neil Ford 134

Pei, I.M. 35, 47–8, 171
Pencil Points 6, 16, 23, 42, 56–8, 107, 117, 120, 128, 143, 155
Pepper, Eleanor 160
photo models
    construction 25, 52, 74, 107, 123, 128, 130, 136
    photography 9, 42, 98, 112–13, 133, 158
Pittsburgh House of Glass 74, 76, 81, 131, 160
Plan-Tech Associates 160

plaster of Paris
    models 9, 41, 53–4, 56, 74, 108, 128, 149, 151–2
    use 58, 60, 62–6, 76, 87, 92–3, 105, 114
plastics 31–2, 53, 69–76, 80–1, 88, 92–3
Plexiglas
    Lever House 1, 7, 81–3, 166
    manufacture 16, 36, 43, 48, 53–5, 74–9, 83, 86–9, 103, 133
    models 35, 85, 88, 130, 137
    new material, 69–73, 87, 92–3, 136
    war 80–1
power tools 4, 9, 19, 21–3, 31, 33
Pran, Catharina 17
Pran, Peter 17, 36
Pratt, Richard 137
Pratt Institute 3, 18
Price, Chester 150

Radio City Music Hall 44–5
Raymond Barger Studios 160
Raymond & Rado 43, 134
realism
    exhibitions 153, 162–3, 169
    model making 8–10, 54, 66, 68, 78, 85, 89, 93, 97, 107
    photography 36, 107, 111–17, 129–37
Reinhard & Hofmeister 62
rendering
    Beaux-Arts 8, 10, 14, 18, 95–8, 105, 145–7
    Chiaroscuro 56, 67–8, 117–19, 123–30
    exhibitions 149–50, 156, 162, 165
    postwar 45, 113, 136
Ricci, Ardolino, and Di Lorenzo 17
Roche-Dinkeloo 43
Rockefeller, Nelson 4
Rockefeller Center 4, 16, 19, 22, 25, 44, 62, 72, 77, 89, 119, 128, 144, 149, 151–2, 158–62, 169
Rogers, Jerry 134
Rohde, Gilbert 70
Rohm & Haas 69–70, 72
Rudofsky, Bernard 26, 43
Rudolph, George Cooper 6, 165
Rush Studios 165
Ruskin, John 53

Saarinen, Eero 1, 17, 25, 36, 47, 163
Saarinen, Eliel 42
Salmon, Thomas 35–6, 48
Santeramo, Joseph 35

Schickmann, R.H. 43
Schultze, Leonard 159
Scott, Michael 74
Seagram Building 1, 81, 87, 169, 171
Semper, Gottfried 53
Severinghaus, Walter 46
Shagden, Joseph 23–4
Shaw, Naess & Murphy 26
Shreve, Lamb & Harmon 26, 64–5, 74
Shuster, Daniel 138
Sick, Charles 48
Sieben, Jacob 19
Skidmore, Owings & Merrill
    model photos 138–9
    practice 4, 6, 15, 36, 38–9, 43–4, 46–7, 81, 85–6, 88, 90, 163–7, 169
Smith, James Robert 36
Speyer, A. James 43, 134, 136, 161
Steinhof, Eugene 41
Stoller, Ezra 6, 37–9, 47, 138–40, 143, 165
Stone, Edward Durell
    Conrad 43–4
    Liebman House 99–108
    model photos 129–31, 134
    New York World's Fair 24
    practice 4–5, 19, 22, 38, 45–7, 49, 77, 141, 158, 160–2, 167, 169
Strain, Howard 32
Stubbins Jr., Hugh 160

Tabler, William B. 43
Teague, Walter Dorwin 23, 25, 30, 153
Thorp, John B. 18
Tigerman, Stanley 50
Twining Models 17, 27
Tyng, Ann 43

Urban, Gretl 151

van Alen, William 159
van Anda, George 130
Van der Gracht & Kilham 26
Vasari, Giorgio 14–15, 48
Villa Savoye 79, 157

Walker, Ralph 159
Waring, Stephen 26
Warnecke, John Carl 43, 49
Weatherhead, Arthur Clason 42
Wenrich, John 150
White, Lawrence 159
Wickham, Peter Raymond 42, 156

INDEX

Woman's Home Companion 6, 72, 130, 134–5, 162
wood
    material 53–8, 60–7, 73, 92, 136
    model making 21–6, 30–1, 41, 45, 48, 75–6
    models 14, 17–19, 27, 79–83, 86–8, 103–8, 130
Woodruff, John Kellog 19

World War II 3, 6, 8, 22, 24, 26–30, 47, 69, 72–3, 111, 120
Wright, Frank Lloyd 131, 160

Yamasaki, Minoru 43

Zeckendorf, William 43
Zoning Law 56, 59, 62, 67, 97, 119